Praise for *The 30 Minute Vegan's Taste* ʅ

"Mark Reinfeld delivers cookery brilliance in *Taste of Europe*. ᴡᴡ ɪᴛɴ culinary finesse, he elevates traditional European dishes to plant-based prestige! Now you can savor delicacies from Spain, Germany, Italy, France—and more—in the comfort of your own vegan kitchen. Mark, you had me at 'Vegan Gelato'!"

> —Dreena Burton, author of *Let Them Eat Vegan* and *eat, drink & be vegan*

"*The 30 Minute Vegan's Taste of Europe* is jam-packed full of vibrant, delicious, healthful recipes that are better than a trip to Europe! This book is a must-have for every kitchen."

> —Julie Hasson, author of *Vegan Diner* and *The Complete Book of Pies*

"This tasty culinary expedition provides a perfect combination of exotic and familiar dishes to enthrall any curious cook. I am eternally grateful to Mark Reinfeld for veganizing these exquisite traditional recipes so we may enjoy them while sustaining a healthful and compassionate diet."

> —Julieanna Hever, MS, RD, CPT, *Plant-Based Dietitian* and author of
> *The Complete Idiot's Guide to Plant-Based Nutrition*

"With Mark Reinfeld's guidance, anyone can produce impressive and delicious vegan meals. Sure to become a classic of healthy and humane cuisine, *Taste of Europe* is packed with easy recipes that will appeal to vegans and meat-eaters alike."

> —Jack Norris, Registered Dietitian, coauthor of *Vegan for Life*

"Mark Reinfeld takes compassionate cooking to a new level with these incredible recipes. *Taste of Europe* makes vegan meals accessible to everyone—and is the perfect cookbook for when you want to impress your meat-eating friends."

> —Virginia Messina, MPH, RD, vegan dietitian, coauthor of *Vegan for Life*

Praise for *The 30 Minute Vegan's* series:

Named a "Top Ten Vegan Cookbook" by *VegNews*, July/August 2010

"This book is filled with delicious, exciting, healthful recipes that are accessible for everyone. You'll love it whether you're a vegan, or you just want to eat like one once in a while."

> —Ellie Krieger, RD, best-selling author of *So Easy: Luscious, Healthy Recipes for Every Meal of the Week* and host of Food Network's *Healthy Appetite*

"Mark and Jennifer are on the cutting edge of healthy dining. This is vegan cuisine at its finest."

 —Cher

"Whether you are vegan or not, this is a very appealing collection of recipes. I know they're going to become part of my culinary life."

 —Deborah Madison, author of *Vegetarian Cooking for Everyone* and *Local Flavors*

"*The 30-Minute Vegan* is a fail-safe cookbook designed to save you time and eliminate stress in the kitchen. With a well-planned collection of fast, simple, and healthy recipes, the duo is determined to keep home dining diverse and your diet in tip-top shape."

 —*VegNews*

"One of the very best vegan cookbooks of all time. Fabulous recipes, healthy food, clear directions, and delicious results!"

 —John Robbins, author of *The New Good Life* and *Diet for a New America*

"*The 30-Minute Vegan* has found a permanent home in my kitchen, where its pages will quickly become worn, torn, and stained."

 —HungryVegan.com

"The vegan's answer to Rachael Ray and Mr. Food, this is recommended for anyone wishing to re-create their favorite Asian restaurant dishes without the meat."

 —*Library Journal*

"For vegetarians who are ready to take the step to vegan and omnivores that would like to add animal-free dishes to their diet, *The 30-Minute Vegan's Taste of the East* offers an array of dishes that will make their experimentation easy. Vegans will find it is an excellent addition to their cookbook libraries."

 —Blogcritics

"There's a . . . 'keep it simple' approach to *Taste of the East*. Murray and Reinfeld must have been thinking weeknight suppers with the 150 recipes they've assembled, which includes hearty noodle and rice bowls, Indian stews, Chinese stir fries and Southeast Asian fusion."

 —*Portland Oregonian*

the 30 Minute Vegan's

TASTE of EUROPE

Other books by Mark Reinfeld:

The 30 Minute Vegan with Jennifer Murray

The 30 Minute Vegan's Taste of the East with Jennifer Murray

The Complete Idiot's Guide to Eating Raw
with Bo Rinaldi and Jennifer Murray

Vegan World Fusion Cuisine with Bo Rinaldi

the 30 Minute Vegan's

TASTE of EUROPE

150 Plant-Based Makeovers of Classics from France, Italy, Spain, and Beyond

Mark Reinfeld

Da Capo
LIFE
LONG

A Member of the Perseus Books Group

Design and production by Trish Wilkinson
Set in 11 point Minion Pro

Cataloging-in-Publication data for this book is
available from the Library of Congress.

First Da Capo Press edition 2013
ISBN: 978-0-7382-1433-7 (paperback)
ISBN: 978-0-7382-1616-4 (e-book)

Published by Da Capo Press
A Member of the Perseus Books Group
www.dacapopress.com

Note: The information in this book is true and
complete to the best of our knowledge. This book
is intended only as an informative guide for those
wishing to know more about health issues. In no
way is this book intended to replace, counter-
mand, or conflict with the advice given to you by
your own physician. The ultimate decision con-
cerning care should be made between you and
your doctor. We strongly recommend you follow
his or her advice. Information in this book is general and is offered with no guarantees on the part
of the authors or Da Capo Press. The authors and
publisher disclaim all liability in connection with
the use of this book.

Da Capo Press books are available at special discounts for bulk purchases in the U.S. by corpora-
tions, institutions, and other organizations. For
more information, please contact the Special Markets Department at the Perseus Books Group,
2300 Chestnut Street, Suite 200, Philadelphia, PA,
19103, or call (800) 810-4145, ext. 5000, or e-mail
special.markets@perseusbooks.com.

10 9 8 7 6 5 4 3 2 1

*To my grandfather Benjamin Bimstein,
master chef, ice carver, and an inspiration for
living life with courage and creativity.*

May all be healthy, happy, and well fed.

Contents

CONTENTS

CONTENTS

Prepare to Rock Your World with the Tastes of Europe!

E urope holds a special place in everyone's heart. The medieval castles; the narrow cobblestone streets, robust farmers' markets; and the richness and history of the arts, culture, and cuisine can awaken the wonder in anyone. It is truly a gift to experience the beauty and romance of the Old Country. I invite you to prepare for an adventure of a lifetime, for through the pages of the *Taste of Europe* you will be guided on a journey of culinary exploration through this magical and wondrous world.

While there are many cookbooks that focus on a single European ethnic cuisine, this book is unique in that veganized regional favorites from many European countries are shared. It's where the joie de vivre meets the dolce vita. The revered cuisines of France, Italy, and Greece; the boldness of Spanish and Portuguese foods; and family favorites from the United Kingdom, Ireland, and Germany are all represented. I've also included a sampling of dishes from Eastern and Northern Europe, such as the cuisines of Romania, Hungary, Poland, Czechoslovakia, Sweden, Finland, and Iceland.

Through Vegan Fusion cuisine, you'll learn that seemingly disparate flavors and ingredients from various cuisines can actually complement one another and enhance your dining experience. With the recipes of the *Taste of Europe*, you can dine on Italian Minestrone and Fettuccine Alfredo by the shores of the Mediterranean, enjoy a Chocolate Fondue from the Swiss Alps, and finish it off with a Ginger Brew from the land of Stonehenge.

From the subtle herbes de Provence to the sharper Hungarian or Spanish paprika, the depth of ingredients and flavor that comes to us through Europe is immense. Please see the Taste of Europe Pantry section (page 245) to learn about some of the more popular regional favorites. Fortunately, virtually all of these ingredients are easily accessible at most markets. There are some specialty items that can be found at your local natural foods store, ethnic market, or online. Please see page xxi for a list of those items to stock up on your next visit to your local natural foods store. And feel free to ask your grocer to carry certain products; you will be surprised how accommodating markets can be. Check out some of the online resources listed in Appendix D.

Veggie Europe—From Pythagoras to Sir Paul McCartney

The earliest records of large portions of a population embracing a vegetarian diet come to us from ancient India, where ahimsa, or nonviolence, became a way of life for many. You might be surprised to discover that there is also a rich history of vegetarianism in Europe, dating back to 500 BC and the times of Pythagoras, the Greek philosopher, scientist, and mystic. Apparently Pythagoras took a trip to India and was greatly influenced by the lifestyle of the sages and philosophers he came across. He brought this knowledge back with him to southern Italy and insisted that all of his students follow a vegetarian diet. In fact, the earliest vegetarians in Europe were called Pythagoreans. This may explain why the cuisine of Italy is perhaps the most vegan-friendly of all of Europe. Other ancient Greek philosophers, including Empedocles, and many of those at Plato's Academy likewise embraced the vegetarian lifestyle.

Fast forward to the Renaissance, when cool bros such as Leonardo da Vinci, Pierre Gassendi, and English writer Thomas Tryon were proponents of the lifestyle. In the nineteenth century and the Age of Enlightenment, England begins to take center stage on the veggie scene. These are the times of poet Percy Bysshe Shelley and Reverend William Cowherd, the latter of whom was one of the forerunners of the Vegetarian Society that formed in England in 1847. In another step forward, almost one hundred years later, Donald Watson coined the term *vegan* and helped form the Vegan Society in England in 1944. Of course, this is an extremely brief history of a robust movement. For a more in-depth exploration, please check out *The Bloodless Revolution: A Cultural History of Vegetarianism from 1600 to the Modern Times* by Tristram Stuart.

Vegan Fusion

The style of my cuisine is Vegan Fusion. This means that I often combine ingredients from different culinary traditions in the same dish or menu. Quinoa is a South American grain, yet it complements a dish of Italian ratatouille or Hungarian stroganoff just as well as does any rice. I also find that wheat-free tamari, a soy sauce used extensively in Asian cuisine, creates a layer of flavor and helps accentuate the flavor of other ingredients, regardless of the ethnicity of the dish.

I highly recommend using organic ingredients whenever possible in these recipes. Organic food is grown without the use of chemical fertilizers and pesticides, most of which have not been fully tested for their long-term effects on humans. For maximum food safety, go organic. Please see Appendix C for more information on organics.

I also recommend using a minimum of processed and packaged ingredients. This is much better for your health and the reduction in packaging is good for the planet. Most European cultures have rich traditions of using fresh local and organic produce. While the image of a Frenchwoman carrying a baguette in her bag is somewhat of a cliché, daily trips to the local olive vender, baker, and produce market are a part of life.

When you eat locally grown foods whenever possible, it ensures optimal flavor and freshness and saves all of the resources involved in shipping over long distances. Growing foods in your own garden or participating in community-supported agriculture programs (CSAs) are the best option if you have the opportunity. It's very rewarding to see something grow from seed to plant. Farmers' markets are the next best choice. Get to know the people growing your food! Many of the recipes in the *Taste of Europe* can be adapted to include whatever ingredients are fresh and available.

Having said that, I would like to point out that many of the recipes in the book contain what I call "transitional" ingredients. These are ingredients that I consider healthier than their animal product equivalent, though not necessarily foods that I would consider healthful enough to include on a daily basis. I refer to them as transitional because I feel that certain products, such as vegan butter, vegan cream cheese, vegan sausages, and even seitan, can greatly help people transition to a plant-based lifestyle by satisfying cravings for animal products. My main goal with the *Taste of Europe* has been to create vegan makeovers of classic European dishes to demonstrate the incredible versatility of plant-based cuisine. These transitional products have certainly been crucial in helping me accomplish this. As an advocate of healthy eating and living, I do encourage you to enjoy these products on special occasions.

A Journey of a Thousand Miles Begins with One Step

This book has deep personal meaning for me. My love of international travel, culture, and cuisine was awakened during extended stays in Europe. During my junior year of college at the London School of Economics, I traveled extensively: I experienced the cuisine throughout England, Wales, Scotland, France, Spain, Portugal, Italy, Switzerland, Germany, Greece, Israel, and the Soviet Union. My wanderlust—and my palate—were awakened!

After graduating from the State University of New York at Albany, I took a year off before entering law school at New York University and returned to the life of the traveler. I worked as an au pair in Paris, hitchhiked from Amsterdam to Germany just in time to witness the opening of the Berlin Wall, witnessed the student revolution in Prague, and was there for a democratic revolution in Nepal. I visited several Eastern European countries, including Poland, Czechoslovakia, Hungary, and Yugoslavia. I concluded the trip with travel through Israel, the Sinai Desert, and India, and a four-week trek to Mount Everest.

This time period also corresponds to when I began my personal journey toward the vegetarian lifestyle. While I was working on a kibbutz in Israel, I would walk through the valley and encounter cows, goats, and chickens. I began to feel that they had just as much of a right to live their lives on the planet as I did. In fact, I started feeling the same love toward them that I felt towards my pet dog. It was then I began to question how comfortable I was eating them.

What sealed the deal was when I was asked to remove chickens and place them in crates so they could be sent to slaughter. After several minutes in that environment I realized that I would not participate in the process of slaughter. That day began my Veg Journey.

My recent return visits to Europe have led to the final offering of the book. The last three-month trip in particular was truly an epic journey of culinary discovery. I learned so much in my research. I offered classes and workshops in England and Paris, participated in the Paris Vegan Days where over eight thousand were in attendance, and met incredible people who passed on secret family recipes and culinary tips that I'm thrilled to be sharing with you. The richness of the European culinary traditions can now be yours for the taking.

Contributing Chefs

While the pantry lists will keep you more than adequately stocked for your culinary travels, there are a few additional elements that will help heighten your experience. I am very happy to be including contributions from some amazing chefs I have had the pleasure of working with. Jennifer Murray, coauthor of *The Complete Idiot's Guide to Eating Raw*, *The 30-Minute Vegan*, and *The 30-Minute Vegan's Taste of the East*, has created a comprehensive resource on European culinary herbs (page xxvii); in it, you'll learn a bit more about various combinations and flavor profiles that have long been used in these regions. Patrick Bremser, former head chef of the Blossoming Lotus restaurant on Kauai, shares his expertise on wine pairing, offering suggestions for types of wines and beers to use in the recipes in this book (page xxxix). Colin Patterson, another former head chef of the Blossoming Lotus, shares a fascinating section on wild mushrooms, ingredients that feature prominently in many European cuisines (page xxxv).

Peace Begins in the Kitchen

Preparing food can be a sacred and healing time for you to connect with nature in your own kitchen. It can be a time when you leave all of your cares at the door and focus on creating delicious meals. It is also so much *fun*! Whether you're preparing a meal for yourself or for twenty, experimenting with different ingredients and culinary traditions is one of life's greatest gifts.

I encourage you to cultivate as much mindfulness, calmness, and love when you prepare your meals, creating an inspiring and uplifting ambiance in the kitchen. Get your groove on by listening to your favorite music. Bring flowers, favorite photos, or other objects of beauty into the space to awaken the creative chef within. May you be inspired by these recipes and the information in this book to take your health and vitality to the next level in the most creative and delicious way possible!

With deep thanks and aloha,
Mark

Want to Know More?

Our company, Vegan Fusion, promotes the benefits of vegan foods for our health, the preservation of our planet, and to create a more peaceful world. In addition to our award-winning cookbooks, we offer workshops, chef trainings and immersions, and vegan culinary retreats around the world. We also offer consulting services, and can assist in menu and recipe development with this Innovative Global Cuisine. For inspiration surrounding the vegan lifestyle, to check out our online culinary course, and to sign up for our free online newsletter, please visit our website: www.VeganFusion.com.

How to Use This Book

Virtually all of the recipes can be completed in less than 30 minutes, including preparation and cooking time. Several recipes do have cooking, baking, freezing, or refrigerating times that exceed this time frame, but the labor time is almost always under 30 minutes in every case. I've also included some of my favorite variations to the recipes, some of which may also take longer than 30 minutes. These are clearly noted.

The clock starts ticking once the ingredients have been gathered and are ready for use. The time doesn't include searching through the cabinets for tools or ingredients. The addition of ingredients that are listed as optional will also add to the preparation time. Read through the recipe carefully, perhaps even twice. Make sure you have everything you need and gather it before you begin. Remember that with practice, everything becomes easier. The more you make a recipe, the faster you will get and the more likely you will be able to fit it into the 30-minute time frame.

In each section, the recipes are listed in the order you might find them on a menu—appetizers, soups, salads, side dishes, entrées, breakfasts, desserts, beverages, and condiments. Within that structure, for the most part recipes are then listed from lighter to heavier. Use these recipes as a starting point for creating your own versions and specialties based on your preferences and whatever ingredients are fresh and available. I'm a strong believer in creative expression in the kitchen; don't just try to stick to the recipe. If you love garlic, add more garlic. If you like it hot, up the quantity of chiles. Never let one or two missing ingredients stop you from making a recipe. There is always something you can substitute; be creative!

Throughout the book, I introduce many of the techniques of vegan natural food preparation. These techniques are also highlighted in Appendix B. For a more thorough exploration, including tips for stocking your kitchen, as well as for an extensive resource guide, please check out *The 30-Minute Vegan*. Be sure to take a look at the Appendix A, too—there you'll find lists of some key ingredients for these recipes, as well as common ingredients for many vegan dishes.

While each country has developed its unique culinary traditions, there are many ingredients that transcend borders. For instance, you will find olive oil is used in several countries. Similarly, those countries bordering the Mediterranean Sea have developed comparable culinary traditions. Please visit the Taste of Europe Pantry (page 245) for a wide selection of these ingredients.

As far as the shelf life of the dishes, I generally recommend enjoying the food the day it is prepared and for the next day or two after that. Some recipes, such as salad dressings and desserts, may last a bit longer. Please check daily to ensure freshness. Store leftovers in a glass container in the refrigerator.

The Theory of Relativity—Different Nutritional Theories

Having completed a master's degree program in holistic nutrition, one of the first things I realized is that there are many conflicting nutritional theories out there, each with their own body of evidence to support their theory. You'll find variations on the ways of eating mentioned throughout the book. Here's a quick overview of some of the more popular nutritional theories:

Raw Foods: Raw foods are nutrient-rich foods that have not been heated above about 116°F. Many feel that heating food beyond a certain temperature begins to diminish the nutrient content in the food. Live food cuisine is a growing trend in the culinary world. Those eating raw foods report feeling increased energy, weight loss, healing, and a host of other benefits. While most of the recipes in this book are cooked foods, I have provided several raw food recipes and those that are adaptable to being raw. In some cases, I provide a cooked and raw variation of a dish so you can compare the different flavors. The raw food recipes in the book are indicated with a ♥.

Gluten Free: Gluten is a protein that is found in wheat and other cereal grains that is responsible for the grains' elasticity. More and more people are being diagnosed with celiac disease—or are simply cutting gluten out of their diet, for overall health. I have used spelt flour in all of the recipes in this book. Spelt is an ancient variety of wheat, which does contain gluten, though in a form that many with wheat allergies can tolerate. Those with celiac disease are unable to tolerate gluten in any form. For a gluten-free flour mix, please see page 260. **Every recipe in this book, with the exception of two recipes using phyllo dough, is either gluten free or can be easily adapted to gluten free.** I have noted on the recipes including a gluten product what to use as a replacement. For the gluten intolerant, please remember to use gluten-free tamari as the soy sauce, and to purchase a gluten-free variety of nutritional yeast—two common ingredients used in the book.

Oil Free: Many people feel that including processed oils in our diet is less than optimal for heart health. If you wish to eliminate processed oils, especially when sautéing, please use the water sauté method discussed on page 253. You can also replace the olive oil called for in the recipes with a higher-heat oil such as grapeseed or coconut.

Low Sodium: If you wish to reduce your sodium intake, please use a low-sodium soy sauce, add salt to taste instead of following the recipe's recommendation, and/or replace the sea salt with kelp granules.

Soy Free: If you wish, you may replace the soy sauce called for in the recipes with coconut aminos, available at your local natural foods store.

Sugar Free: Refined white sugar is implicated in many illnesses. For several dessert recipes, I list organic sugar as an ingredient to indicate my recommendation to use an alternative to white sugar. Please see the sweetener chart on page 262 for some healthful alternatives to white sugar and visit your local natural foods store to discover several natural sweeteners on the market.

Specialty Items

Although most foods can be purchased at your supermarket, some items may require a trip to the natural foods store. Here is a list of the ingredients to stock up on to complete the recipes.

Arrowroot powder: A powdered starch made from the root of the arrowroot plant. Used as a thickener in sauces, soups, and desserts. Dissolve arrowroot with an equal amount of cold water before adding to the mixture being thickened.

continues

Specialty Items continued

Brown rice pasta: The premier choice for gluten-free pasta. Tinkiyada brand is recommended.

Coconut oil: Made from the popular coconut.

Egg replacer: Because flaxseeds are highly nutritious, the recipes in this book use ground flaxseeds as an egg replacer. The standard ratio is 1 egg = 1 tablespoon of ground flaxseeds + 3 tablespoons of water. Feel free to replace the flaxseeds with another egg replacer.

Gardein products: This company produces several animal product analogues that can be used in many of the dishes in the book, to replace the tofu, tempeh or seitan called for in the recipe. They have products that replicate beef, turkey, chicken, and fish. Please visit Gardein.com for a complete list of products.

Kudzu root: A starchy tuber used to thicken sauces.

Miso paste: A salty paste made by fermenting soybeans, grains, and other beans. Purchase unpasteurized for maximum nutritional benefits.

Nutritional yeast: A plant-based culture consisting of up to 50 percent protein. The Red Star brand is a source of B vitamins, including B_{12}. It imparts a nutty and cheeselike flavor to dishes. Go for the large-flake variety.

Raw apple cider vinegar: The raw variety is said to contain the highest nutritional value.

Organic sugar: See page xxi.

Quinoa: Botanically a seed, though commonly referred to as the ancient grain of the Incans, quinoa is high in protein and may be used to replace rice in any of the recipes in the book.

Salt: Consider purchasing gourmet salts such as Celtic or Himalayan, which are higher in mineral content than most commercial salts. You can also experiment with smoked salts, which add an additional depth of flavor to your dishes.

continues

Specialty Items continued

Silken firm tofu: A creamy variety of tofu that is wonderful for puddings and sauces; see page 249.

Tempeh: A soy product similar to tofu, though with a heartier texture and nuttier flavor. Turtle Island brand recommended (see page 250).

Vegan butter: Try Earth Balance brand.

Vegan cheese: Try Daiya brand or Follow Your Heart.

Vegan mayonnaise: Use Vegenaise, or make your own (page 261).

Vegan sausages: Tofurky and Field Roast have good products.

Wheat-free tamari: A by-product of the miso-making process, this is the recommended soy sauce for all of the recipes in the book.

White spelt flour or gluten-free flour mix: Bob's Red Mill has a wonderful gluten-free baking mix that can be used one for one to replace the flour called for in the recipes. For gluten-free baking, you will also want to pick up xanthan gum as a specialty product. This is a substance to replace the gluten in other flours that can contribute elasticity to the recipes.

Sidebars and Symbols

Throughout the pages you will see the following sidebars and symbols:

Quicker and Easier: While virtually all of the recipes in this book may be considered quick and easy, these dishes are even more simple to prepare.

If You Have More Time: These recipes and variations of recipes take longer than 30 minutes. Give them a try when you have more time to explore them!

Chef's Tips and Tricks: We share the secrets that make your life in the kitchen easier and more enjoyable.

Chef Patrick Recommends: Suggestions from Chef Patrick Bremser, our resident sommelier for the type of wine or beer to use in a recipe.

♥ Indicates a recipe that is 95 percent or more raw, or can be easily adapted to raw. See page xx for information on raw foods.

🕐 This recipe or variation may take longer than 30 minutes if you count baking, refrigerating, or freezing time. Some recipes may take longer than 30 minutes until you are comfortable with the steps of the recipe. With practice you will find yourself preparing them at a much quicker pace.

Chef's Tips and Tricks

Keys to Success in a 30-Minute Kitchen:
Guidelines for the Efficient Chef

Preparing food is an art form; these tips will help you have great success in the kitchen and will enable you to enjoy yourself. If you're having a good time, this good juju will be imparted to the food and everyone will enjoy it!

- Read each recipe thoroughly. Look up words and ingredients you are unfamiliar with. Understand the process involved. Understand when multitasking is necessary rather than waiting for each step to be complete before moving on to the next step.
- Before beginning any preparation, create a clean work area. Gathering the ingredients in the recipe before you begin ensures that you have everything you need, know what you will be using as a substitute, and eliminates time spent searching through cabinets. Gather your measuring spoons and cups, tools, and appliances. Preparing food in a clean and organized space is always easier.
- Having the proper tools is essential to being able to whip food up quickly. It may increase your cooking time if you don't have tools such as a garlic press, zester, citrus juicer, or blender. Work up to a fully stocked kitchen.

continues

Chef's Tips and Tricks continued _____

- Although the recipes are designed to taste their best by following the exact measurements, eventually you will learn to discover acceptable approximations. At some point you will be able to look at two different cloves of garlic and know that one is about 1 teaspoon, and the other is about 1 tablespoon. In cases like these, don't worry too much about measuring everything with ultimate precision. With baking, however, measurements need to be precise since leavening is involved.
- Some herbs, such as parsley, cilantro, or fennel, don't need to be plucked from the thin part of their stems before mincing or chopping. Just keep them bundled together and chop into the whole bunch at once. The thin parts of the stems generally have the same flavor, and once minced, basically taste the same.
- Cut stacks of veggies rather than each individual piece. Don't separate celery stalks when you can cut into the whole bunch at once. The same goes for heads of lettuce and cabbage. Stack tomato, potato, or onion slices and cut them simultaneously.
- The easiest way to sift flour is with a fine-mesh strainer. For accuracy, always sift baking soda, baking powder, cocoa powder, and any spices that have lumps.
- You don't need to peel organic carrots, cucumbers, potatoes, zucchini, or beets unless specified; just wash them well. This is not only quicker, but also helps preserve the nutritional content of the food.
- Many of the recipes, particularly the soups, call for adding vegetable stock or water to a pan that already has vegetables cooking in it. You can save on cooking time by heating the stock or water in a separate pot while you get the other ingredients ready. This way, when you add the liquid to the vegetables, it will already be at the temperature of the rest of the ingredients and will avoid the cooling and reheating that occurs when a colder liquid is added.
- Most blenders have cup and fluid ounce measurements right on the pitcher, so no need to dirty more measuring cups.
- One of the most important tips to help cut down on preparation time is to set aside an hour or so on one of your least busy days for advance prepping. Having prepped ingredients on hand makes it easier to create meals on the go. Here you can cut vegetables and store them in a glass container in the fridge. You can also cook a squash, grain, or pot of beans. You can then use these foods in recipes over the next few days. Consider preparing a pot of rice in the morning and using it for the evening meal.

European Herbs and Spices

by contributing chef Jennifer Murray

Fresh herbs can fragrance a room, add flavor to a meal, and even make you feel like a master gardener (truth is, they grow like weeds). Did you know that they can also fortify your immune system, ease stress, and eliminate digestive issues, along with a host of other nutritional and medicinal qualities? Many of the culinary herbs we use today have their origins in the European continent, where they have been utilized over thousands of years in folk medicine and rituals; as gifts, garlands, and adornments; and to prevent contact with harmful substances. Many major medical research institutions across the country and the world have been conducting studies for decades on the significant medicinal properties of herbs that most of modern civilization has relegated to common culinary purposes.

In addition to sharing commonly known nutritional properties such as abundant vitamins, minerals, and chlorophyll, herbs have their own unique blends of healthful properties. All of these plants are carrying loads of valuable antioxidants that reduce damage to the body basically by gobbling up free radicals for you. This selfless service is invaluable in preventing everything from the common cold to aging.

Much of the healing potential of herbs lies in their volatile, or essential, oils, which are designed to fight off illnesses within their plant of origin. When the plant feels stressed by environmental, bacterial, or viral causes, it increases its supply of these oils as a lifesaving technique to combat the stress it is under. And they can do the same for you.

Luckily, getting good amounts of these herbs into your culinary repertoire has become quite simple in our modern world. Most grocery stores keep fresh herbs in stock in the produce department (or you can try asking them to do so). When blended, the herbs shrink down to very small quantities. You may find yourself interested in growing your own herb garden just to keep up with your newfound demand for these delicious and healing plants. Once you start looking, there is no end to what you can add fresh herbs to. Try sprinkling them over your salad, sandwiches, or toast; add them to dressings and sauces; blend your own pestos and green smoothies, chutneys, and beverages; and try adding them to grain dishes or curries after they are done cooking.

> Take notice: Although herbs are for the most part harmless, pregnant or nursing women should check with their doctor before incorporating large amounts of fresh herbs in their diet.

Note: Many herbs come in both fresh and dried varieties. Fresh herbs are essential to making delicious, flavorful foods. Dried herbs usually have an altered flavor that may not be considered a suitable substitute for the fresh variety, although they certainly have many appropriate uses of their own. When substituting dried herbs for fresh, cut the quantity to one-third (e.g., 1 tablespoon minced fresh parsley = 1 teaspoon dried).

Basil: Also referred to as "sweet basil," is used extensively in Italian and Mediterranean cooking and has been cultivated for over two thousand years. Aside from its most common uses in pestos and tomato sauce, basil has a rich folklore. In the Middle Ages, and in some countries today, it symbolizes love. Opal basil, with its dark purple leaves, can be used interchangeably with sweet basil. Although it has a hardier leaf, the flavor is very similar.

Bay leaf, a.k.a. laurel or bay laurel: Most commonly used in sauces, stews, and soup stock, and generally added as a whole leaf, then removed before the food is served. It adds a savory, deep undertone to the dish.

Bouquet garni: A pungent herbal bouquet tied with string and used in French cuisine when simmering foods. Most often contains thyme, parsley, and bay leaves, but may also include tarragon, basil, rosemary, and other herbs.

Chervil: A staple of French cuisine as part of the fines herbes blend. Used in light sauces and dressings. Has a fragrance like myrrh.

Chives: An onion-like herb with tall, green blades like scallions that are easiest to cut with kitchen scissors. Best raw or when added at the end of preparing a dish, chives go great with potatoes and for garnishing soups. One of the fines herbes of French cuisine. Also try with marjoram, rosemary, mint, and parsley.

Dill: A biblical herb, has very aromatic leaves that are used fresh or dried. Use sparingly when dried as it imparts a strong flavor. The seeds and flowers of the plant are also used. Common in European and North African cuisine. Try with cucumber, cabbage, and plant-based cream sauces.

Fennel: Indigenous to the Mediterranean shores, this highly aromatic plant is used as a vegetable (the bulb), an herb (the feathery stems), and a spice (the seeds). In all forms, fennel has a flavor and aroma similar to those of anise.

Fines herbes: Used extensively in French cuisine. Includes fresh parsley, chives, tarragon, and chervil; may also include marjoram.

Herbes de Provence: Another staple of French cuisine that typically contains dried thyme, rosemary, marjoram, basil, savory, and bay leaf. In modern cooking, herbes de Provence may also include lavender flowers and tarragon. Thyme usually imparts the dominant flavor of the blend.

Lavender: An unlikely member of the mint family, this herb is praised for its floral aroma and sweet, singular taste. Although usually used in baked goods, honeys, and other sweet foods, lavender is occasionally used in savory food spice blends such as herbes de Provence, and as a tea (or tisane). To use, either add dried flower buds directly or steep in hot water first, discard, and use the tea.

Lemon verbena: An herb with a strong, lemony flavor used by the Spanish and Portuguese and in the popular Louisa tea in Greece. Although it can be used in vegetable dishes, lemon verbena is most commonly an ingredient of herbal tea, which is where you are most likely to find it in a grocery store (inside the tea bags).

Marjoram: Has a slightly sweet, citrus flavor, very similar to oregano but milder. Used in Italian cuisine and in the French herbes de Provence mix. Marjoram is a lovely addition to soup stock.

Mint: A lovable fresh herb of dessert plate fame; can just as easily be incorporated in salads, curries, beverages, or cooling pestos or chutneys. Medicinally, mint is highly prized for its ability to soothe an aching tummy, usually as tea. Peppermint, as well as less common varieties such as chocolate mint, are generally preferred for culinary purposes over the more mentholated taste of spearmint.

Oregano: Has a strong flavor used widely in Mediterranean cuisines, particularly Italian. Oregano was the symbol of joy and happiness for the ancient Greeks and Romans, who used it ceremoniously in marriage rituals. Much of its lore is attributed to the beauty and aromatic fragrance of the mountains upon which it grows.

Parsley: Comes in two forms. Curly leaf has a more delicate flavor and is generally relegated to use as a garnish and breath freshener. Italian parsley (or flat-leaf parsley) is the most popular herb in the world. It has a stronger flavor than the curly variety and is preferred for culinary purposes. Try in salads, sprinkled over soups, or in pesto.

Rosemary: With such a strong, pungent flavor, usually used sparingly. Italians particularly like these fresh thin leaves (like pine needles) that can be minced or added along with the whole stem and removed at the end of the cooking process. The stem itself can also be used as a BBQ skewer for grilled veggies (with or without the needles still attached).

Saffron: The most expensive spice in the world, due to two factors: First, each saffron crocus contains only three of its colorful stigmas, and second, those stigmas must be harvested individually, by hand. Found in Spanish and other European cuisine, saffron adds a distinctive flavor and bright orange color.

Sage: Green, velvety leaves used fresh or made into a dried herb called rubbed sage. Although of European origin, sage is also used in stuffing, the quintessential American holiday food.

Savory: A strongly flavored herb with a peppery taste; comes in a summer and a winter variety, the latter being more suited to slow-cooked foods such as soups and stews. Thyme can be considered a reasonable substitution if savory is not available.

Tarragon: Comes in Spanish and French varieties. With a slightly sweet, aniselike flavor, tarragon is favored in French cuisine. Part of common blends such as fines herbes, herbes de Provence, and bouquet garni, tarragon is also used to flavor herbal white wine vinegar.

Thyme: A savory herb with small leaves that imparts a strong flavor to dishes. Used commonly in Greek and African cuisine, thyme makes a lovely addition to salad dressings, soups, and sauces. Thyme accompanies tarragon and oregano as part of bouquet garni and is also a major component of herbes de Provence. Lemon thyme is a variety, having a lighter, brighter, citrus flavor.

Spices Popular in Eastern European Cuisine

Allspice: Familiar in the West as a spice similar to cinnamon and used in baked goods and sweet treats, allspice berries were also traditionally used in stews and slow-cooked foods.

Caraway: With a strong, sharp, but slightly sweet flavor, used in breads, sauces, sauerkraut, and other pickled foods.

Celery seeds: Tiny seeds of the celery plant. These have a very strong celery flavor to them, so use sparingly or the intense flavor will be overpowering. We love to use celery seed for depth in soups, stocks, and sauces where meat stocks are generally used.

Cinnamon: A highly prized, sweet, pungent spice that has been used for ages in Eastern European cuisine in everything from beans and bread to cakes and beverages.

Cloves: A pungent spice with an extremely strong, intense taste. Cloves are generally used in sweets, with fruit, or in beverages.

Coriander: The seeds of the cilantro plant, with a much different, more floral, sweet flavor. In European cuisine, coriander seeds are generally found in sweet foods and fruit dishes.

Mace: Similar to nutmeg in flavor. Mace is the outer cover of the nutmeg seed. We like to use mace in baked goods as it imparts an unusual, distinct flavor noticed by all who eat it.

Mustard seeds: Available in black, brown, and yellow varieties with quite different flavors. Mustard seeds are most famously used as a condiment when mixed with salt and vinegar. The seeds can also be used in breads, sautés, and sauerkraut.

Nutmeg: A familiar sweet, warm spice used to flavor baked goods as well as beverages, stews, and sweet breads.

Paprika: This bright red powder is used to color as well as flavor dishes. Made from ground red peppers, paprika in the West is generally mild, as the Spanish kind is used. The Hungarian paprika peppers used in dishes such as goulash are spicier, darker, and more pungent. Be sure to experiment with the smoked varieties as well.

Pepper: The most popular spice in the world. Black pepper is pungent and spicy. White pepper is made from the core of the pepper berry and must be used sparingly, as it has a stronger flavor than black pepper. Red chile peppers are also frequently dried, ground, and used in flavoring savory foods.

Poppy seeds: Very small black seeds with a delicate though distinct flavor. Most commonly seen in breads (especially sprinkled on top) as well as in confections.

Sesame seeds: Small white seeds most commonly seen removed from their grayish-white hull, but are edible both ways. With a nutty flavor and high oil content, sesame can be ground into a butter (tahini), pressed into oil, or used whole either raw or toasted.

Chef's Tips and Tricks

Herb Water

Looking to spice up a glass of water? Add a few sprigs of fresh herbs such as rosemary, parsley, cilantro, basil, or thyme and allow to sit for up to 20 minutes. This will infuse a lovely flavor into the water, which will impart some of the herb's micronutrients as well as help you drink more of the life-giving liquid.

Wild Mushrooms

by contributing chef Colin Patterson

Once you go wild you never go back. . . .

Wild, foraged mushrooms are amazing not just because they are a culinary delight, but because they are crucial to healthy soil and are the largest biological entities on the planet. One forager referred to them as "nature's Internet," the essential wiring of the Gaian consciousness. As a chef, I can tell you from firsthand knowledge that wild foods have a different quality you can feel and taste; the ancient biodiversity creates a depth that cultivated ingredients rarely have.

Here are nine heavy hitters that I use frequently in the Northwest, which are usually available when in season across the country. Please be aware, however, that most wild mushrooms are not edible. Consult with an expert if you have any questions on the type of mushroom you are harvesting.

Morel

There are three types:

Natural black morels (available early May to late June) have a thick flesh and grow in undisturbed lands. **Coninca** or **burn morels** (available late May to early July) have a thinner flesh and grow where a fire has happened from the previous year. **Blonde gray morels** (available July to mid September) have a firm, drier flesh and are gray in color.

These mushrooms all have a honeycomb-like structure that must be cooked thoroughly to be consumed. The bigger they get, the more likely they are to attract worms, so sometimes they must be dunked in warm water and cut in half to thoroughly clean them.

Morels make delicious sauces. Their rich flavor and pocket shape makes them perfect for anything thick, such as mushroom gravy. If you want to make a regular salad extraordinary, smoke them and then roast with olive oil and salt until they're a little crispy. You will have a flavor explosion.

Porcini or King Bolete

The two types of porcini are **Spring King bolete** (mid May to early July) and **Fall King bolete** (September to mid October).

These truly are the king of mushrooms. Superrich elegant flavor, amazing texture, and culinary diversity make the porcini my personal favorite. They are great raw or cooked, grilled, sautéed, roasted, fresh or frozen; they are equally wonderful pureed in sauces, and when dried, they make the best stock. In fact, they have such a beautiful flavor, there's no need to overpower it with lots of seasoning or covering them with sauces. Simply sauté the mushroom with a little salt and call it good.

Chanterelle

There are three major types of chanterelles: **summer chanterelle**, with a bright orange flesh (July to early September); **golden chanterelle**, the most prevalent and with a light yellow color (August to early December); and **white chanterelle**, with white flesh (August to October).

These are the most abundant of the wild mushrooms, with a delicate flavor and dense texture. Their consistency varies depending on size and moisture content; it's a good idea to cut them thinly and cook them for a while to help break down their tough structure. For this reason, chanterelles are excellent in sauces and mixed in with other dishes that have longer cooking times.

Lobster

This is a thick porous mushroom that gets its name from its red/orange color and funky shape that resembles the shell of a lobster (available September to mid-November).

Lobster mushrooms, with their hint of flavor of the sea, are a fun culinary ingredient because they easily take on flavor, and so are good marinated or added to stews or curries. Saffron makes a perfect match due to the similar color of the two ingredients and because the lobster mushrooms will greatly absorb the flavor of the exotic spice (see page xxx).

Matsutake or Pine

This wonderful mushroom has a white, dense flesh with a distinct cinnamon flavor and aroma (available September to November). Matsutake is the most prized mushroom in Japan; it has an intense flavor and is wonderful for brothy soups. Its intoxicating aroma makes it a great candidate to infuse into anything hot (which you'd then want to serve immediately to get the full taste experience). One of my favorite ways to eat it is by making a broth of leeks, matsutake, kombu, and tamari and serve it with soba noodles, fresh *shiso*, and lemon juice. . . . *Bon appétit* or *douzo meshiagare*! Soul food, Japanese style.

Oyster

These wonderful fungi have a delicate texture and cook quickly, which makes them great for lighter dishes. I like to marinate them in a little fresh lemon juice and mirin (a rice wine).

Shiitake

Shiitakes have a wonderful rich flavor and immune-boosting properties that have made them a favorite in Japanese cooking. The stems are quite woody, so I generally remove them before cooking (note that the stems are great for stock). Try marinating shiitakes in tamari and ginger, then grilling them . . . yum!

Portobello

While not a wild mushroom per se, portobellos are a typical favorite in the veggie world because of their dense texture. Great sautéed and grilled, they are the perfect substitute for porcini. If you want to elevate the texture, peel the skin off the top of the cap and scoop out the gills with a spoon before using.

Truffle

Truffles are fungi, like mushrooms, but grow underground and associate with tree roots. Truffles are all about aroma, so are best infused into things and served hot. If you have the opportunity to work with these expensive little beauties, it is best to shave them as thinly as possible, either at the end to finish a dish or in a sauce cooked slow and gentle. For most of us, truffle oil is a great alternative and works well in popcorn, soups, salad dressings, and at the end to finish a dish.

Vegan Wine and Beer Pairing

by contributing chef Patrick Bremser

Pairing both amazing feasts and simple meals with a beverage of choice can be a daunting task. We have all experienced a sensational pairing or two with our meals and a few that should have not crossed our palate. And because of those one or two excruciatingly distasteful swashes, we often pass the pairing baton to those who say they know more than we. Alas, the secrets these beverages hold in their masterful pairing are simpler than you may realize! They just take a little understanding.

Pairing wines and beers with vegan fare takes a little special awareness and focus. To really understand the components of a good match on your palate, you need to first look at the components of your cuisine. For a dish to be mouthwatering, it is balanced in its tastes and flavors. According to the different culinary traditions of the world, these flavors and tastes are classified as salty, sour, bitter, sweet, astringent, savory, and pungent. These are also the same taste qualifiers for beers and wines. These tastes dance on the palate, affecting the way you mentally and physically perceive your meal.

Depending on the season and healthful needs of your body, your palate may crave specific tastes and flavors. It is good to remember that the event of pairing wonderful beverages with your delectable cuisine is a dance that is different in each new bite. Give yourself a little flexibility when playing with new combinations of foods and beverages. Everyone has a different palate and preferences. If the food makes the beverage dance across your palate, and the beverage makes the food dance across it, you have got it!

A couple key factors have helped me very quickly and easily gauge whether a beverage is in the running to be paired with a particular dish. One test you can perform in the store when selecting a beverage involves regionality: when eating what they eat, drink what they drink. This requires a little understanding about what locale your beverage, dish, and ingredients are from. If you are making a classically Italian dish, you will have much more success with an Italian wine than with a British ale. Drink a Chianti with your tomato-based lasagna—the Tuscans have been enjoying that combination for centuries! Drink your crisp ale with some tempeh and vegetables off the grill. Get to know the region your dish is from and the beverages those folks enjoy. You will hardly go wrong listening to the history of regional pairings.

As you look into the different regions, especially Europe, you can also begin to see another key factor that contributes to your successful pairing adventure. Many ingredients are shared over latitudinal lines or areas with similar climate conditions. For example, tomatoes can be found in the cuisines of many of the Mediterranean countries. As Turkey, Greece, Italy, France, and Spain all use similar ingredients, where are the taste and flavor differences?

Here you have to look more deeply into your dish: What are the main ingredients building the key flavors? What are the flavor points that stand out above the others? Is it sour? Salty? Sweet? And how is that flavor best balanced so that all the tastes shine?

This is a good general guide:

Sweet foods, such as desserts or sweet flavors within a dish, are best complemented with beverages that are equally as sweet or sweeter than the dish.

A predominant sour flavor in your dish is best complemented with beverages of equal tartness or with dry wines.

Salty flavors in your dish work best with contrasting flavors of acidic, sweet, and bubbly beverages. Bitter and astringent flavors within a dish are wonderfully contrasted with beverages that are slightly acidic, such as dry white wines, thus bringing out their natural sweetness.

When looking at the main differences between vegan and nonvegan food and beverage pairing, you are left with only one small difference: fat quantity. Nonvegan wine pairing leans heavily on the play of fats from animal products and its experience of richness on the palate. In vegan fare, most of your fats are from single oils and nuts. They function the same as the fats in animal products, just with different flavor nuances. Classically, wine and cheese are said to be the easiest pairing because the fat from the dairy coats the taste buds, actually leaving the palate unable to distinguish the specific tastes of the wine. Fats in general play wonderfully on the palate as the balancing counterpart for the taste element of acidity. A perfectly balanced vinaigrette is extraordinary, as it highlights the flavors in the salad instead of overpowering the palate with its acidity.

Throughout the culinary traditions of Europe, foods and specific beverages have been enjoyed together for centuries. The geographical and cultural differences have helped play foundry roles in this culinary dance. When we add the essential tastes of salty, sour, sweet, bitter, astringent, and savory to the map of the European subcontinent, we get a diverse view of culinary cosmology, including beverages. Each little nook in the Bordeaux region of France has its own varietal of wine and specific fruits, vegetables, and herbs that grow best in that area. Weather also plays a giant role in the history of these culinary traditions. Let's look at a couple of these popular regions:

Italy: Italians quite possibly could be the most passionate people in the world about their food and wine. I think only the French would challenge that perspective! Over the twenty main regions of Italy, countless varietals of grapes have been cultivated for wine making. Italy spans a breadth of geography from frozen alpine peaks of the north to the scorching island of Sicily in the south. On an Italian wine label, the grape varietal and the region is always noted, making wine pairing easier. With a little research on the origin of your dish, you are sure to pick a good pairing.

France: The French are the originators of modern cuisine. They take food and beverage pairing quite seriously. Each of France's twelve major grape-growing regions have their specific varietals. For instance, in Bordeaux, the only permitted varietals to be grown are the Cabernet Sauvignon, Cabernet Franc, Merlot, Petit Verdot, Malbec, and Carménère. Alas, in France, the labels on their wines do not include varietals, only the regions. Knowing the regions and what varietals are specific to them is your first step in French wine pairing. From there, the combinations are endless!

Greece: Greeks have the longest noted history of wine deeply embedded in their culture, dating back over six thousand years. It is the home of *Vitis vinifera*, the ancestor of all other grape varietals. Greek mythology tells stories of Dionysus, the god of wine and harvest. In the ten main growing regions across Greece, a *culinista* will find some of the most underappreciated wines in the world. Wine in Greece is a food affair, as it is in Italy. Both reds and whites tend to fall on the dry side of the spectrum, making them great wines to be enjoyed with foods, as their light acidity brings out the natural sweetness of the dish. Pair according to the predominant flavors in your dish.

Germany: Germans have a long history with both wine and beer. In the 1400s, the German Beer Purity Law declared beer could only be made with water, hops, and barley. It was repealed in 1988 to include wheat, yeast, and cane sugar. German wine history dates back over a millennium earlier! The geography and cooler northern weather of Germany forced the development of more frost tolerant varietals, something the varietals of Greece and Italy do not need. One of the most common German varietals is the Riesling. Because of its versatility, Riesling wines cover a broad spectrum from dry to sweet characteristics, making them some of the most food-friendly grapes available. The beers of Germany are just as varied as the wines in France. As a general rule, lighter beers work with the lighter foods and the darker beers work with the heavier foods. The most common German beer is the Hefeweizen, and it is best enjoyed with lighter, more acidic foods. Watch the sweetness arise across your palate!

United Kingdom and Ireland: Wine grapes have been brought to the British Isles by many dignitaries and heads of state for centuries. Alas, because of the region's mostly northern geography, the grapes just have not survived as well as they have among its southern cousins. Barley and wheat, on the other hand, are staples within the culture of the islands. As with the German beers, the variations on the lager, porter, stout, brown ale, and bitter are as many as there are brewers!

Spain and Portugal: The Iberian Peninsula has a long history with viniculture, dating back over five thousand years. The arid landscape and extreme temperature variations make growing conditions tough for just about anything. These conditions shine through in the wines, making them generally dry, acidic, and in some grapes such as the Garnacha, almost dusty. This creates wonderful food wines. The wines of Spain and Portugal tend to open the flavors of a dish like sunshine on blossoms. All labels include the grape varietal.

Fortified wines such as port and sherry are specific wines that have gone through either a complete or a partial fermentation process that has been stopped by the addition of brandy or another grape-based spirit. In the case of port, the partial fermentation leaves a residual sugar content that is determined by the individual producers. As for pairing food with a fortified wine, the sweetness and alcohol content play significant roles. The heat of the high alcohol content is only matched with a higher fat content in the food. Classically, these fortified wines were not served with food; rather, they were enjoyed as digestifs before or after a meal. Follow the basic taste rules to try pairing them with other dishes. Only your palate knows best!

Eastern Europe: Over the mountainous edges of Eastern Europe, we can find little nooks and crannies of microclimates that produce extraordinary wines and beers. Most of the cuisine native to the chilly and rough terrain of Romania, Hungary, Poland, Bulgaria, and the Czech Republic are simple foods that warm the body to the core. These wines and beers have been hidden to us until recently, when commerce began spreading westward. Enjoy a Hungarian Tokaji with a thick, creamy dessert!

Over the course of your pairing adventures, the most important part to remember is that you are the best gauge for what tastes great to you. Open yourself to playing and trying out different beverages with your dishes. Take the leap when you are shopping. There are endless options that are reasonably cost efficient and make extraordinary pairings.

Chef's Tips and Tricks

Vegan Wines and Beer

Many commercially available beers and wine are filtered with animal product ingredients such as isinglass (from fish bladder), gelatin, egg whites, or seashells. Most Guinness beer, for instance, does use isinglass in the refining process. The Guinness Extra Stout, made in North America, does not contain isinglass and is therefore suitable for vegans. Please check with the company to insure that your beverage is vegan. You can also visit www.Barnivore.com, a website with a comprehensive vegan beer and wine guide.

PART ONE

ITALY

One can have no smaller or
greater mastery than mastery of oneself.
—LEONARDO DA VINCI

What can you say about the country that put the *eat* in *Eat, Pray, Love*? The imprint of so much history is always present in Italy as modern skyscrapers share space with ancient Roman ruins. The cuisine of Italy is one of the most well exported in the world and you can find an Italian restaurant in pretty much every corner of the globe.

Italy also has a rich vegetarian tradition that continues to this day. In fact, most vegan travelers will find Italy to be the most accommodating country to visit in Europe. Perhaps that's why this is the largest section of the *Taste of Europe*. (It was actually tempting to fill the entire book with Italian recipes, there were so many to choose from!) Italy is also birthplace of one of the most famous vegetarians, Leonardo da Vinci, who was one of the main driving forces of the Italian Renaissance.

Italy's documentation of its love of food traces itself back to the fourth century BC. Since then there have been many cookbooks that place an emphasis on vegetables. In the early 1600s, Giangiacomo Castelvetro wrote *A Brief Account of All Vegetables, Herbs, and Fruit*, a compendium of Italian veggies and fruits with suggestions on how to prepare them. He also emphasized vegetables as the main portion of the meal, instead of a small side dish. To say he was ahead of his time is an understatement!

1

In the late 1700s, Vincenzo Corrado wrote *The Courteous Cook*, which placed a strong emphasis on vegetarian food. Clearly influenced by Pythagoras, he considered a plant-based diet to be more natural to humans.

As with most of the European countries, Italy's cooking is influenced by its neighbors. Northern Italy has German influences, while the southern and western portions often nod to French and Mediterranean cuisines. In eastern Italy, you'll find food with Austrian, Hungarian, Croatian, and Slovenian flavors.

The Italian pantry is brimming with home-style ingredients. Farm-fresh vegetables are used to create sauces that are passed down from generations. Expect to find spinach, potatoes, tomatoes, peas, bell peppers, broccoli, corn, onions, squash, mushrooms, cabbage, carrots, beets, artichokes, garlic, eggplant, pumpkin, spring onions, scallions, asparagus, fennel, zucchini, radicchio, endive, arugula, pepperoncini, cauliflower, capers, and an abundance of chile peppers.

Popular herbs and spices include basil, thyme, oregano, rosemary, parsley, mint, myrtle, anise, nutmeg, clove, black pepper, cinnamon, and saffron. As far as condiments go, balsamic vinegar is a biggie. Fruits include grapes, olives, lemons, oranges, melon, watermelon, and raisins. Common legumes include lentils, cannellini beans, white beans, fava beans, and chickpeas. For nuts, there are pine nuts and almonds. Grains include wheat, rice, and buckwheat. For beverages, there is a multitude of wines, and of course espresso, espresso, and more espresso.

Your Italian vegan culinary tour includes a sampling of recipes from many regions throughout the country. Be sure to have your espresso smoothie on hand to power you through the adventure. You can start your feast with Bruschetta or Spinach Polenta. Enjoy classic soups such as Fire-Roasted Minestrone or Tuscan White Bean Soup. You will find animal-free versions of traditional dishes, including Tempeh Neatballs and Spaghetti, Tofu Scaloppine, Tofu Cacciatore, and the iconic eggplant parmesan. You can impress your guests with your gnocchi or raw ravioli and serve with either of the two pesto recipes included.

It goes without saying that Italy is heaven on earth for pasta lovers (there are even establishments called *spaghetterie*, where they specialize in the famous pasta). So as would be fitting for any Italian section, there is a selection of several pasta dishes including Fettuccine Alfredo, Orzo with Roasted Zucchini, and Angel Hair with Roasted Garlic and Arugula, to name a few. Vegan desserts are on the forefront of the revolution as it is so simple to create dairy- and egg-free versions of traditional favorites. Here you will find three types of gelato, Baked Walnut Fig Crumble, and a vegan tiramisu, which will put the *buono* in your *buono appetito*!

When in Rome . . . The Italian Feast

Meals are serious business in Italy. The siesta is built into the daily fabric of life in Italy as a time to rest after a big long meal with friends and family. Three or four courses are usually served, sometimes more, each with its own protocol. Holiday meals can last to three to four hours. Here is a sample schedule for a full-on Italian Feast. Please remember not to have your *contorno* before your *secondo*.

Apertivo—get your juices flowing with an aperitif

Antipasto—a "before the meal" hot or cold appetizer

Primo—first course, usually a pasta, risotto, gnocchi, or soup

Secondo—main dish

Contorno—side dish, such as salad or cooked vegetables

Formaggio e Frutta—the first dessert, of cheese and fruit

Dolce—the sweet, cakes or cookies

Caffè—coffee or espresso

Digestivo—after-dinner liqueurs

After all of this . . . it's siesta time, for sure!

Bruschetta

Once the fare of medieval Italian peasants, and now served at the poshest of dinner parties, bruschetta is roasted bread that has been rubbed with olive oil, salt, and pepper and is served with various toppings. Take your pick from any or all of these enticing selections and see the variations for even more suggestions. Serve as a starter for any occasion or as a light lunch with Fire-Roasted Minestrone (page 9), Creamy Florentine Soup (page 11), or Tuscan White Bean Soup (page 12).

SERVES 6 TO 8

1 baguette

About 3 tablespoons olive oil

Sea salt

Freshly ground black pepper

Crushed red pepper flakes

About 2 tablespoons Italian Spice Mix (page 51; optional)

HEIRLOOM TOMATO SALAD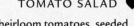

2 heirloom tomatoes, seeded and chopped into ½-inch chunks (2 cups)

1 to 2 teaspoons minced fresh garlic

2 tablespoons chiffonaded basil

2 teaspoons olive oil (optional)

1 teaspoon balsamic vinegar

1 teaspoon freshly squeezed lemon juice

¼ teaspoon minced hot chile pepper or crushed red pepper flakes, or to taste

¼ teaspoon sea salt

A pinch of freshly ground black pepper

1. Preheat the oven to 375°F. Slice the baguette into ½-inch slices. Drizzle with oil, and sprinkle with salt, pepper, and crushed red pepper flakes to taste, and Italian Spice Mix, if using. Bake for 10 minutes, or until crisp.

2. Meanwhile, prepare your toppings. Combine all the heirloom tomato salad ingredients in a bowl and mix well. Combine all the tapenade ingredients in another bowl and mix well.

3. Combine all of the green olive puree ingredients in a blender or food processor and blend until smooth. Transfer to a small bowl.

4. To serve, place the bruschetta on a platter with small bowls of the toppings. Or you can top the bruschetta with the different toppings. It's your call!

TAPENADE

½ cup finely minced kalamata olives

1 to 2 teaspoons minced fresh garlic

¼ teaspoon minced and seeded hot chile pepper

1 tablespoon capers

½ teaspoon minced fresh thyme or marjoram

½ teaspoon freshly squeezed lemon juice

1 tablespoon olive oil (optional)

1 teaspoon chiffonaded basil

1 teaspoon finely minced fresh flat-leaf parsley

GREEN OLIVE PUREE

1½ cups green olives

2 tablespoons olive oil

2 to 3 garlic cloves

⅛ teaspoon freshly ground black pepper

2 teaspoons freshly squeezed lemon juice

A pinch of crushed red pepper flakes

Variations

- Other toppings may include the shiitake topping from the Linguini with Clam-Free Sauce (see page 23), Pesto Magnifico (page 31), Cashew Cream (see page 90), Caponata (page 7), or White Bean Dip (page 6).
- Add 1 tablespoon of the Italian Spice Mix (page 51) to the tapenade.

Chef's Tips and Tricks

The heirloom tomato salad is a perfect example of a simple dish where the quality of ingredients crucial to success can make or break the meal. Go for a high-quality olive oil, aged balsamic vinegar, and a nice Celtic sea salt or smoked salt (see page xxii) to take it to the highest heights.

White Bean Dip

Here we have the hummus of Italy, made with white beans instead of chickpeas. You can be sure that this dip delivers with all of the gusto of its Middle Eastern counterpart, with its symphony of herbs and a hint of garlic. Create a superb start to any Italian feast and serve with fresh cut veggies or crackers, or as a topping for Bruschetta (page 4). Or you can go rogue and serve warm with Buono Appetito Pesto Risotto (page 30) and Broccoli Rabe with Garlic and Red Pepper (page 19).

SERVES 4 TO 8

2 (15-ounce) cans cannellini beans, drained and rinsed well, or 3½ cups cooked (see page 257)

¼ cup olive oil

1 garlic clove, pressed or minced

2½ tablespoons freshly squeezed lemon juice

½ teaspoon sea salt

⅛ teaspoon freshly ground black pepper

¼ teaspoon crushed red pepper flakes, or ½ teaspoon seeded and diced hot chile pepper

1 tablespoon chiffonaded basil

2 teaspoons finely chopped fresh flat-leaf parsley

½ teaspoon finely chopped fresh oregano

½ teaspoon finely chopped fresh sage

½ teaspoon finely chopped fresh thyme

¼ teaspoon finely chopped fresh rosemary

1. Place the beans, olive oil, garlic, lemon juice, salt, pepper, and crushed red pepper flakes in a food processor and process until smooth.

2. Transfer to a bowl with the remaining ingredients and mix well. Allow to sit for at least 5 minutes before serving.

Variations

- Add ¼ cup of diced sun-dried tomatoes and/or ¼ cup of diced kalamata olives along with the herbs.

- To serve warm as a side dish, before placing the beans in the food processor, place them in a pot over medium-high heat and cook for 3 minutes, stirring frequently and adding small amounts of water or vegetable stock to prevent sticking. Transfer to the food processor and follow the recipe as above.

Caponata 🕐

This eggplant-based dish traces its origins to Sicily, the largest island in the Mediterranean. There are numerous regional variations of this recipe, one of which even includes octopus. This version is fortunately octopus-free. Be sure to rinse the eggplant after sweating to wash off the extra salt. Serve as an appetizer on Bruschetta (page 4) or as a side dish with Angel Hair with Roasted Garlic and Arugula (page 21) or Linguini with Clam-Free Sauce (page 23).

SERVES 4 TO 6

1 pound eggplant, cut into ½-inch cubes (5 cups)

Sea salt for sweating eggplant

2 tablespoons olive oil

1 yellow onion, sliced thinly (1½ cups)

¾ cup thinly sliced celery

4 to 5 garlic cloves, pressed or minced

¼ cup sliced fennel

3 tomatoes, seeded and chopped into ½-inch chunks (3 cups)

2 tablespoons balsamic or red wine vinegar

3 tablespoons capers

¼ cup chiffonaded fresh basil

2 tablespoons finely chopped fresh flat-leaf parsley

2 teaspoons organic sugar (optional)

1¼ teaspoons sea salt, or to taste

½ teaspoon freshly ground black pepper

¼ to ½ teaspoon crushed red pepper flakes

¼ cup pine nuts, toasted (see page 249)

1. Arrange the eggplant cubes in a single layer on a baking sheet or casserole dish and sprinkle liberally with salt. Allow to sit for at least 5 minutes and up to 30 minutes if you have the time, before rinsing with water and draining well. (See box.)

2. Place the oil in a large sauté pan over medium-high heat. Add the onion, celery, garlic, and fennel, and cook for 3 minutes, stirring frequently.

3. Add the tomatoes, eggplant, and the remaining ingredients, except the pine nuts, and cook for 20 minutes, stirring frequently and adding small amounts of water if necessary to prevent sticking.

4. Garnish with the pine nuts before serving.

continues

Caponata *continued*

Variations

- Replace the tomatoes with two 14.5-ounce cans of fire-roasted tomatoes, drained.
- Add 2 tablespoons of Italian Spice Mix (page 51) along with the onion.
- Replace the pine nuts with toasted walnuts (see page 249) or slivered almonds.

Chef's Tips and Tricks

Sweating the Eggplant

This appetizing culinary term refers to a technique that is said to help tenderize the eggplant and remove some of its natural bitterness. Simply sprinkle a liberal coating of salt on top of slices of eggplant and allow them to sit in a glass dish or on a plate for up to 30 minutes. Water beads will form on the surface. Rinse well before using.

Depending upon the eggplant, this may not be necessary. The thinner Japanese eggplants generally do not need this step.

Fire-Roasted Minestrone

The poster child of Italian cuisine, minestrone is the quintessential one-pot soup of Italy. Typically tomato based, with lots of veggies and pasta, this version uses fire-roasted tomatoes for a unique flare. You will need to be pretty quick on the chopping to fit this into 30 minutes; begin chopping the vegetables while the stock heats. If you don't have all the herbs fresh, don't fret. You can replace them with dried herbs, use 2 tablespoons of the Italian Spice Mix (page 51), or simply use whichever ones you do have on hand. Enjoy an epic soup and salad by serving with Radicchio and Endive with Shaved Fennel and Italian Vinaigrette (page 13).

SERVES 6 TO 8

2 tablespoons olive oil

1 yellow onion, chopped (1¼ cups)

½ cup chopped fennel bulb (optional)

3 large garlic cloves, pressed or minced

1 tablespoon finely chopped fresh oregano

1 tablespoon finely chopped fresh marjoram

1 tablespoon finely chopped fresh sage

1 teaspoon minced fresh rosemary

½ teaspoon dried thyme

1 cup thinly sliced celery

2 (14.5-ounce) cans fire-roasted tomatoes, undrained

2 bay leaves

4 to 5 cups heated vegetable stock (page 253) or water, depending on desired consistency

1 cup potato that has been chopped small

1 cup thinly sliced carrot

1 cup chopped green beans or zucchini

1 (15-ounce) can chickpeas, drained and rinsed, or 1¾ cups cooked (see page 257)

continues

1. Place the olive oil in a large stockpot over medium-high heat. Add the onion, fennel, garlic, oregano, marjoram, sage, rosemary, thyme, and celery, and cook for 2 minutes, stirring frequently. Add the tomatoes, bay leaves, and vegetable stock and stir well.

2. Add the potato, carrot, and green beans. Cook for 10 minutes, stirring occasionally

3. Add the beans and pasta and cook for 8 minutes, or until just soft, stirring occasionally. Add the remaining ingredients, remove the bay leaves, and stir well.

continues

9

Fire-Roasted Minestrone *continued*

⅓ cup rice pasta, such as elbow,
   penne, or fusilli

2 tablespoons chiffonaded fresh
   basil

2 tablespoons finely chopped fresh
   flat-leaf parsley

1½ teaspoons sea salt

½ teaspoon freshly ground black
   pepper

1 tablespoon balsamic vinegar

½ teaspoon crushed red pepper
   flakes

3 tablespoons nutritional yeast
   (optional)

Variations

- There are as many ways to make mine-strone as there are soccer fans in Rome . . . and there are a lot of soccer fans in Rome!
- Replace the chickpeas with cannellini, kidney, or your favorite beans.
- Replace the fire-roasted tomatoes with finely chopped fresh tomatoes and use 5 cups of stock instead of 4 cups.
- Replace the carrot, potato, and green beans with any of your favorite vegetables, such as mushrooms, parsnip, broccoli, cauliflower, or cabbage.
- Top each serving with a simple mushroom sauté. Heat 2 teaspoons of olive oil in a small sauté pan over medium-high heat. Add ½ cup of diced yellow onion and two minced garlic cloves and cook for 2 minutes, stirring frequently. Add 1 cup of thinly sliced mushrooms, such as cremini or shiitake, and cook for 5 minutes, stirring frequently.

Chef's Tips and Tricks

No fresh herbs handy? Not a problem!

You can replace any of the fresh herbs with their dried equivalent. Use 1 teaspoon of dried for every tablespoon of fresh. If using the dried spices, add them along with the thyme at the beginning of the cooking process, instead of at the end.

Creamy Florentine Soup

This is a dish to show the connoisseurs of Italian cuisine how we do creamy soups vegan style. The secret lies in blending the soup along with the flavorful pine nuts, also called pignoli, which have been enjoyed by humans in Europe since Paleolithic times, long before *David* was a twinkle in Michelangelo's eye. Serve with Buono Appetito Pesto Risotto (page 30) and a mixed green salad with Italian Vinaigrette (page 14)

SERVES 6

2 tablespoons olive oil

1 yellow onion, chopped small (1½ cups)

1¼ cups thinly sliced celery

4 garlic cloves, pressed or minced

½ cup chopped fennel bulb

5 cups heated vegetable stock (see page 253) or water

16 ounces frozen spinach, thawed, or 4 cups tightly packed fresh, rinsed and drained well

¾ cup pine nuts

¼ cup finely chopped fresh basil

¼ cup nutritional yeast

3 tablespoons finely chopped fresh flat-leaf parsley

2 teaspoons minced fresh rosemary

1 teaspoon sea salt

½ teaspoon dried thyme

¼ teaspoon freshly ground black pepper

¼ teaspoon crushed red pepper flakes

2 cups fresh or frozen corn

1. Place the oil in a large pot over medium-high heat. Add the onion, celery, garlic, and fennel and cook for 5 minutes, stirring frequently.
2. Add the vegetable stock and spinach, lower the heat to medium, and cook for 10 minutes, stirring occasionally. Add the remaining ingredients, except the corn, and cook for 5 minutes.
3. Transfer small batches of the soup to a large blender and carefully blend well. Return to the pot, add the corn, and cook for 5 minutes before serving.

Variations
- For a deeper and richer flavor, toast the pine nuts (see page 249).
- Replace the pine nuts with macadamia nuts or cashews.
- Replace the pine nuts with 1 cup of unsweetened soy or coconut milk.

Tuscan White Bean Soup

Oh, the rolling countryside of Tuscany! The farmlands, the vineyards, the ancient cities poised on hills! Tuscan cuisine, with its focus on fresh garden vegetables, is one of the most healthful in Italy. This heart-healthy soup captures some of the romance of this special region. Enjoy with Rice Pilaf with Fennel and Saffron (page 78) and Horta (page 181).

SERVES 6

2 tablespoons olive oil

1 yellow onion, chopped small
    (1½ cups)

1 cup thinly sliced celery

4 garlic cloves, pressed or minced

2 teaspoons dried oregano, or
    1 tablespoon fresh, chopped finely

1 teaspoon fresh thyme, or
    ½ teaspoon dried

2 carrots, cut into ¾-inch slices
    (1½ cups)

10 cremini mushrooms, quartered
    (1¼ cups)

1 large zucchini, cut into ¾-inch slices
    (1½ cups)

2 tomatoes, seeded and chopped into
    ½-inch chunks (2 cups)

5 cups heated vegetable stock
    (see page 253) or water

1 (15-ounce) can cannellini beans,
    drained and rinsed, or 1¾ cups
    cooked (see page 257)

3 tablespoons chiffonaded fresh basil

1 tablespoon finely chopped fresh
    sage (optional)

1½ teaspoons sea salt, or to taste

¼ teaspoon freshly ground black
    pepper

¼ teaspoon crushed red pepper
    flakes

1 tablespoon wheat-free tamari or
    other soy sauce (optional)

1. Place the oil in a large pot over medium-high heat. Add the onion, celery, and garlic and cook for 3 minutes, stirring frequently. Add the oregano, thyme, carrots, mushrooms, zucchini, and tomatoes, and cook for 5 minutes, stirring occasionally and adding small amounts of stock or water if necessary to prevent sticking. Add the vegetable stock and cannellini beans and cook for 10 minutes, stirring occasionally.

2. Place 3½ cups of the soup in a blender and blend until creamy. Be sure to use mostly vegetables and beans, with enough liquid to blend. Return to the pot and stir well.

3. Add the remaining ingredients and cook for 5 minutes, stirring occasionally. For a true Tuscan experience, serve with fresh warm bread.

Variations
- Add 1 cup of corn and/or 2 cups of thinly sliced spinach after blending.
- Replace the tomatoes with a 14.5-ounce can of fire-roasted tomatoes.
- Replace the zucchini and carrots with broccoli and cauliflower.

Radicchio and Endive with
Shaved Fennel and Italian Vinaigrette ♥

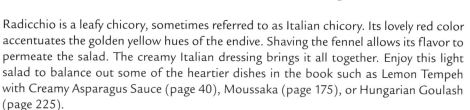

Radicchio is a leafy chicory, sometimes referred to as Italian chicory. Its lovely red color accentuates the golden yellow hues of the endive. Shaving the fennel allows its flavor to permeate the salad. The creamy Italian dressing brings it all together. Enjoy this light salad to balance out some of the heartier dishes in the book such as Lemon Tempeh with Creamy Asparagus Sauce (page 40), Moussaka (page 175), or Hungarian Goulash (page 225).

SERVES 4

1 large Belgian endive, bottom removed

½ pound radicchio, rinsed, drained, and chopped small

1 avocado, peeled, pitted, and cut into small cubes

1 fennel bulb, shaved (¼ to ½ cup; see box)

10 to 12 cherry tomatoes, halved

¼ cup pine nuts, toasted (see page 249)

continues

1. Divide the endive into four portions and arrange on the outer edge of each salad plate. Place the chopped radicchio in the center of the plate and top with avocado, cherry tomatoes, and shaved fennel.
2. Place the dressing ingredients in a blender and blend until creamy.
3. Drizzle the dressing over the salad and garnish with pine nuts before serving.

continues

Chef's Tips and Tricks

To shave the fennel, quarter the bulb and remove the core. Using a vegetable peeler, simply shave off pieces of the fennel from the outer portion until you have the desired amount.

Radicchio and Endive with Shaved Fennel and Italian Vinaigrette *continued*

ITALIAN VINAIGRETTE

Makes 1 cup dressing

½ cup olive oil

2 tablespoons red wine vinegar

1 tablespoon freshly squeezed
   lemon juice

¼ cup water

2 teaspoons agave or coconut
   nectar (see page 262) or pure
   maple syrup

1 tablespoon minced fresh basil

1 tablespoon minced fresh flat-leaf
   parsley

½ teaspoon dried oregano

¼ teaspoon dried thyme

¼ teaspoon sea salt, or to taste

⅛ teaspoon freshly ground
   black pepper

1 small garlic clove

1 teaspoon wheat-free tamari or
   other soy sauce (optional)

⅛ teaspoon crushed red pepper
   flakes

Variations

- Replace the radicchio and endive with arugula, spinach, or mixed salad greens.
- Get elaborate with your salads and add your favorite chopped veggies, such as celery, zucchini, bell peppers, cabbage, artichoke hearts, or olives.
- Replace the pine nuts with toasted walnuts, pecans, sunflower seeds, or pumpkin seeds (see page 249).

Gnocchi

Pleasing palates since Roman times, gnocchi are the dumpling of Italy. These vegan gnocchi are made from just two ingredients—potatoes and flour. Top with drizzled olive oil, salt and pepper, vegan butter, Roasted Tomato and Garlic Sauce (page 35), or Toasted Walnut Pesto (page 22).

MAKES 1 DOZEN GNOCCHI

2 russet potatoes, cut into ½-inch cubes (3 cups)

½ to 1 cup flour (try white spelt)

Variations

- Replace the potatoes with sweet potatoes.
- For squash gnocchi, add 1 cup of cooked squash to the potato.

1. Bring a large pot of water to a boil. Place a steamer basket in a separate medium-size pot filled with 1 inch of water. Place over high heat and bring to a simmer. Place the potatoes in the steamer basket and cook covered until just soft, about 15 minutes.

2. Transfer the potatoes to a large bowl and mash well. Make sure there are no big chunks. Add the flour and mix well. Transfer to a flour-dusted cutting board or other clean, dry surface. Roll into a log about 1 inch in diameter. Cut off twelve pieces to create your gnocchi. If you have more time, you can press the pieces over a gnocchi board, or roll over a large fork to create the traditional grooves. The grooves are what help the gnocchi absorb the sauce.

3. Place the gnocchi in the pot of boiling water and cook for 5 minutes. Carefully remove with a slotted spoon.

Chef's Tips and Tricks

Gnocchi aren't difficult to make, but here are two tips that will help you:

The key to the perfect gnocchi lies in the consistency of the potato. Too moist and they will not hold their form when placed in the water. If you have more time, bake your potatoes instead of steaming them.

True gnocchi aficionados will want to purchase a gnocchi board to create the perfect markings that are on the traditional dish. A ricer is also a worthy investment, to grate the potatoes in the perfect fashion. See Appendix D for information on where to purchase.

Raw Ravioli with Sun-Dried Tomato Sauce ♥

I'm not sure the pope would give his blessing to this out-of-the-box version of the Italian staple. In fact, they might not even let you into the Vatican with this in your lunchbox. Using thinly sliced zucchini, beets, turnips, or watermelon radish as the "pasta," and a raw cheeselike filling of cashews and pine nuts, a magical dish is born. Serve as an appetizer before you feast on Tempeh Neatballs (page 34), Eggplant Parmesan Stacks (page 38), or Tofu Cacciatore (page 32).

MAKES 18 RAVIOLI WITH FILLING AND SAUCE LEFT OVER

2 medium-size zucchini

Chiffonaded fresh basil or finely chopped fresh flat-leaf parsley

Diced black or kalamata olives

NOTTA RICOTTA FILLING

¾ cups raw cashews or macadamia nuts

¼ cup pine nuts

3 tablespoons water

1 tablespoon freshly squeezed lemon juice

1 tablespoon olive oil (optional)

1 tablespoon nutritional yeast

1 tablespoon finely chopped fresh basil

1 tablespoon finely chopped fresh flat-leaf parsley

¼ teaspoon sea salt, or to taste

⅛ teaspoon freshly ground black pepper

¼ teaspoon crushed red pepper flakes

2 teaspoons Italian Spice mix (page 51; optional)

1. Soak the cashews and pine nuts in about 2 cups of water for 10 minutes. Soak the sun-dried tomatoes in ¼ cup of hot water for 5 minutes.
2. Meanwhile, slice each zucchini into eighteen ¹⁄₁₆-inch-thick rounds, using either a mandoline or a sharp knife. Set aside.
3. Prepare the sauce by placing all its the ingredients, including the sun-dried tomatoes and soaking water, in a blender and blending until creamy.
4. Prepare the Notta Ricotta: Drain and rinse the soaked nuts well. Transfer to a food processor or strong blender with the remaining Notta Ricotta ingredients and process until smooth. If you are using a blender, you many need to add additional water.
5. Create the ravioli by placing a small amount of Notta Ricotta in the center of a zucchini slice. Top with an additional zucchini slice and seal by pinching the two slices together along the edges. Repeat with the remaining zucchini. To serve, drizzle with sauce and garnish with basil and diced olives.

continues

continued

SUN-DRIED TOMATO SAUCE

Makes 1 cup sauce

3 sun-dried tomatoes soaked in
¼ cup hot water

1 tomato, seeded and chopped into
½-inch chunks (1 cup)

2 teaspoons olive oil

2 teaspoons freshly squeezed
lemon juice

1 teaspoon balsamic vinegar

⅛ teaspoon crushed red pepper
flakes

¼ teaspoon sea salt

A pinch of freshly ground black
pepper

Variations

- You can bump up the flavor of the Notta Ricotta by adding 1 teaspoon each of finely chopped fresh rosemary, oregano, thyme, and/or sage.
- Use the Spanikopita filling (page 173) instead of the Notta Ricotta.
- Top with Pesto Magnifico (page 31).
- Add ½ teaspoon of Tapenade (page 5) to each ravioli.

Chef's Tips and Tricks

For added flavor, and to keep this dish raw, you can place the zucchini slices on a dehydrator tray, lightly drizzle with olive oil, and a pinch of sea salt, and freshly ground black pepper. Dehydrate at 115°F for 30 minutes, or until the zucchini are just soft before filling with the Notta Ricotta.

Alternatively, if you do not tell the raw police, you can place the zucchini slices on a baking sheet, drizzle lightly with olive oil, and season with a pinch of sea salt (try smoked salt) and ground black pepper, and bake at 350°F for 10 minutes before filling with Notta Ricotta.

Spinach Polenta

Prepare to experience soul food, Italian style! The grits of Italy, polenta is a creamy and delectable cornmeal that can be used in countless ways. This version uses fresh spinach and herbs to create an Italian flair. Use as few or as many of the herbs that the recipe calls for as you wish. Be careful when stirring the polenta; it has a tendency to bubble up and splatter, so you may wish to use an oven mitt. Serve on its own or top with Roasted Tomato and Garlic Sauce (page 35) or Toasted Walnut Pesto (page 22).

SERVES 4 TO 6

2 tablespoons vegan butter or coconut or olive oil

¼ cup sliced green onion

2 garlic cloves, pressed or minced

½ teaspoon minced fresh rosemary

½ teaspoon dried oregano

½ teaspoon dried thyme

3 cups soy, rice, or almond milk

1½ teaspoons sea salt, or to taste

¾ cup uncooked polenta

¾ cup finely chopped, tightly packed spinach, rinsed and drained well

3 tablespoons finely chopped fresh basil

3 tablespoons pine nuts (optionally toasted; see page 249)

2 teaspoons balsamic vinegar

¼ teaspoon freshly ground black pepper, or to taste

¼ teaspoon crushed red pepper flakes

¼ cup grated vegan mozzarella-style cheese (optional)

1. Oil an 8-inch casserole dish well.
2. Place the vegan butter in a pot over medium-high heat. Add the onion, garlic, rosemary, oregano, and thyme, and cook for 5 minutes, stirring frequently. Add the soy milk and salt, and bring to a boil. Slowly whisk in the polenta. Carefully whisk for 5 minutes, stirring constantly.
3. Lower the heat to low, add the remaining ingredients except the vegan cheese, if using, and cook for 5 minutes, carefully stirring occasionally. Add the vegan cheese, if using, and cook for 3 minutes, stirring occasionally.
4. Transfer to the prepared casserole dish. You can serve the polenta as is, or allow to cool. You can speed this up in a freezer or refrigerator. Once cooled sufficiently, about 10 minutes in the freezer or 20 minutes in the refrigerator, break out your cookie cutters to make creative designs, or cut into triangles, squares, circles, or rectangles.
5. Once cooled and cut, the polenta can then be grilled or sautéed.

Variations

- Add ¼ cup of soaked, drained, and thinly sliced sun-dried tomatoes and/or ¼ cup of thinly sliced kalamata olives.
- Replace the dried herbs with 1½ tablespoons of Italian Spice Mix (page 51).
- Replace the pine nuts with chopped pecans or walnuts.

Broccoli Rabe with Garlic and Red Pepper

Also known as rapini or broccoletti, broccoli rabe is a popular food in southern Italy and other Mediterranean countries and was brought to the United States in the 1920s by Italian farmers. The red of the pepper creates a striking contrast to the deep green of the rabe. Serve as part of a bountiful Italian feast along with Tofu Scaloppine (page 37) and Linguine with Clam-Free Sauce (page 23).

SERVES 4 TO 6

1 pound broccoli rabe, its very bottom trimmed

2 to 3 tablespoons olive oil

6 to 8 garlic cloves, minced or pressed

1 large red bell pepper, seeded and julienned

½ cup thinly sliced fennel bulb (optional)

¼ teaspoon sea salt, or to taste

⅛ teaspoon freshly ground black pepper, or to taste

¼ teaspoon crushed red pepper flakes

1 tablespoon balsamic vinegar

1 tablespoon freshly squeezed lemon juice

2 tablespoons vegan butter (optional)

Black and white sesame seeds

1. Place a steamer basket in a medium-size pot filled with 1 inch of water. Place over medium-high heat and bring to a simmer. Place the broccoli rabe in the steamer basket and cook covered for 5 minutes. Remove from the heat.

2. Meanwhile, pour the olive oil into a large sauté pan over medium-high heat. Add the garlic, red bell pepper, and fennel, if using, and cook for 5 minutes, stirring frequently.

3. Add the broccoli rabe and gently stir well. Cook for a few more minutes, or until the broccoli rabe is just tender, gently stirring occasionally. Add the remaining ingredients and gently stir well.

4. To serve, lay the broccoli rabe on a plate and top with the pepper mixture. Garnish with sesame seeds before serving.

Variations

- Add 1 cup of thinly sliced shiitake mushrooms along with the red pepper.
- Replace the broccoli rabe with broccoli, cauliflower, asparagus, zucchini, or kale.
- Roast the red pepper and add at the final step. To roast peppers, preheat an oven or toaster oven to 400°. Rinse the peppers and place on a well-oiled baking sheet. Place in the oven and cook until the skin of the peppers is charred and bubbly, approximately 35 minutes. A quicker method is to roast on the broil setting. Flip the pepper periodically to ensure even cooking. Remove from the oven and place in a covered bowl for 10 minutes. Peel off the skin and remove the seeds. It's important for all the skin to be bubbly, to make peeling them easier. They may also be roasted over an open flame. In all instances, you are looking for a charred skin.
- Replace the sesame seeds with toasted pine nuts, chopped cashews, or chopped macadamia nuts (see page 249).

Orzo with Roasted Zucchini

Orzo is a barley-shaped pasta that is also referred to as *risoni*, the Italian word for "barley." It has a light, delicate flavor that complements the almost buttery flavor of the roasted zucchini in this simple and colorful dish. This light dish can be served with Tofu Scaloppine (page 37), Tuscan White Bean Soup (page 12), or Tempeh Neatballs (page 34).

SERVES 6

2 cups uncooked orzo (5 cups cooked)

1½ teaspoons sea salt, or to taste

2 zucchini, chopped into ½-inch chunks (2½ cups)

1¾ cups sliced cremini or shiitake mushrooms

1 cup seeded and diced red bell pepper

4 garlic cloves, pressed or minced

¼ cup thinly sliced fennel bulb (optional)

3 tablespoons olive oil

¼ cup sliced kalamata olives

2 tablespoons finely chopped fresh flat-leaf parsley

2 tablespoons chiffonaded fresh basil

2 tablespoons balsamic vinegar

2 teaspoons wheat-free tamari or other soy sauce (optional)

2 teaspoons dried oregano

1 teaspoon dried thyme

½ teaspoon freshly ground black pepper

¼ teaspoon crushed red pepper

¼ cup sliced green onion (optional)

1. Preheat the oven to 375°F. Bring 8 cups of water to a boil in a medium-size pot over high heat. Add the orzo and ¾ teaspoon of the sea salt, lower the heat to medium, and cook until the orzo is just soft, about 12 minutes. Drain well and place in a large bowl.

2. Meanwhile, place the zucchini, mushrooms, red bell pepper, garlic, and fennel, if using, plus the remaining ¾ teaspoon of sea salt and 2 tablespoons of olive oil in a large casserole dish and gently stir well. Bake for 15 minutes, stirring occasionally to ensure even cooking.

3. Remove from the oven and transfer the zucchini mixture to the bowl with the orzo and remaining ingredients. Stir well before serving. Can be served warm or cold.

Variations

- To make this gluten-free, replace the orzo with gluten-free pasta of your choosing, such as penne or rigatoni.
- Add ½ cup of chopped artichoke hearts and/or ½ cup of chopped hearts of palm in step 3.
- Add 1 cup of corn along with the zucchini.
- Add ½ cup of shredded vegan mozzarella cheese.
- Add 1 tablespoon of minced fresh sage and 1 teaspoon of minced fresh rosemary.

Angel Hair with Roasted Garlic and Arugula

Calling this dish a garlic lover's pasta would be an understatement. "Garlic worshipper's pasta" would be more accurate. Feel free to adjust the quantity to suit your fancy. The heat of the pasta gently cooks the arugula when it is tossed in, so no need to cook it separately. Enjoy as part of a Fusion meal with Escalavida Grilled Vegetables (page 108) and Provençal Vegetable Salad (page 67).

SERVES 4

10 ounces angel hair pasta

1 teaspoon sea salt, or to taste

¾ cup sun-dried tomatoes

14 to 18 garlic cloves, chopped roughly

¾ cup diced fennel bulb (optional)

⅛ teaspoon freshly ground black pepper

¼ teaspoon crushed red pepper flakes

2 tablespoons olive oil

3 cups baby arugula, rinsed, drained well, and chopped roughly

½ cup grated mozzarella-style vegan cheese (optional)

½ cup chiffonaded fresh basil

¼ cup thinly sliced kalamata olives

2 tablespoons nutritional yeast

2 cloves minced fresh garlic (optional)

1. Preheat the oven to 375°F. Bring water to a boil and cook the pasta according to the package instructions, adding ¾ teaspoon of salt to the boiling water. Drain well and place in a large bowl. You can add some vegan butter or olive oil to the pasta to prevent sticking.
2. Soak the sun-dried tomatoes in 1 cup of hot water for 15 minutes, or until soft, drain well, and slice into thin strips.
3. Meanwhile, place the garlic, the fennel, if using, ¼ teaspoon of salt, and the pepper, crushed red pepper flakes, and olive oil in a small casserole dish and mix well. Bake for 12 minutes, or until the garlic is just soft and golden brown.
4. Place in a small bowl with the sliced sun-dried tomatoes and the remaining ingredients and mix well. Add to the pasta and gently toss well. Add additional salt and pepper to taste before serving.

Variations
- Replace the angel hair pasta with rigatoni, penne, linguine, or fettuccine.
- Add 1 cup of seeded and diced red bell pepper along with the garlic.
- Add ½ cup of sliced artichoke hearts and/or 1 tablespoon of capers in step 4.
- Garnish with ¼ cup of pine nuts or walnuts, raw or toasted (see page 249).
- Add 2 tablespoons of finely chopped fresh flat-leaf parsley, 1 teaspoon of fresh oregano, and ½ teaspoon minced fresh rosemary in step 4.

Penne Pasta with Toasted Walnut Pesto and Cherry Tomatoes

Pesto is one of my favorite dishes to prepare. Originating in Genoa in northern Italy, its fame has spread far and wide. Pesto was traditionally made in a mortar and pestle with basil, pine nuts, garlic, and olive oil. This version uses toasted walnuts. Serve the pesto as a spread on wraps, a sauce on pasta, or a dip for vegetables. You name it.

SERVES 4 TO 6

12 ounces penne pasta

1 teaspoon sea salt (optional)

1 pint cherry tomatoes, halved

Black and white sesame seeds

TOASTED WALNUT PESTO

Makes about 1 cup pesto

4 ounces fresh basil (2 cups)

¾ cup walnuts, toasted
(see page 249)

½ cup olive oil

1 tablespoon freshly squeezed
lemon juice

1 large garlic clove

¼ teaspoon sea salt, or to taste

¼ teaspoon freshly ground black
pepper, or to taste

2 tablespoons nutritional yeast
(optional)

1. Bring 8 cups of water to a boil over medium-high heat. Meanwhile, combine the pesto ingredients in a food processor or strong blender and process until smooth. If you use a blender, you may need to add more oil, depending upon its strength.
2. Cook the pasta according to the package instructions, optionally adding the salt to the boiling water. Drain well and place in a large bowl.
3. Add the pesto to pasta and gently stir well. Top with cherry tomatoes and a pinch of sesame seeds before serving.

Variations
- So many variations are possible and the combination of fresh herbs, garlic, and lemon uplifts all that it comes in contact with!
- Add 1 teaspoon of minced jalapeño and 2 tablespoons of diced red onion to the pesto before processing.
- Replace the walnuts with pine nuts, cashews, pecans, pistachios, or macadamia nuts, raw or toasted.
- Replace the basil with fresh cilantro.
- Replace the basil with 1¼ cups of fresh flat-leaf parsley, ½ cup of basil, and 1 tablespoon each of fresh sage, oregano, and rosemary.
- Add more or less olive oil depending upon how you wish to use the pesto. Add less for a thicker spread; add more if you wish to use for more pasta or a sauce on steamed vegetables. If you add more olive oil, adjust the salt and pepper to taste.

Linguine with Clam-Free Sauce

This was one of my most beloved dishes as a child. It was a revelatory moment when I discovered the possibility of a vegan version. The shiitake mushrooms serve as clams and *arame* seaweed imparts the flavor of the sea. Once the pasta is cooked and drained, you can optionally toss it with a little olive oil to prevent sticking. Serve with Broccoli Rabe with Garlic and Red Pepper (page 19) and Radicchio and Endive with Shaved Fennel and Italian Vinaigrette (page 13).

SERVES 4

14 ounces linguine

1¾ teaspoons sea salt, or to taste

2 tablespoons *arame*

½ cup hot water

2 tablespoons olive oil

6 garlic cloves, pressed or minced

3 cups fresh shiitake mushrooms, cut into ½-inch cubes

½ cup dry white wine (see box)

1½ tablespoons freshly squeezed lemon juice

1½ cups unsweetened soy, rice, or macadamia milk (see page 259)

3 tablespoons nutritional yeast

2 tablespoons vegan butter (optional)

¼ teaspoon freshly ground black pepper

¼ teaspoon crushed red pepper flakes

3 tablespoons finely chopped fresh flat-leaf parsley

Pine nuts

1. Cook the pasta according to the package instructions, optionally adding 1 teaspoon of sea salt to the boiling water. Drain well.
2. Meanwhile, soak the *arame* in hot water. Pour the olive oil into a large sauté pan over medium-high heat. Add the garlic and cook for 2 minutes, stirring constantly. Add the shiitakes, white wine, and lemon juice, and cook for 5 minutes, stirring frequently and adding small amounts of water or vegetable stock if necessary to prevent sticking.
3. Add the soy milk, nutritional yeast, the vegan butter, if using, and the remaining ¾ teaspoon of salt, pepper, crushed red pepper flakes, and the *arame* and its soak water, and cook for 5 minutes, stirring occasionally.
4. To serve, divide the pasta among individual plates, top with the shiitakes and sauce, and garnish with the parsley and pine nuts.

Variations

- For an even creamier sauce, blend ¼ cup of cashews with the soy milk before adding.
- Add ½ cup of grated vegan mozzarella-style cheese along with the soy milk.
- You can replace the shiitakes with reconstituted dried shiitakes or other mushrooms such as cremini or oyster.
- Replace the linguine with your pasta of choice, such as spaghetti or angel hair.

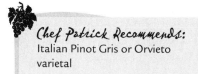

Chef Patrick Recommends:
Italian Pinot Gris or Orvieto varietal

Pasta Primavera with Alder-Smoked Tofu

Pasta primavera was created by Italian immigrants in North America and with ancient origins dating back to the mid-1970s. *Primavera* means "spring" and is a celebration of herbs and colorful vegetables of the season. Please don't be intimidated by the inclusion of smoked tofu. I wanted to provide a recipe where you can experiment with your new smoker. Alder is a popular wood used for smoking in European cuisine. If you have yet to experience the joys of using a smoker, be not dismayed; you can always marinate the tofu with a bit of liquid smoke. Serve with Caponata (page 7) or Raw Ravioli with Sun-Dried Tomato Sauce (page 16).

SERVES 6 TO 8

SMOKED TOFU

14 ounces extra-firm tofu

2 tablespoons wheat-free tamari or other soy sauce

1½ tablespoons smoke chips (such as alder, hickory, or cherry)

PASTA

16 ounces pasta, such as tricolored fusilli or bowties, penne, or tagliatelle

½ teaspoon sea salt (optional)

Nutritional yeast (optional)

VEGETABLE MEDLEY

3 cups small broccoli florets

1 cup thinly sliced carrot

1 red bell pepper, seeded and diced (1 cup)

½ cup thinly sliced green onion

2 tablespoons chiffonaded basil

1 tablespoon finely chopped fresh flat-leaf parsley

1. Place a steamer basket in a large pot filled with ½ inch of water. Place over high heat and bring to a simmer. Slice the tofu into three cutlets and slice each cutlet in half. Place in the steamer basket and cook covered for 5 minutes. Transfer the tofu to a shallow dish and drizzle with the soy sauce, making sure to coat each cutlet. Allow to sit in the soy sauce for 5 minutes.

2. Place the wood chips in the smoker according to the manufacturer's instruction. Add the tofu and smoke over medium heat for 15 minutes.

3. Meanwhile, bring a large pot of water to a boil over high heat. Add the pasta, and the salt, if using, and cook according to the package instructions. Drain well.

4. Use the same steamer basket used for the tofu to steam the broccoli and carrot until just tender, about 5 minutes. Place in a large bowl with the bell pepper, green onion, basil, and parsley, and mix well.

5. Prepare the primavera dressing by combining all of its ingredients in a small bowl and whisking well.

6. Chop the tofu into ½-inch cubes and add to the vegetables along with the pasta and dressing. Gently toss before serving. Top with nutritional yeast, if using, and enjoy warm or cold.

continues

continued

PRIMAVERA DRESSING

¼ cup olive oil

2 tablespoons balsamic vinegar

1 tablespoon freshly squeezed lemon juice

1 teaspoon pure maple syrup

1 teaspoon vegan Dijon or stone-ground mustard

2 teaspoons wheat-free tamari or other soy sauce

1 teaspoon hot sauce (optional), store bought or homemade (see page 243)

½ teaspoon sea salt

¼ teaspoon freshly ground black pepper

¼ teaspoon crushed red pepper flakes

Variations

- If you do not have a smoker, you can roast the tofu. Preheat the oven to 375°F. Place 1½ tablespoons of wheat-free tamari or other soy sauce, 1 tablespoon of olive oil, and ½ teaspoon of liquid smoke in a casserole dish and mix well. Add the tofu and bake for 20 minutes. Remove from the oven, slice into cubes, and follow the above instructions.
- If you broke out the smoker, try smoking other vegetables such as onion, mushrooms, and/or cherry tomatoes, and add to the pasta.
- Add 1 tablespoon of chiffonaded fresh sage along with the herbs.
- Add 1 tablespoon of Italian Spice Mix (page 51) along with the herbs.
- Add ½ cup of thinly sliced fennel bulb along with the vegetables.
- Replace the alder chips with others such as hickory, cherry, or mesquite.

Fettuccine Alfredo

Talk about successful self-promotion! Alfredo di Lelio, a Roman chef in the early 1900s, named a cheese and butter pasta dish after himself and the rest is history. What would Alfredo say about the vegan revolution that has swept the culinary world and veganized his prized creation? I'll let you be the judge after tasting this rich and satisfying dish. Serve as part of a Mediterranean feast with Escalivada Grilled Vegetables (page 108) and Provençal Vegetable Salad (page 67).

SERVES 4 TO 6

28 ounces fettuccine pasta, such as brown rice

¾ teaspoon salt (optional)

ALFREDO SAUCE

3 cups unsweetened soy milk

½ cup cashews (¾ cup if not using the vegan cheese)

¼ cup nutritional yeast

1 large garlic clove

2 teaspoons wheat-free tamari or other soy sauce

1 teaspoon sea salt, or to taste

¼ teaspoon freshly ground black pepper

¼ teaspoon crushed red pepper flakes

2 tablespoons freshly squeezed lemon juice

1¼ cups grated mozzarella-style vegan cheese (optional, but your friends will thank you if you add it)

3 tablespoons chiffonaded fresh basil

2 tablespoons finely chopped fresh flat-leaf parsley

½ cup finely chopped green onion

1. Bring a large pot of water to a boil on high heat. Add the pasta, and salt, if using, and cook uncovered according to package instructions. Drain well.

2. Meanwhile, prepare the sauce. Place the soy milk, cashews, nutritional yeast, garlic, tamari, salt, pepper, and crushed red pepper flakes in a blender and blend until creamy. Transfer to a pot and place over medium heat. Cook for 5 minutes, stirring frequently.

3. Lower the heat to low, add the lemon juice and the vegan cheese, if using, and cook for 5 minutes, stirring occasionally. Add the basil and parsley and mix well.

4. Combine the pasta and sauce in a large bowl and gently mix well. Top with the green onion before serving.

Variations
- Add 1 teaspoon of fresh oregano, and ½ teaspoon each of fresh thyme, minced fresh sage, and minced fresh rosemary.
- Add 1 tablespoon of Italian Spice Mix (page 51).

Manicotti

Oh the joy to create a vegan version of another one of my favorite childhood meals! Although mancotti is traditionally a cheese-filled pasta noodle smothered in tomato sauce, you will definitely not miss the dairy in this manicotti. Read through the instructions thoroughly before beginning this culinary adventure. You will need to move fast to get this done in 30 minutes, as there are a lot of moving pieces. You can also prepare the dish on one day and bake and serve it the next day. Serve with Radicchio and Endive with Shaved Fennel and Italian Vinaigrette (page 13) and Glazed Roasted Root Vegetables (page 133), and finish off with Strawberry Rose Granita (page 43).

SERVES 6 TO 8

8 ounces manicotti noodles (14)

½ teaspoon sea salt (optional)

3½ cups tomato sauce or homemade (see page 35)

¾ cup grated vegan mozzarella-style cheese

TOFU FILLING

2 teaspoons oil

1 small yellow onion, minced (1 cup)

3 garlic cloves, pressed or minced

14 ounces extra-firm tofu, crumbled

½ cup grated vegan mozzarella-style cheese (optional)

¼ cup nutritional yeast

3 tablespoons creamy tahini

3 tablespoons chiffonaded basil

2 tablespoons finely chopped fresh flat-leaf parsley

2 teaspoons wheat-free tamari or other soy sauce (optional)

1 teaspoon sea salt

¼ teaspoon freshly ground black pepper

½ teaspoon crushed red pepper

2 teaspoons fresh oregano

1 teaspoon dried thyme

1 tablespoon Italian Spice Mix (page 51) or Herbes de Provence (page 94) (optional)

1. Preheat the oven to 450°F and lightly oil a baking sheet. Bring a large pot of water to a boil on high heat. Add the pasta, and the salt, if using, and cook until al dente (slightly soft with a bit of firmness), about 10 minutes. Transfer to a colander and run under cold water until cool. Transfer the pasta to the prepared baking sheet.

2. Meanwhile, prepare the filling. Place a sauté pan over medium-high heat. Place the oil and onion in the pan and cook for 3 minutes, stirring constantly. Add the garlic and cook for 1 minute, stirring frequently. Add the remaining filling ingredients and mix well.

3. Spread ½ cup of the tomato sauce on the bottom of a 9 by 13-inch casserole dish. Using a spoon, fill each manicotti with about 2 rounded tablespoons of filling and place in the casserole dish. Repeat with the remaining manicotti. Top with the remaining sauce and vegan cheese, and bake covered for 20 minutes.

Variations

- Add 1 cup rinsed and chopped spinach along with the onion.
- Use shells instead of manicotti.

Pesto Pizza

On my visit to Rome, the question wasn't, "What's for dinner?" It was, "What type of pizza do you want for dinner?" Traveling farther south to the bustling city of Naples, the birthplace of pizza as we know it, I finally experienced it—pizza nirvana. You would be amazed at the incredible variety of toppings, both savory and sweet, to delight your vegan palate. Here we have an aromatic pesto on top of this simple and quick-cooking crust. See the variations for suggestions to create a designer pizza extravaganza. Enjoy your creation as part of a light meal with Creamy Florentine Soup (page 11) and Radicchio and Endive with Shaved Fennel and Italian Vinaigrette (page 13).

MAKES 4 SMALL PIZZAS

CRUST

1¾ cups white spelt flour

¼ cup cornmeal

¼ cup oil

1 tablespoon ground flaxseeds mixed with 3 tablespoons water

¼ cup plus 2 tablespoons water

2 tablespoons minced fresh herbs, such as basil, flat-leaf parsley, oregano, and thyme

½ teaspoon sea salt

¼ teaspoon freshly ground black pepper

¼ teaspoon crushed red pepper flakes

Pesto Magnifico (page 31)

2 tomatoes, sliced thinly

Diced kalamata olives

1. Preheat the oven to 425°F. Oil a baking sheet or pizza stone well.
2. Prepare the crust: Place the flour and cornmeal in a large bowl and whisk well. Combine the remaining crust ingredients in a small bowl or measuring cup, mix well, and add to the bowl containing the flour mixture. Mix well and form into a ball. Place the dough on a cornmeal-dusted, clean, dry surface and roll into a thick log. Slice into four equal-size pieces.
3. Using a rolling pin or your hands, form individual pizzas about 6 inches in diameter. Place on the prepared baking sheet or pizza stone and bake for 15 minutes.
4. Meanwhile, prepare the pesto. To serve, spread the pesto on each pizza, top with tomatoes and olives, and enjoy!

continues

continued

Variations

- You can also place the pesto and toppings on the pizza before baking. This will create a softer crust.
- If you have more time, you can double the recipe to create a single 16-inch pizza.
- The sky is the limit with the amount of designer pizzas you can create. Here are but a few ideas:
  - Roasted Tomato and Garlic Sauce (page 35) and arugula.
  - Notta Ricotta (page 16) or Cashew Cream (page 90) with grilled portobello mushroom (page 252).
- Create ethnic pizzas:
  - French—serve with Tarragon Cream (page 76) and slices of Braised Tempeh with Herbes de Provence (page 80).
  - German—serve with tomato sauce topped with Beer-Braised Greens (page 189), sauerkraut, and slices of Baked Vegan Schnitzel (page 196) or Notwurst (page 197).
  - Spanish—serve with Romesco Sauce (page 114) and Escalivada Grilled Vegetables (page 108).
  - Hawaiian—add smoked tofu (see page 24) and grilled pineapple (see page 252) along with the pesto topping.

Buono Appetito Pesto Risotto

Where Bollywood meets the leaning tower of Pisa, our 30-minute risotto uses basmati rice instead of the traditional Arborio rice (see variation). The pesto addition to the dish is heavenly. I knew my vegan pesto had arrived when it received the seal of approval from Lucia, the non-English-speaking cook for the villa I visited outside of Rome. Cigarette dangling from her mouth, and still stirring her pasta sauce, she seemed surprised there was no cheese. You will be, too, especially with the addition of nutritional yeast, which adds the cheeselike flavor to the dish. Serve with Tofu Scaloppine (page 37) and Broccoli Rabe with Garlic and Red Pepper (page 19) for a glimpse of Dante's *paradiso*!

SERVES 4 TO 6

4½ cups vegetable stock (see page 253) or water

1 tablespoon olive oil

1 cup diced yellow onion

1 cup uncooked white basmati rice

¾ cup white wine (see box) or additional vegetable stock

½ cup unsweetened soy or rice milk

2 tablespoons nutritional yeast

2 tablespoons freshly squeezed lemon juice

¾ teaspoon sea salt, or to taste

⅛ teaspoon freshly ground black pepper

½ cup grated vegan mozzarella-style cheese (optional)

1. Place the vegetable stock in a small pot over high heat and cook for 2 minutes. Lower the heat to low. Meanwhile, place a large sauté pan over medium-high heat. Place the oil and onion in the sauté pan and cook for 5 minutes, stirring constantly. Add the rice to the onion mixture and stir well to coat with oil.

2. Add the wine, if using, and stir well. Add 1½ cups of the hot stock, lower the heat to medium, and stir well. Cover the pot. Stir every few minutes until the liquid is almost all absorbed. Add another cup of stock, stir well, and return the cover to the pot. Continue this process until all the stock is used and the rice is just soft and chewy. Add more stock if necessary. Add the remaining ingredients, including the soy milk, and stir well.

3. While you are cooking the rice, prepare the Pesto Magnifico by placing all of its ingredients in a food processor or blender and process until creamy. You may need to add more oil or water, if using a blender, to reach the desired creaminess. Add to the risotto and mix well before serving.

continues

continued

PESTO MAGNIFICO

Makes ¾ cup pesto

1 cup tightly packed fresh basil

¼ cup pine nuts

1 clove garlic

3 to 4 tablespoons olive oil

1 tablespoon freshly squeezed lemon juice

½ teaspoon sea salt

⅛ teaspoon freshly ground black pepper

2 teaspoons nutritional yeast

¼ teaspoon crushed red pepper flakes, or seeded and diced hot chile pepper

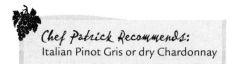

Chef Patrick Recommends:
Italian Pinot Gris or dry Chardonnay

Variations

- So many are possible.
- Replace the pesto with an equal amount of cooked and lightly salted squash or pumpkin, optionally adding vegan butter to taste.
- You can add the following with or without the pesto:
- Add ½ teaspoon of saffron threads (see page xxx) soaked in ¼ cup of hot water for 15 minutes before adding to the dish (use the threads and their soaking water).
- Add 1 cup of sliced mushrooms and 1 cup of rinsed and chopped spinach.
- Replace the onion with ½ cup of diced shallots and 2 minced garlic cloves.
- Add ½ cup of diced sun-dried tomato, ¼ cup of diced olives, 2 tablespoons of chiffonaded fresh basil, 1 tablespoon of finely chopped fresh flat-leaf parsley, 2 teaspoons of minced fresh oregano, and 1 teaspoon of fresh thyme.
- Of course, you can go traditional, if you have more time, by using Arborio rice and more stock.

Chef's Tips and Tricks

With origins in Venice and the surrounding area, the perfect risotto is definitely an art form. There are lots of variables involved. The amount of liquid ultimately used in the dish will depend on the heat of the stove, the amount of evaporation, how long the dish is covered, the temperature of the stock, and so on. For best results, keep the pan covered as much as possible and make sure the stock is kept hot. And when in doubt, stir, stir, and stir some more.

Tofu Cacciatore

Nothing says, "That's amore" like a good cacciatore. While *cacciatore* means "hunter" in Italian, the only hunting this dish requires is for veggies in your garden or produce section. It is traditionally made with tomato, mushrooms, and onions. If you have more time, try this with Roasted Tomato and Garlic Sauce (page 35). Serve with Spinach Leek Rice (page 169) and Horta (page 181).

SERVES 4 TO 6

TOFU MARINADE

2 tablespoons olive oil

1½ tablespoons wheat-free tamari or other soy sauce

14 ounces extra-firm or super-firm tofu

¼ cup plus 2 tablespoons Italian flour mix 1 (recipe follows) or bread crumbs

ITALIAN FLOUR MIX 1

¼ cup spelt, garbanzo, or rice flour

2 teaspoons dried parsley

¼ teaspoon garlic powder

¼ teaspoon onion powder

1 teaspoon dried basil

¼ teaspoon dried oregano

¼ teaspoon dried thyme

⅛ teaspoon sea salt

1. Preheat the oven to 400°F. Place the olive oil and soy sauce for the tofu marinade in a 9 by 13-inch casserole dish. Slice the tofu into ½-inch cubes, place in the marinade, and allow to sit for 5 minutes, flipping occasionally.
2. Prepare the Italian flour mix by combining all of its ingredients in a small bowl and stirring well. Alternatively, if using bread crumbs, place the bread crumbs in a small bowl. Dip each piece of tofu in the flour mix, coating both sides, and return it to the casserole dish. Bake for 15 minutes.
3. Meanwhile, prepare the cacciatore sauce by placing the oil in a large sauté pan over medium-high heat. Add the onion and garlic and cook for 3 minutes, stirring frequently. Add the pepper and mushrooms and cook for 3 minutes, stirring frequently.
4. Lower the heat to medium. Add the red wine, tomato sauce, and remaining ingredients and cook for 10 minutes, stirring occasionally. Add the tofu and gently stir well before serving.

continues

continued

CACCIATORE SAUCE

1 tablespoon olive oil

1 yellow onion, sliced thinly (1¼ cups)

3 garlic cloves, minced or pressed

1 red bell pepper, seeded and chopped (1 cup)

6 large cremini or button mushrooms, quartered

1 cup red wine (see box)

3 cups tomato sauce (see box)

1 tablespoon capers

1 tablespoon balsamic vinegar

½ teaspoon sea salt, or to taste

¼ teaspoon freshly ground black pepper

¼ teaspoon crushed red pepper flakes

Variations

- If you wish, you can sauté the tofu in oil instead of baking it once it is breaded. Simply heat a large sauté pan over medium-high heat. Pour in a liberal amount of oil and add the tofu pieces. Cook for 3 to 5 minutes before gently flipping. Cook for an additional 3 to 5 minutes. Add to the tomato sauce as in the above recipe.
- Experiment with different types of mushrooms, such as portobello, shiitake, or oyster.
- Add 1 cup of chopped carrot or parsnip along with the red pepper.
- Replace the tofu with tempeh and marinade for an additional 10 minutes.

Chef Patrick Recommends:
Italian, Chianti varietal

Chef's Tips and Tricks

Want to spice up a store-bought jar of tomato sauce? Try adding fresh Italian herbs. For a 16-ounce jar, try adding 2 tablespoons each of finely chopped basil and flat-leaf parsley, 2 teaspoons of oregano, and 1 teaspoon of thyme. You can also add 2 tablespoons of the Italian Spice Mix (page 51).

Tempeh Neatballs

One of the first dishes I learned to prepare as a child was meatballs and spaghetti. It is such a delight to be able to share this cow-friendly version. Tempeh replaces the meat and the oat flour holds it all together. Top with Roasted Tomato and Garlic Sauce (page 35) or your favorite pasta sauce. Serve with your pasta du jour or make your own tempeh ball hero sandwich.

SERVES 6 TO 8

2 tablespoons olive oil

½ cup finely diced yellow onion

3 garlic cloves, minced or pressed

16 ounces tempeh, diced finely

¼ cup oat flour

3 tablespoons nutritional yeast

1 tablespoon wheat-free tamari or other soy sauce

1 tablespoon balsamic vinegar

2 tablespoons minced fresh basil

2 tablespoons minced fresh flat-leaf parsley

2 teaspoons minced fresh rosemary

2 teaspoons dried oregano

1 teaspoon ground fennel (optional)

½ teaspoon sea salt

¼ teaspoon freshly ground black pepper

¼ teaspoon crushed red pepper flakes

Oil for sautéing

1 (12-ounce) jar pasta sauce or Roasted Tomato and Garlic Sauce (page 35)

1. Combine all the ingredients, except the oil for sautéing and the pasta sauce, in a large bowl and mix well. Form into ten equal-size balls (think golf ball size) and set aside.
2. Pour the oil into a large sauté pan over medium-high heat. Add the tempeh balls and cook until slightly crispy and browned, about 7 minutes, gently flipping to ensure all sides are cooked.
3. Lower the heat to simmer, add the tomato sauce, and cook for 5 minutes, gently stirring occasionally.

Variation

- You can also bake the tempeh balls. Preheat the oven to 375°F. Place the balls on a well-oiled baking sheet and bake for 10 minutes. Gently flip and bake for an additional 10 minutes. If you wish you can flip every 5 minutes, rolling the balls on a different side with each flip.

Roasted Tomato and Garlic Sauce

Tomato sauce is perhaps the most iconic symbol of Italian cuisine. Roasting the vegetables creates an added depth of flavor, compared to the traditional sauté and simmer method. Make a double batch and use for all your pasta sauce needs, including Tempeh Neatballs (page 34), Eggplant Parmesan Stacks (page 38), Tofu Cacciatore (page 32), Gnocchi (page 15), and more.

MAKES 6 CUPS SAUCE

2 tablespoons olive oil

½ cup red wine (see box)

8 medium-size tomatoes, seeded and chopped into ½-inch chunks (6 cups)

1 yellow onion, diced (2 cups)

6 to 8 large whole garlic cloves

½ cup chopped fennel bulb (optional)

2 teaspoons sea salt

½ teaspoon freshly ground black pepper

2 tablespoons tomato paste

3 tablespoons finely chopped fresh basil

3 tablespoons finely chopped fresh flat-leaf parsley

1 tablespoon roughly chopped fresh oregano

2 teaspoons fresh thyme

2 teaspoons minced fresh rosemary (optional)

2 teaspoons agave nectar or sweetener of choice (see page 262)

1½ tablespoons balsamic vinegar

1½ teaspoons minced fresh sage (optional)

¼ teaspoon crushed red pepper flakes

1. Preheat the oven to 450°F. Place the olive oil, wine, tomatoes, onion, garlic, fennel, if using, and 1 teaspoon sea salt and the black pepper in a large casserole dish and stir well. Roast in the oven for 15 minutes.

2. Place the contents of the casserole dish in a blender, blend until smooth, and transfer to a large pot over medium-high heat.

3. Add the remaining ingredients, including the remaining salt, and cook for 5 minutes, stirring frequently.

continues

Chef Patrick Recommends:
Italian, Chianti varietal

Roasted Tomato and Garlic Sauce *continued*

Variations

- Although fresh tomatoes are superior, it's okay to use canned tomatoes in a pinch. For this recipe, use 28 ounces of whole canned tomatoes. Drain well and set the juice aside before roasting. Add the juice to the blender, along with the rest of the ingredients.
- For a Bolognese sauce, add 14 ounces of crumbled extra-firm tofu or crumbled tempeh and mix well
- Use whichever of the dried and fresh herbs you have on hand. Remember that 1 teaspoon dried is roughly equal to 1 tablespoon fresh in most substitutions.
- Add 1 large zucchini, sliced thickly, along with the tomatoes.
- Add 1 tablespoon or more of Italian Spice Mix (page 51) if substituting for some of the fresh herbs.

Tofu Scaloppine

Scaloppine refers to breaded and sautéed cutlets. This recipe opts for an animal-friendly version that uses tofu and is topped with a tangy cream sauce with artichoke hearts and capers. Serve with Orzo with Roasted Zucchini (page 20) and Radicchio and Endive with Shaved Fennel and Italian Vinaigrette (page 13).

SERVES 4

TOFU MARINADE

2 tablespoons olive oil

2 tablespoons wheat-free tamari or other soy sauce

14 ounces extra-firm or super-firm tofu

ITALIAN FLOUR MIX 2

½ cup spelt or gluten-free flour (see note about gluten-free, page xx)

1 tablespoon minced fresh basil

1 teaspoon each dried parsley, oregano, and thyme, or 1 tablespoon Italian Spice Mix (page 51)

⅛ teaspoon sea salt

¼ teaspoon freshly ground black pepper

TOPPING

4 tablespoons vegan butter

2 tablespoons minced garlic

2 tablespoons freshly squeezed lemon juice

¼ cup chopped artichoke hearts

1 tablespoon capers

¼ teaspoon sea salt, or to taste

¼ teaspoon freshly ground black pepper, or to taste

2 tablespoons chopped fresh flat-leaf parsley

1½ cups unsweetened soy creamer, or 1 cup unsweetened soy or rice milk

1. Set the oven to BROIL. Place the olive oil and soy sauce in a 9 by 13-inch casserole dish and stir well. Slice the tofu lengthwise into three cutlets and slice each of these cutlets in half to yield six cutlets. Place the cutlets in the casserole dish and broil for 5 minutes, flipping after 2 minutes.

2. Combine Italian flour mixture 2 ingredients in a small bowl and mix well. Dip each cutlet into the breading mixture and return it to the casserole dish. Broil for 7 minutes. Flip the cutlets and broil for an additional 7 minutes. Place on a serving platter or individual plates.

3. Meanwhile, place the vegan butter in a large sauté pan over medium-high heat. Add the garlic and cook for 2 minutes, stirring frequently. Lower the heat to medium. Add the remaining ingredients, except the soy creamer and parsley, and cook for 5 minutes, stirring occasionally. Add the soy creamer and stir well. Set over low heat.

4. Top each cutlet with the contents of the sauté pan and garnish with parsley before serving.

Variations

- Replace the tofu with tempeh and marinade for an additional 10 minutes.
- Add ¼ cup of soaked, drained, and thinly sliced sun-dried tomatoes.
- Replace the parsley with fresh basil or 1 tablespoon of minced fresh dill.

Eggplant Parmesan Stacks

A southern Italian dish that has become almost synonymous with vegetarian cooking, Eggplant Parmesan is actually one of the first vegetarian dishes I learned how to prepare. If you have the time, use the Roasted Tomato and Garlic Sauce (page 35). This version creates decorative stacks that make for a classy presentation. Serve with Angel Hair with Roasted Garlic and Arugula (page 21) and mixed wild greens with Toasted Hazelnut Vinaigrette (page 188).

SERVES 4

2 tablespoons ground flaxseeds

½ cup water

1 tablespoon olive oil

¾ teaspoon sea salt

¼ teaspoon freshly ground black pepper

1 cup dried bread crumbs

1 large eggplant, cut into twelve ½-inch rounds

2 cups tomato sauce (see page 35)

1½ cups grated vegan mozzarella-style cheese

1. Preheat the oven to 425°F. Oil a baking sheet well. Place the flaxseeds, water, olive oil, salt, and pepper in a shallow dish and mix well. Place the bread crumbs in another shallow dish.

2. Dip each eggplant slice into the flaxseed mixture, making sure to coat both sides, then into the bread crumbs, also making sure to coat both sides. Place the slices on the prepared baking sheet.

3. To assemble your stacks, stack the ingredients on a clean cutting board in the following order: eggplant slice, 1 to 2 tablespoons of sauce, 1 tablespoon of grated cheese, eggplant slice, 1 to 2 tablespoons of sauce, 1 tablespoon of grated cheese, eggplant slice, 1 to 2 tablespoons of sauce, 1 tablespoon of grated cheese.

4. Transfer to a lightly oiled baking sheet. Bake until the eggplant is tender and cooked through, about 20 minutes, and serve hot.

continues

continued

Variations

- For a gluten-free version, use gluten-free bread crumbs.
- Spice up the bread crumbs with 2 tablespoons of minced fresh herbs, such as a combination of basil, flat-leaf parsley, and oregano.
- Add a zucchini layer to your stacks in addition to the eggplant by slicing a large zucchini into ½-inch rounds and following the same instructions given for the eggplant.
- Once the eggplant is breaded, sauté the slices in safflower oil for 10 minutes, flipping once or twice. Place on paper towel to drain the excess oil. Assemble as in step 3 and bake only until the cheese melts, about 5 minutes.
- Create a casserole by following the layering instructions in step 3 and placing the ingredients in an 8-inch casserole dish instead of creating stacks.

If You Have More Time

There is a great debate in the culinary world as to whether current varieties of eggplant need to sweat. If you are in the "sweat all eggplant" school of thought, sweat the slices for 10 to 20 minutes before using in the recipe (see page 8).

Lemon Tempeh with Creamy Asparagus Sauce

This is a hearty dish with a veritable symphony of flavor. If you have more time, allow the tempeh to sit in the white wine and fresh lemon juice marinade for up to 20 minutes. The asparagus sauce gets its creaminess from blended, toasted pine nuts. If you have more time, steam the tempeh for 5 minutes (see page 250) before using in the recipe. Serve with Orzo with Roasted Zucchini (page 20) and Beer-Braised Greens (page 189).

SERVES 4 TO 6

TEMPEH MARINADE

¼ cup freshly squeezed lemon juice

1 tablespoon olive oil

¼ cup white wine (see box)

¼ teaspoon sea salt

¼ teaspoon freshly ground black pepper

1 garlic clove, pressed or minced (optional)

16 ounces tempeh, sliced into eight ¼-inch-thick cutlets

1. Preheat the oven to 375°F. Place all of the marinade ingredients, except the tempeh, into a 9 by 13-inch casserole dish and mix well. Add the tempeh and allow to sit for 5 minutes, flipping once to ensure an even coating. Bake for 20 minutes.

2. Meanwhile, prepare the asparagus sauce: Pour the olive oil into a large sauté pan over medium-high heat. Add the onion and garlic and cook for 3 minutes, stirring frequently. Add the asparagus and white wine and cook for 3 minutes, stirring frequently. Add the vegetable stock and cook for 5 minutes, stirring frequently. Add the remaining ingredients, except the basil and parsley, and mix well.

3. Transfer the contents of the sauté pan to a strong blender and carefully blend until creamy. Return the mixture to the sauté pan. Add the basil and parsley and mix well.

4. To serve, place a liberal amount of sauce on each plate, add the tempeh cutlets, top with a small amount of sauce, and garnish each serving with a lemon wedge and few toasted pine nuts.

continues

continued

CREAMY ASPARAGUS SAUCE

1 tablespoon olive oil

¾ cup thinly sliced yellow onion

3 garlic cloves, pressed or minced

1 pound asparagus, ends removed,
    cut into ½-inch pieces (3¼ cups)

½ cup white wine (see box)

1 cup vegetable stock (see page 253)
    or water

¼ cup pine nuts, toasted
    (see page 249)

2 tablespoons nutritional yeast
    (optional)

1 tablespoon freshly squeezed
    lemon juice

2 teaspoons wheat-free tamari or
    other soy sauce

1¼ teaspoons sea salt, or to taste

¼ teaspoon freshly ground
    black pepper

¼ teaspoon crushed red pepper
    flakes

2 tablespoons chiffonaded fresh
    basil

2 tablespoons finely chopped
    fresh flat-leaf parsley

Lemon wedges

Toasted pine nuts

Variations

- Replace the tempeh with tofu.
- Replace the asparagus with an equal amount of chopped broccoli or cauliflower.
- Add 2 tablespoons of vegan butter and/or ¼ cup of grated vegan mozzarella-style cheese after you return the blended sauce to the sauté pan, and mix well.
- Add 1 tablespoon of Italian Spice Mix (page 51) along with the onion and garlic.
- Add 1 teaspoon each of minced fresh rosemary, sage, thyme, and oregano before blending.
- Replace the pine nuts with macadamia nuts or cashews.

Chef Patrick Recommends:
Italian, Verdicchio or dry Chardonnay

Frittata with Artichoke Hearts and Sun-Dried Tomatoes

Real men eat vegan frittata. Traditionally made with eggs, and considered by some to be the omelet of Italy, this recipe is made with silken tofu and strongly flavored with some of the heavy-hitting Mediterranean ingredients. If you use an ovenproof pan such as cast iron, you can do your sautéing and baking in the same pan. If not, use a well-oiled 9-inch pie dish for the baking portion. Serve as part of a Fusion brunch with Buckwheat Galettes with Tarragon Cream (page 76) and Horchata (page 123).

SERVES 4 TO 6

14 to 18 sun-dried tomatoes
 (about ½ cup)
1 tablespoon olive oil
1 cup diced yellow onion
3 garlic cloves, pressed or minced
1 (12.3-ounce) package silken
 firm tofu
10 ounces extra-firm tofu
¼ cup unsweetened soy milk
3 tablespoons nutritional yeast
1 tablespoon freshly squeezed
 lemon juice
1 tablespoon wheat-free tamari or
 other soy sauce
1½ teaspoons balsamic vinegar
¾ teaspoon ground turmeric
1 teaspoon sea salt
¼ teaspoon freshly ground
 black pepper
¼ teaspoon crushed red pepper flakes
1 cup quartered artichoke hearts
2 tablespoons chiffonaded
 fresh basil
1 tablespoon finely chopped fresh
 flat-leaf parsley
½ teaspoon minced fresh rosemary
1 teaspoon minced fresh oregano
½ teaspoon dried thyme (optional)
½ cup grated vegan mozzarella-style
 cheese (optional)

1. Preheat the oven to 425°F. Soak the sun-dried tomatoes in 1 cup of hot water until soft, 5 to 10 minutes. Drain well, and chop into small pieces.
2. Meanwhile, place a sauté pan over medium-high heat. Place the oil, onion, and garlic in the pan and cook for 3 minutes, stirring constantly.
3. Place the tofu, soy milk, nutritional yeast, lemon juice, tamari, vinegar, turmeric, salt, pepper, and crushed red pepper flakes in a food processor and process until creamy.
4. Transfer to the sauté pan with the remaining ingredients, including the artichoke hearts and sun-dried tomatoes, and mix well.
5. Place the pan in the oven (if you are not using an ovenproof pan, transfer to a well-oiled 9-inch pie dish) and bake for 20 minutes. For optimal flavor and if you have more time, bake for an additional 10 minutes and allow to set until firm, about 5 minutes, before serving. Serve warm or cold.

Variation
- Add 1 cup of diced mushrooms, peppers, or zucchini to the sauté pan after the onion has cooked for a few minutes. Cook for an additional 3 minutes before adding the ingredients from the food processor.

Strawberry Rose Granita

The original Italian ices, made in the comfort of your own home! This dish takes just moments to prepare; although it does require additional time for freezing and scraping, the results are the ultimate in a chilled slushy dessert. Be sure to use a standard 9 by 13-inch casserole dish. If you use a smaller (or thicker) casserole dish, it will take longer to freeze. Serve on its own or top with fresh fruit. This makes a particularly refreshing snack after a heartier meal that may include Lemon Tempeh with Creamy Asparagus Sauce (page 40) or Eggplant Parmesan Stacks (page 38).

MAKES 3 CUPS GRANITA

1 pound fresh organic strawberries, chopped, or whole frozen strawberries (3 cups) (see note)

¾ cup water

½ cup organic sugar (see page xxi)

1 tablespoon freshly squeezed lemon juice

2 teaspoons rose water (see note)

Mint leaves

1. Place all the ingredients, except the mint leaves, in a strong blender and blend well.
2. Transfer to a 9 by 13-inch casserole dish and place in the freezer. Freeze for 30 minutes and scrape the sides with a fork. Return to the freezer. Scrape the entire granita every 30 minutes and return to the freezer for up to 3 hours.
3. Garnish with mint leaves before serving.

Variations

- Replace the strawberries with an equal amount of other fruit, such as blueberries, peaches, or nectarines. Adjust the sweetener to taste, depending upon the sweetness of the fruit.
- Watermelon Mint Granita—replace the strawberries with seeded watermelon and replace the lemon juice with lime juice. Add 2 teaspoons of mint extract.
- Mocha Granita—omit the lemon juice and rose water. Replace the fruit and water with 3 cups of coffee and ¼ cup of unsweetened cocoa powder.

Chef's Tips and Tricks

Please purchase only organic strawberries. See page 270 to discover why nonorganic strawberries are placed on the list of the Dirty Dozen.

Make sure the rose water you are using is food grade. Some rose waters contain rose oil, and are meant as a perfume instead of for culinary uses. Heritage is a company that has a readily available food-grade rose water.

Orange Anise Biscotti Bites

Biscotti are traditionally a twice-baked biscuit, originating in the town of Prato and were the snack of choice for Pliny the Elder (who is said to have impeccable taste, so we can take his word for it). This quick and easy version takes a lot less time than the typical 90 minutes. For gluten-free biscotti, replace the flour with gluten-free flour (see page 260). Serve with an Espresso Smoothie (page 49) while contemplating the subtleties of Bernini's statues.

MAKES 12 TO 14 BITES

DRY

2½ cups white spelt flour (for more info on gluten-free flour, see page 260)

¾ cup evaporated sugar cane (an organic sugar; see note)

1 teaspoon baking powder

⅛ teaspoon sea salt

½ teaspoon ground aniseed

WET

¼ cup freshly squeezed orange juice

2 tablespoons ground flaxseeds mixed with 6 tablespoons water

4 tablespoons coconut oil or vegan butter or shortening

Zest of 1 orange (1 teaspoon)

½ teaspoon vanilla extract

1. Preheat the oven to 425°F. Oil a baking sheet well or line with parchment paper. Place the dry ingredients in a large bowl and whisk well.
2. Place the wet ingredients in another bowl and mix well. Add the wet ingredients to the dry and mix well.
3. Form twelve to fourteen equal-size balls and place on the prepared baking sheet. Press down to form cookies about ½ inch tall.
4. Bake for 15 minutes. Allow to cool for 5 minutes before placing on a cooling rack or large plate.
5. For more traditional biscotti, you can form into one 8- by 10-inch loaf and bake for 5 minutes. Slice into ½- or ¾-inch bars. Bake again for 10 minutes.

Variations
- Hazelnut Biscotti—add ¼ cup ground hazelnuts and ½ teaspoon hazelnut extract.
- Lemon Mint Biscotti—replace the orange juice with 2 tablespoons of freshly squeezed lemon juice and 2 tablespoons of water, replace the orange zest with ½ teaspoon lemon zest, and add 1 tablespoon of chiffonaded mint leaves.
- Coconut Biscotti—add ½ cup of dried coconut to the dry ingredients, add ⅓ cup of coconut milk to the wet, and be sure to use coconut oil instead of the vegan butter listed in the recipe. You can also add 1 teaspoon of coconut extract.
- Chocolate Biscotti—dip the cooled biscotti in Swiss Chocolate Fondue (page 240).
- Replace the vanilla extract with raspberry, coffee, almond, or coconut extract, or your favorite.

Vegan Gelato

Perhaps one of the most rewarding culinary journeys in Italy is to track down the perfect vegan gelato, where the gelato shops offer a vibrant Technicolor display of options. Start with these three versions and go on to devise countless creations of your own. Invest in an ice-cream maker if you are serious about your gelato. See the note below on how to prepare without this handy device. Enjoy after any meal you wish to end in culinary bliss.

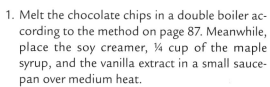

MAKES ABOUT 1 QUART GELATO

CHOCOLATE ALMOND BUTTER

1 cup vegan dark chocolate chips

2 cups soy creamer

¼ cup pure maple syrup or agave nectar, plus ¼ cup of pure maple syrup

2 teaspoons vanilla extract

3 tablespoons arrowroot powder dissolved in ¼ cup cold water

½ cup almond butter

1. Melt the chocolate chips in a double boiler according to the method on page 87. Meanwhile, place the soy creamer, ¼ cup of the maple syrup, and the vanilla extract in a small saucepan over medium heat.
2. Add the arrowroot mixture and whisk until the creamer thickens, about 3 minutes. Add the melted chocolate chips, and stir until a uniform consistency is attained.
3. Place in an ice-cream maker and freeze according to the manufacturer's instructions.
4. Combine the remaining ¼ cup of maple syrup and the almond butter in a small bowl. Add to the gelato and run through the ice-cream maker before serving.

STRAWBERRY BANANA HEMP

1 cup hemp milk

1 cup coconut milk (use regular, not light)

1 vanilla bean, ends trimmed off, or 1 tablespoon vanilla extract

½ cup mashed ripe banana

½ cup agave nectar or pure maple syrup

1 cup organic strawberries

2 tablespoons amaretto (optional)

3 tablespoons arrowroot powder dissolved in ¼ cup cold water

1. Place all the ingredients, except the arrowroot mixture, in a blender and blend well.
2. Transfer the mixture to a pot over high heat and bring to a boil. Lower the heat to medium, add the arrowroot mixture, and cook for 5 minutes, stirring frequently.
3. Place in an ice-cream maker and freeze according to the manufacturer's instructions.

continues

Vegan Gelato *continued*

 ESPRESSO MAGNIFICO

½ cup water

2 tablespoons ground espresso

2 cups soy creamer

¾ cup coconut milk (use regular, not light)

½ cup agave nectar or pure maple syrup

1 teaspoon coffee extract

3 tablespoons arrowroot powder dissolved in ¼ cup cold water

1. Bring the water to a boil in a small pot. Add the espresso and remove from the heat.
2. Allow to steep for 15 minutes. Strain well and place in a pot over medium-high heat with all the ingredients, except the arrowroot mixture, and bring to a boil. Lower the heat to medium, add the arrowroot mixture, and cook for 5 minutes, stirring frequently.
3. Place in an ice-cream maker and freeze according to the manufacturer's instructions.

Chef's Tips and Tricks

If you are without an ice-cream maker, place the gelato in a glass container and freeze for 3 hours. Remove from the freezer and allow to thaw until it is just soft. Place in a food processor and process before serving.

Baked Walnut Fig Crumble

One of the first foods to be cultivated by humans, and especially popular with the ancient Romans, figs have been gracing our menus for over eleven thousand years. Walnuts and figs go together like Romulus and Remus. This is Italian comfort food at its finest. For a luscious dessert or midnight snack, serve warm with vegan ice cream or Cashew Cream (page 90) and a drizzle of chocolate sauce from the Bread Pudding (see page 201).

SERVES 6 TO 8

FILLING

4 cups chopped fresh figs

½ cup raisins

½ cup chopped walnuts

2 teaspoons vanilla extract

¼ cup water or fruit juice

½ cup organic brown sugar or sweetener of choice (see page 261)

½ teaspoon ground cinnamon

¼ teaspoon ground cardamom

⅛ teaspoon ground nutmeg

Pinch of sea salt

TOPPING

2 cups rolled oats

½ cup flour (try gluten-free)

¼ cup fruit juice or water

¼ cup organic brown sugar or sweetener of choice

4 tablespoons melted vegan butter

2 tablespoons melted coconut oil or more fruit juice or water

¼ teaspoon ground cinnamon

⅛ teaspoon ground nutmeg

Pinch of ground cardamom

Pinch of sea salt

1. Preheat the oven to 400°F. Oil an 8-inch casserole dish well.
2. Place the filling ingredients in a large bowl and mix well. Transfer to the prepared casserole dish.
3. Combine the topping ingredients in a large bowl and mix well. Crumble on top of the filling. Bake for 20 minutes. If you have more time, and for a crisper crumble, bake for an additional 5 minutes. Enjoy warm, top with vegan ice cream such as Coconut Bliss, and bliss out!

Variations

- If using dried figs, use ½ cup of fruit juice and soak the figs while you prepare the rest of the recipe. You may also add 1 to 2 tablespoons of rum or brandy to help soften the figs.
- Replace the walnuts with pecans, hazelnuts, macadamia nuts, or your favorite.
- Replace the figs with berries, peaches, mango, or pineapple.
- Replace the vegan butter with coconut oil.

Tiramisu Parfait

Tiramisu is to Italian desserts what the Sistine Chapel's ceiling is to interior design. It typically takes hours to prepare. This quick and easy version is sure to satisfy the most discriminating of palates. It has all of the elements of a decadent dessert, but is made in a fraction of the time. For the most successful tiramisu, you will need to find good solid vegan cookies or cake that can withstand being dipped in the espresso without dissolving. If you have more time, make the Orange Anise Biscotti Bites (page 44) to use in this recipe. Serve in parfait glasses at the end of your feast, which may include such Italian classics as Gnocchi (page 15) and Eggplant Parmesan Stacks (page 38).

SERVES 6

CREAM LAYER

2 cups raw cashews

1¼ cups almond, coconut, hemp, or soy milk (see page 259)

¼ cup agave nectar, organic sugar, or sweetener of choice to taste (see page 261)

4 teaspoons vegan butter

2 teaspoons vanilla extract

2 teaspoons coffee extract

1 to 2 teaspoons of super finely ground coffee

A pinch of sea salt

ESPRESSO COOKIE LAYER

¾ cup prepared espresso

12 (2-inch) vegan cookies or pieces of vegan cake, such as ladyfingers or Orange Anise Biscotti Bites (page 44)

1 teaspoon unsweetened cocoa powder

2 tablespoons shaved dark chocolate (see note)

1. Create the cream layer by placing all of its ingredients in a strong blender or food processor and processing until very creamy. Add additional almond milk, 1 tablespoon at a time, if necessary, depending upon the strength of your blender, to create a creamy, light, and fluffy topping that is not liquidy.

2. Assemble each parfait by dipping two cookies into the espresso and placing at the bottom of a parfait glass. Pour any extra espresso into the glasses. Add ¼ cup to ½ cup of the cream layer to each glass and press down with a spatula. If you wish, you can create a second layer by repeating this step.

3. Top with a dusting of cocoa powder and shaved chocolate.

Variations
- Add ¼ cup Kahlúa to the cream layer.
- Create a double-layered parfait by using half as much in each layer.

Chef's Tips and Tricks

Break out your Microplane zester, or use the small grater section of your grater to shave your favorite chocolate as the final topping.

Espresso Smoothie

Espresso is the life blood of Europe. And no one does espresso quite like the Italians. After drinking my fourth cup in a day, at eleven o'clock at night, I knew I had arrived. You might be surprised to discover that espresso actually has less caffeine than regularly brewed coffee, as the longer brewing time in brewed coffee extracts more caffeine. Enjoy this nectar when you are looking for an extra boost.

MAKES TWO 12-OUNCE SMOOTHIES

2 to 3 shots espresso

1½ cups soy or other nondairy milk of choice

1 large ripe banana

2 tablespoons almond or peanut butter

4 ice cubes

1 tablespoon pure maple syrup, dark agave nectar, or sweetener of choice, or to taste

Pinch of ground cinnamon

Pinch of ground anise (optional)

Place all the ingredients in a strong blender and blend until smooth.

Variations

- Experiment with different types of nondairy milks, such as hemp, rice, almond, or oat.
- Go mocha by adding 2 tablespoons of unsweetened cocoa powder.
- Add more banana for a thicker beverage.
- You can also use frozen banana instead of ice cubes.
- Replace the anise with ground cardamom or nutmeg.

Chef's Tips and Tricks

Pasta

Italy is the pasta capital of the universe. The countless varieties of pasta are typically divided into two general categories: fresh (usually made with eggs) or dried. The flour used is traditionally durum flour or durum semolina. With the resurgence of the interest in gluten-free cooking, there are now many pastas created with brown rice (my favorite is Tinkyada, a wonderful brand) as well as quinoa, corn, and Jerusalem artichoke flours.

The cooking method as most people know is to cook the pasta in boiling water. If you add a small amount of sea salt to the water, it will bring out flavor in all of the pasta. (Some Italian grandmothers are said to recommend adding enough salt to the water until it has the flavor of the ocean.) The cooking time is determined by the type of pasta. The final consistency of choice is al dente—cooked until just soft, and still firm. Follow the package instructions for best results. If your sauce is ready when the pasta is, do not rinse the pasta, as the starch on its surface will help the sauce stick to the pasta.

Quicker and Easier Italy

Italian Spice Mix

Make this simple mixture in advance to add a taste of Italy to your favorite dishes.

MAKES ½ CUP SEASONING

3 tablespoons dried basil
2 tablespoons dried parsley
1 tablespoon dried marjoram
1 tablespoon dried oregano
1 teaspoon dried thyme
1 teaspoon garlic powder

▶ Combine all the ingredients in a small bowl and mix well. Store in a spice jar in a cool, dry place.

You can also add any or all of the following: 1 tablespoon of dried rubbed sage, 2 teaspoons of dehydrated onion flakes, ½ teaspoon of ground rosemary, 1 teaspoon of crushed red pepper flakes, and 1 teaspoon of ground fennel seed.

Balsamic Reduction

Reducing balsamic vinegar creates a versatile syrup that has the sweetness and rich flavor of the balsamic vinegar without the tang. The most simple recipe calls for pouring 2 cups of a high-quality balsamic vinegar into a heavy-bottomed saucepan. Bring to a boil, lower the heat to low, and simmer uncovered, stirring occasionally, until the liquid is syrupy and reduced to about ½ cup. You can enhance the flavor of the reduction by adding any or all of the following ingredients: 2 tablespoons of Sucanat or organic brown sugar (see page 261), a few sprigs of fresh herbs such as rosemary or thyme, a dozen whole peppercorns, 2 whole garlic cloves, and/or ¼ cup of chopped onion. If adding the herbs, peppercorns, garlic, or onion, strain the mixture well through a fine sieve before it has had a chance to cool. The mixture will thicken as it

continues

Balsamic Reduction continued _____

cools. You can also make a wonderful and simple reduction by using 1 part red wine and 1 part balsamic vinegar. This will keep for months in a glass jar in the refrigerator. Pour into a squeeze bottle and drizzle over salads, vegetables, or entrées.

For an epic **Italian Dipping Sauce** for bread, artichoke hearts, or even steamed veggies, combine the following in a small bowl and mix well: ½ cup of olive oil; 1 tablespoon of balsamic vinegar; 1 tablespoon of minced fresh flat-leaf parsley; 1 tablespoon of nutritional yeast (optional); 1 clove garlic, minced; 1 teaspoon of minced fresh oregano; ½ teaspoon of dried thyme; ¼ teaspoon of minced fresh rosemary; ½ teaspoon of sea salt, or to taste; ¼ teaspoon of crushed red pepper flakes; and ⅛ teaspoon of freshly ground black pepper.

Caprese Salad: Slice an heirloom tomato into thick slices. Top each slice with a fresh basil leaf and a slice of vegan mozzarella-style cheese. Drizzle with a high-quality olive oil and balsamic vinegar, and top with a pinch of sea salt and freshly ground black pepper.

Tofu or Tempeh Parmesan: Slice a 14-ounce block of extra-firm tofu into thirds or an 8-ounce block of tempeh in half. Marinate and roast according the instructions on page 252. Top with tomato sauce and grated vegan mozzarella-style cheese. Return to the oven and bake for 10 more minutes at 375°F, or until the cheese melts.

Credits: Mark Reinfeld

PART TWO

FRANCE

What wisdom can you find that is greater than kindness?

—Jean-Jacques Rousseau

rance holds such a special place in the foodie world that for many it sets the gold standard of culinary excellence. The French influence is so strong that many of the familiar modern-day food-related terms are of French origin. All of us have dined in a restaurant, café, or bistro, and ordered an entrée or (frequently misspelled) hors d'oeuvres from a menu.

The Cordon Bleu, with origins in late nineteenth-century France, is the largest culinary institution in the world. You might have heard of one of its prized students, Julia Child. She attended the school in the late 1940s and was a pioneer in introducing classic French cuisine to the American palate. I felt Julia's spirit when I taught my first vegan classes in Paris at the Gentle Gourmet B&B.

Once seen as the nemesis of vegan travelers, France is far more veg friendly these days, at least in the major cities. The vegan movement is definitely alive and well in Paris, where vegetarian and vegan options abound. Activists, such as contributing chef Deborah Pivain and her children Alex and Caroline, created Paris Vegan Days, an annual celebration of all things vegan.

As in many European countries, the cuisine of France is as varied as there are numerous distinctive regions, each with its own culinary traditions and local specialties. Travel to the shores of Brittany or Normandy; through the Loire Valley, Provence, or Burgundy; to the south of France along the Mediterranean; and on to the mountainous regions of the Alps, and you will be treated to a wide variety of dishes and flavors. The influences of Spain, Italy, Germany, Switzerland, and Belgium can all be felt as you approach the borders of these countries.

In your travels through France, you will come across such vegetables as leeks, shallots, carrots, potatoes, French green beans (haricots verts), eggplant, zucchini, turnips, olives, and garlic. The fungi truffles are popular, as well as mushroom varieties chanterelle, oyster, and porcini.

Your dishes will be flavored with such herbs as tarragon, lavender, chervil, marjoram, bay leaves, thyme, sage, rosemary, savory, basil, fennel, and oregano. The famous herbes de Provence contains a mixture of herbs typical to the southern regions of France, and became commercially available under that name in the 1970s. While the blends may vary, common ingredients include thyme, savory, fennel, basil, and lavender. The recipe on page 94 shows you how to make your own blend.

Popular fruits include oranges, lemons, tangerines, grapefruit, tomatoes, apricots, peaches, grapes, apples, pears, plums, and berries such as strawberries, raspberries, black berries, black currants, and red currants. Buckwheat as well as wheat are grains grown in the country. For nuts, chestnuts are king.

France is known for its rich butter- and cream-laden cooking. With the advent of vegan butter and nondairy cheeses, milks, and creams, many of these classic dishes are now accessible for the adventurous chef. I have included a wide array of cuisine in this section. Here you will find veganized versions of classic dishes, such as French Onion Soup, quiche, bourguignon, and bouillabaisse, as well as previously off-limits sauces such as béarnaise, béchamel, mornay, and hollandaise. Experience meat-free versions of foie gras, escargots, and even frog's legs (officially Kermit safe!). The pièce de résistance, of course, is dessert, with a selection of crepes chocolat, lavender truffles, a raw pear tart, and a cooked and raw version of chocolate mousse. Bon appétit!

Faux Gras

This pâté is a much gentler version of the authentic foie gras, and is made with walnuts and mushrooms. I provide a raw and a cooked recipe so you can experience two different versions of this classic dish. Serve this goose-friendly version over crackers, on its own, or as part of the Italian Bruschetta (see page 4).

COOKED VERSION: MAKES 1 CUP PÂTÉ

2 tablespoons olive oil

½ cup diced yellow onion

¼ cup thinly sliced celery

2 garlic cloves, pressed or minced

½ cup chopped walnuts

¼ cup diced carrot

¼ cup thinly sliced and chopped leek

¾ cup diced shiitake mushrooms

½ teaspoon hot chile pepper, or
    ¼ teaspoon cayenne pepper,
    or to taste

¼ cup white wine (see box) or
    vegetable stock (see page 253)

4 teaspoons water

1 tablespoon freshly squeezed
    lemon juice

1 teaspoon chopped fresh thyme

½ teaspoon minced fresh rosemary

¾ teaspoon sea salt

¼ teaspoon freshly ground black
    pepper

½ teaspoon wheat-free tamari or
    other soy sauce (optional)

¼ to ½ teaspoon truffle oil

2 tablespoons vegan mayonnaise
    (Vegenaise or homemade; see
    page 261; optional)

1. Place a small sauté pan over medium-high heat. Place the oil, onion, celery, and garlic in the pan and cook for 2 minutes, stirring constantly. Add the walnuts, carrot, leek, mushrooms, and chile pepper and cook for 3 minutes, stirring frequently and adding small amounts of vegetable stock if necessary to prevent sticking.

2. Add the wine and cook for 5 minutes, stirring frequently. Add the remaining ingredients except the vegan mayonnaise, if using, and cook until the carrot is just soft, about 3 minutes.

3. Transfer to a food processor with the vegan mayonnaise and process until smooth before serving.

Chef Patrick Recommends:
French, Sauvignon Blanc

continues

Faux Gras *continued*

RAW VERSION ♥: MAKES 1 CUP PÂTÉ

¾ cup walnuts

¾ cup diced mushrooms

2 tablespoons finely diced yellow onion

2 tablespoons plus 1 teaspoon olive oil

1 garlic clove

¼ cup diced carrot

¼ cup thinly sliced and chopped leek

2 tablespoons water

½ teaspoon hot chile pepper, or ¼ teaspoon cayenne pepper, or to taste

1 tablespoon freshly squeezed lemon juice

1 teaspoon chopped fresh thyme

½ teaspoon minced fresh rosemary

½ teaspoon sea salt

¼ teaspoon freshly ground black pepper

1 teaspoon wheat-free tamari or other soy sauce (optional)

¼ to ½ teaspoon truffle oil

1. Soak the walnuts in a small bowl with enough water to cover. Allow to sit for 20 minutes. Drain and rinse well.
2. Transfer to a food processor with the remaining ingredients and process until smooth.

Snail-Free Escargot (or EscarNo)

At some point in the course of human history, someone thought it was a good idea to eat snails and the French took to the idea. This version of the classic French dish uses mushrooms instead. I know, you can thank me later. For best results, cook them in a large sauté pan with a lid. To fool your guests, serve in a classic porcelain escargot dish, which has rounded indents (available at most kitchen supply stores). Feast on this dish as an appetizer on its own or topped with Pesto Magnifico (page 31), or as a side dish along with Braised Tempeh with Herbes de Provence (page 80) or Rainbow Steamed Vegetables with Spicy Béchamel Sauce (page 81).

MAKES 16 VEGAN ESCARGOTS

18 cremini mushrooms

FILLING

2 teaspoons olive oil

¼ cup minced shallot

Mushroom stems (about ¾ cup rounded)

Pinch of sea salt

Pinch of freshly ground black pepper

¼ teaspoon ground nutmeg

Pinch of cayenne pepper (optional)

SAUCE

1 teaspoon olive oil

1 tablespoon minced shallot

3 to 4 garlic cloves, pressed or minced

½ cup white wine (see box)

1 tablespoon freshly squeezed lemon juice

2 tablespoons vegan butter

1 teaspoon vegan Dijon mustard

⅛ teaspoon sea salt

⅛ teaspoon ground white pepper or freshly ground black pepper

1 tablespoon finely chopped fresh flat-leaf parsley

1. Clean the mushrooms with a mushroom brush or a clean, slightly damp cloth. Remove the stems. Cut off the very bottom portion of the stems and discard. Dice the remaining stems, plus two whole mushrooms, and set aside for use in the filling.
2. Prepare the filling: Place a small sauté pan over medium-high heat. Place the oil and shallot in the pan and cook for 2 minutes, stirring constantly. Add the diced mushrooms and the remaining filling ingredients and cook for 3 minutes, stirring frequently. Stuff the mushrooms with the filling.
3. Prepare the sauce: Place a large sauté pan over medium-high heat. Place the oil, shallots, and garlic in the pan and cook for 2 minutes, stirring constantly. Lower the heat to medium, add the wine, lemon juice, and vegan butter, and stir well. Add the remaining sauce ingredients, except the parsley, and stir well.
4. Carefully add the stuffed mushrooms, stuffed side up, and cook for 10 minutes, gently stirring and basting the mushrooms frequently. Top with fresh parsley before serving.

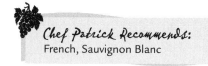

Chef Patrick Recommends:
French, Sauvignon Blanc

French Onion Soup

The humble onion forms the base of this delectable soup. I say *humble*, though *ancient* is also an apt description. Cultivated since the Bronze Age, onions have been a favorite food of humans for over seven thousand years. The key to success in this dish is to cook the onions long enough for them to caramelize a bit, when the natural sweetness is released. If you have the classic ovenproof bowls, now is certainly the time to use them, as they contribute greatly to the experience. For a light lunch, serve with a fresh baguette and Provençal Vegetable Salad (page 67).

SERVES 6 TO 8

2 tablespoons olive oil or vegan butter

2 large yellow onions, sliced thinly (4 cups)

1 teaspoon sea salt, or to taste

½ teaspoon freshly ground black pepper

¾ cup red wine, or 1 cup sherry (see box)

1 tablespoon balsamic vinegar

6 cups vegetable stock (see Chef's Tips)

3 sprigs thyme

2 bay leaves

5 sprigs flat-leaf parsley

1 cup grated vegan mozzarella- or Cheddar-style cheese, or ½ cup nutritional yeast, or to taste

CROUTONS

½ baguette

2 tablespoons olive oil

¼ teaspoon sea salt

¼ teaspoon freshly ground black pepper

1. Prepare the soup: Place the olive oil in a large pot over medium-high heat. Add the onions, salt, and pepper, and cook for 5 minutes, stirring constantly. Add the wine and vinegar and cook for 10 minutes, stirring frequently and adding small amounts of vegetable stock if necessary to prevent sticking.

2. Lower the heat to medium, add the vegetable stock and herbs to the pot, and cook for 15 minutes, stirring occasionally.

3. Meanwhile, prepare the croutons: Set the oven to BROIL and oil a baking sheet. Slice the baguette into ½-inch slices and place on the prepared baking sheet. Baste with olive oil and sprinkle with salt and pepper. Broil for 5 minutes, or until the bread is crispy.

4. To serve, remove the bay leaves and thyme sprigs. Pour the soup into oven-safe bowls, add a baguette slice, and sprinkle the top with vegan cheese. Place under the broiler until the cheese melts, about 5 minutes. If you do not have oven-safe bowls, simply top with the cheese before serving.

continues

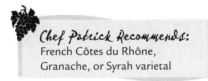

Chef Patrick Recommends:
French Côtes du Rhône, Granache, or Syrah varietal

continued

Variations

- Add 3 cloves of garlic, pressed or minced, to the soup and/or on top of the bread before broiling.
- Add 1 tablespoon of Italian Spice Mix (page 51) to the bread.
- Add 1 sliced portobello mushroom along with onions.
- Add 1 tablespoon of smoked paprika along with the onions

Chef's Tips and Tricks

The vegetable stock is quite important in this dish. If you have more time, make your own stock (see page 253). If you are using a store-bought brand, I recommend using organic, vegan, vegetable-flavored bouillon cubes (one for every 2 cups of water).

Creamy Roasted Chestnut Soup

Chestnuts are grown in abundance on the French island of Corsica and are a common snack and ingredient throughout Europe. While feasting on roasted chestnuts by the gardens of the Louvre in Paris, I wondered how I could incorporate these tasty treats into this book; the result is this rich and creamy soup. Be sure to roast extra chestnuts for a snack, and because some of them may not be usable for the soup (see note). If you start with roasted chestnuts, or if you use store-bought chestnuts, you can easily finish the dish within 30 minutes. Enjoy warm with the Buckwheat Galettes and Tarragon Cream (page 76).

SERVES 6 TO 8

2 teaspoons oil

1 yellow onion, diced (1½ cups)

3 to 4 garlic cloves, pressed or minced

1 cup diced shiitake or chanterelle mushrooms

5½ cups heated vegetable stock (see page 253) or water

About 40 chestnuts in the shell (2 cups chopped), or 1 (14.8-ounce) jar roasted chestnuts

½ cup diced carrot

¾ cup seeded and diced red bell pepper

2 tablespoons freshly squeezed lemon juice

2 tablespoons finely chopped chives

2 teaspoons finely chopped fresh marjoram, or 1 teaspoon dried

1¾ teaspoons sea salt, or to taste

¼ teaspoon freshly ground black pepper

⅛ teaspoon cayenne pepper

1. Preheat the oven to 500°F. Carefully, and I mean very carefully, use a sharp knife to slice an X into the top of each chestnut. Place on a baking sheet and bake for 20 minutes, until the shell is slightly blackened and the chestnut flesh is golden brown.

2. Meanwhile, place a large pot over medium-high heat. Place the oil, onion, garlic, and mushrooms in the pot and cook for 5 minutes, stirring constantly. Add the vegetable stock and cook for 10 minutes. Keep over low heat until the chestnuts are ready.

3. Carefully peel the chestnuts, place them in a blender with 3 cups of vegetable stock, and blend until creamy. Transfer to the pot.

4. Add the remaining ingredients, increase the heat to medium-high, and cook for 7 minutes, stirring occasionally. Depending upon the starchiness of the chestnuts, you may wish to add more stock to reach the desired consistency. If so, season with additional salt and pepper to taste.

continues

continued

Variations

- Serve with a dollop of Vegan Sour Cream (see page 226).
- Add 2 teaspoons of finely chopped fresh sage, and 1 teaspoon of fresh thyme.

Chef's Tips and Tricks

Once your chestnuts are roasted, clean them well of any shell or inner skin. Select only those that are golden brown and just firm for use in the recipe. Discard any that are overly hardened, moldy, or bruised.

French Lentil Soup with Thyme

French lentils, also known as Puy lentils, originate in the Puy region of France. Grown in volcanic soil, they are a highly prized treasure (as far as lentils go) for their strong, peppery flavor. The Tempeh Bacon adds to the texture and layered flavoring of the dish. Make sure to wait until the lentils are completely cooked before adding the salt, or the lentils may be tough. Heating the vegetable stock before adding it to the soup will help keep this dish in the 30-minute range. Serve with Rice Pilaf with Fennel and Saffron (page 78) and Celeriac with Morel Mushroom Sauce (page 70).

SERVES 6

2 tablespoons olive oil

1 yellow onion, chopped small (1¼ cups)

¾ cup thinly sliced celery

3 garlic cloves, pressed or minced

1 teaspoon Herbes de Provence (page 94, optional)

1 cup dried French lentils

7 cups heated vegetable stock (see page 253) or water

1 cup thinly sliced carrot

2 teaspoons fresh thyme

1 teaspoon minced fresh marjoram

2 tablespoons finely chopped fresh flat-leaf parsley

1 teaspoon sea salt, or to taste

¼ teaspoon freshly ground black pepper

⅛ teaspoon cayenne pepper

2 teaspoons wheat-free tamari or other soy sauce (optional)

1 (6-ounce) package Fakin' Bacon or Tempeh Bacon (see page 251) (optional)

1. Preheat the oven to 400°F. Oil a baking sheet. Place the olive oil in a large pot over medium-high heat. Add the onion, celery, garlic, and herbes de Provence, if using, and cook for 3 minutes, stirring frequently.

2. Add the lentils and vegetable stock, and cook covered for 15 minutes, stirring occasionally. Add the carrot and cook for 7 minutes, stirring occasionally. Add the remaining ingredients, except the Fakin' Bacon, and stir well.

3. Meanwhile, place the Fakin' Bacon on the prepared baking sheet and bake for 10 minutes. Flip and bake for an additional 10 minutes. Remove from the oven and chop into small pieces. Set aside.

4. To serve, pour the soup into serving bowls and top with the Fakin' Bacon pieces. If you are not using the Fakin' Bacon, add additional salt and pepper to taste.

Variations

- Replace the carrot with seeded and chopped bell pepper, mushrooms, or cabbage.
- Replace the parsley with fresh basil or 1 tablespoon of dill.
- Top the soup with some crumbled Tofu Feta (page 163).
- If you have more time, replace the lentils with split peas, ideally soaking them for several hours or overnight, rinsing, and draining well, before using in the dish. Add extra soup stock if necessary to reach the desired consistency.

Vegan Bouillabaisse

A traditional stew that typically includes several varieties of seafood and traces its origins back to 600 BC, when ancient Greeks were chilaxing in the harbor town of Marseille, in the Provence region of France. This innovative version uses the sea vegetable *arame* to create the flavor of the sea. If you have more time, you can prepare a bouquet garni (see box). Serve as part of a French feast with Rice Pilaf with Fennel and Saffron (page 78) and Provençal Vegetable Salad (page 67).

SERVES 4 TO 6

14 ounces extra-firm tofu

¼ cup freshly squeezed lemon juice

1 cup white wine (see box)

1 tablespoon olive oil

¾ cup diced shallot

¾ cup thinly sliced celery

¼ cup finely chopped or thinly sliced fennel bulb

2 garlic cloves, pressed or minced

½ teaspoon seeded and diced hot chile pepper

1 cup diced shiitake mushrooms

3 cups heated vegetable stock (see page 253) or water

2 bay leaves

½ cup *arame*

½ teaspoon saffron threads

2 teaspoons fresh thyme

1 tablespoon finely chopped fresh flat-leaf parsley

1 cup seeded and chopped tomato

1¾ teaspoons sea salt

¼ teaspoon freshly ground black pepper

Finely chopped fresh flat-leaf parsley, for garnish

1. Slice the tofu into three cutlets and stack them on top of each other. Slice the cutlets three times widthwise and four times lengthwise. Place the cubes in a shallow dish with the lemon juice and ½ cup of the wine. Allow to sit for 10 minutes, gently stirring occasionally to ensure even coating.

2. Meanwhile, place a large pot over medium high heat. Add the oil, shallot, celery, fennel, garlic, chile pepper, and shiitake mushrooms and cook for 3 minutes, stirring constantly.

3. Lower the heat to medium, add the remaining ½ cup of wine and the vegetable stock, bay leaves, *arame*, and saffron, and stir well. Add the thyme and parsley, and cook for 10 minutes, stirring occasionally

4. Add the tofu and its marinade ingredients and cook for 10 minutes, gently stirring occasionally. Add the tomatoes, salt, and pepper and stir well. Remove the bay leaves, garnish with parsley, and bon appétit!

continues

Chef Patrick Recommends:
French rosé, or California-style Chardonnay

Vegan Bouillabaisse *continued*

Variations

- Roast the tofu for 15 minutes at 400°F before adding to the bouillabaisse.
- You can used dried shiitake instead of fresh. Soak three or four dried shiitake in 1 cup of boiling water, until they are soft enough to chop, about 10 minutes. Use the soaking water to replace some of the vegetable stock.
- If you have more time, allow to cook for an additional 20 minutes over low heat for added flavor.

Chef's Tips and Tricks

Bouquet Garni

Use sprigs of thyme instead of the loose leaves, and tie the bay leaf, parsley, and thyme together with a piece of culinary string.

Provençal Vegetable Salad ♥

A fun and refreshing raw food dish prepared with seasonal fresh vegetables. The dressing, delicately flavored with traditional French herbs, is *magnifique* on any salad, or steamed or roasted vegetables. Serve as a side with Seitan Bourguignon (page 84), Quiche Monet (page 85), or Tofu "Scallops" with Saffron Herb Butter (page 82).

SERVES 4 TO 6

PROVENÇAL DRESSING

1 tablespoon Herbes de Provence (page 94)

3 tablespoons olive oil

1 tablespoon freshly squeezed lemon juice

1 garlic clove, pressed or minced

2 teaspoons red wine vinegar

2 teaspoons vegan Dijon mustard

1 teaspoon pure maple syrup or agave or coconut nectar (see page 261)

½ teaspoon sea salt

¼ teaspoon freshly ground black pepper

¼ teaspoon crushed red pepper flakes

⅛ teaspoon truffle oil (see page xxxviii) (optional)

SALAD

2 medium-size tomatoes, seeded and chopped into ½-inch chunks (2 cups)

1 cup seeded and chopped cucumber

2 tablespoons finely chopped fresh flat-leaf parsley

1 cup chopped green beans

1 cup corn

¼ cup thinly sliced green onion

¼ cup chopped olives (optional)

1. Prepare the dressing: Combining all of its ingredients in a small bowl and whisk well.
2. Prepare the salad: Combine the remaining ingredients in a large bowl and mix well. Pour the dressing over the vegetables and mix well.
3. For best results, chill for at least 10 minutes before serving.

Pommes Frites

Freedom fries to some, French fries to others, these ubiquitous treats are found on menus throughout Europe. In fact, *pommes frites* are one of the staple food groups for vegan travelers in France. See below for how different countries serve this popular dish. If you have more time, and for a crisper fry, leave them in the oven for an extra 10 minutes. Serve as a side with Tofu "Scallops" with Saffron Herb Butter (page 82), Seitan Bourguignon (page 84), or Scrambled Tofu with Chives and Wild Mushrooms (page 86).

SERVES 4 TO 6

4 medium-size russet potatoes (about 3 pounds) (see page 246)

3 tablespoons olive oil

1 teaspoon sea salt

½ teaspoon freshly ground black pepper

1. Preheat the oven to 450°F. Oil one or two baking sheets well.
2. Cut the potatoes into ½-inch-thick slices, then cut each slice into ½-inch-wide strips. Place in a bowl with the remaining ingredients and gently mix well to ensure even coating with the oil.
3. Transfer to the prepared baking sheet and bake until just soft, about 15 minutes.
4. Serve with ketchup or any of the following condiments.

Variations

- Experiment with different potatoes, yams, sweet potatoes, and even parsnips. The baking times are about the same. Cook until a knife can easily pass through the vegetable.
- For garlic fries, add three minced or pressed garlic cloves to the olive oil.
- Serve with a ketchup mayonnaise consisting of equal parts of ketchup and vegan mayonnaise (Vegenaise or homemade; see page 261).
- For cheese fries, serve topped with grated vegan cheese or Mornay sauce (page 81).
- For Italian flair, add 1 tablespoon of Italian Spice Mix to the oil (page 51).
- For Belgian *frites*, serve with vegan mayonnaise (Vegenaise or homemade; see page 261).
- For British style—salt and vinegar flavored—add 1 tablespoon or more of malt or other vinegar after baking and before serving.
- For Greek accents, serve with Tzatziki (page 162).

Green Beans with Beurre Blanc

French cuisine is known for its reliance on rich and decadent ingredients such as butter and cream. Fortunately, with the advent of vegan butter, vegans can now enjoy the flavors of traditional French cuisine on those special occasions. *Beurre blanc* refers to a white sauce. This one is made with white wine and vegan butter. Serve as a side with Braised Tempeh with Herbes de Provence (page 80), or Quiche Monet (page 85).

SERVES 4 TO 6

1 pound green beans, stems removed

1 tablespoon olive oil

3 garlic cloves, minced

¼ cup diced shallot

2 tablespoons freshly squeezed lemon juice

1 tablespoon white wine vinegar

½ cup white wine (see box)

½ teaspoon sea salt

¼ teaspoon freshly ground black pepper

Pinch of cayenne pepper

3 tablespoons vegan butter

¼ cup slivered almonds, toasted (see page 249)

Chef Patrick Recommends:
French, Sauvignon Blanc

1. Place a steamer basket in a medium-size pot with 1 inch of water in the pot. Place over medium-high heat and bring to a simmer. Add the green beans and cook covered until just tender, about 5 minutes. Remove from the steamer basket and place in a colander and run under cold running water until cooled, or in a bowl of ice to stop the cooking process. Drain well.

2. Meanwhile, place the olive oil in a large sauté pan over medium-high heat. Add the garlic and shallot, and cook for 3 minutes, stirring constantly.

3. Lower the heat to medium, add the remaining ingredients, except the green beans, vegan butter, and almonds, and cook for 5 minutes, stirring frequently.

4. Add the green beans and cook until they are just heated through, about 3 minutes, gently stirring well with tongs. Remove the green beans and place on a serving platter.

5. Remove the pan from the heat. Whisk in the butter to emulsify the sauce. Pour over the green beans and top with the almonds.

Variations

- Replace the green beans with an equal amount of broccoli or cauliflower flowerets.
- Replace the almonds with chopped hazelnuts or pecans.
- The sauce is also *très chic* as a topping for steamed vegetables—just complete the recipe without the vegetable, then ladle over your favorite steamed veggies.

Celeriac with Morel Mushroom Sauce

Celeriac is celery root, though it is a different plant than the celery that we are accustomed to. With a flavor similar to that of celery and parsley, it's phenomenal roasted and in sautés. Morel mushrooms (see note on page 71) have a beautiful honeycomb appearance and are a highly prized delicacy. If you cannot find fresh morels, you can use the dried ones. Put these two rock stars together and voilà! Serve with Vegan Bouillabaisse (page 65) and Rice Pilaf with Fennel and Saffron (page 78) or use as a filling in Buckwheat Galettes (page 76).

SERVES 6

1 cup fresh morel mushrooms, woody stem removed

¼ cup olive oil

¾ cup sliced shallot

3 to 4 garlic cloves, minced or pressed

1 celeriac, peeled and sliced into thin wedges (about 5 cups) (see box)

2 cups vegetable stock (see page 253) or water

2 tablespoons nutritional yeast (optional)

2 tablespoons white spelt flour

¾ teaspoon sea salt, or to taste

½ teaspoon freshly ground black pepper

⅛ teaspoon cayenne pepper, or to taste

3 tablespoons minced fresh chives

1 tablespoon minced fresh tarragon (optional)

1. Clean the morels well by gently running them under cold water to remove any dirt. Place in a colander to drain.
2. Place 2 tablespoons of the olive oil in a large sauté pan over medium-high heat. Add the shallot and garlic, and cook for 3 minutes, stirring frequently. Add the celeriac and cook for 5 minutes, stirring frequently and adding small amounts of water if necessary to prevent sticking.
3. Add the morel mushrooms, vegetable stock, and nutritional yeast, if using, and cook for 5 minutes stirring frequently.
4. Create a roux by combining the flour with the remaining 2 tablespoons of olive oil in a small bowl and mixing well to form a paste.
5. Add the roux to the sauté pan and cook for 5 minutes, stirring frequently. The sauce will begin to thicken. Add the remaining ingredients and stir well before serving.

Variations
- Replace the morels with shiitakes, oyster mushrooms, or cremini.
- Replace the celeriac with an equal amount of potatoes.
- Replace the tarragon with fresh minced dill or 2 tablespoons of finely chopped basil or flat-leaf parsley.

Chef's Tips and Tricks

After you peel the celeriac, slice it in half, then into quarters. Remove the soft inner core before slicing into thin wedges for the recipe.

To use reconstituted dried morels, place ½ cup or a ¾-ounce package of the mushrooms in 1 cup of hot water. Allow to sit for 5 minutes. Drain, rinse well, and return the mushrooms to a bowl with 2 cups of hot water or vegetable stock. Use the second batch of soaking water for the recipe instead of the vegetable stock listed above.

Asparagus Hollandaise

A fierce battle rages as to whether this sauce is of French or Dutch origin. Around since the 1600s, it's one of the five main base sauces of French haute cuisine. Whatever the history, this rich sauce is traditionally made by an emulsion of eggs and butter. This version uses vegan mayonnaise and butter to create the decadence for those special soirees. Serve along with Braised Tempeh with Herbes de Provence (page 80), or Mediterranean Pistachio-Crusted Tofu (page 229) and Saffron Quinoa Pilaf (page 231).

SERVES 4 TO 6

1 large bunch asparagus

2 tablespoons vegan butter

1 tablespoon nutritional yeast

¼ teaspoon ground turmeric

¾ cup vegan mayonnaise (Vegenaise or homemade, see page 261)

⅛ teaspoon sea salt

⅛ teaspoon ground white pepper

Pinch of cayenne pepper (optional)

1 tablespoon unsweetened soy milk or creamer

1½ tablespoons freshly squeezed lemon juice

Paprika

Black sesame seeds

1. Place a steamer basket in a medium-size pot with 1 inch of water in the pot. Place over medium high heat and bring to a simmer. Add the asparagus and cook covered until just tender, about 6 minutes. Remove from the heat, drain well, and place on a serving platter

2. Meanwhile, place the vegan butter in a small sauté pan over low heat. Once the butter melts, lower the heat to a simmer. Add the remaining ingredients, except the lemon juice, and cook for a few minutes, whisking constantly (keep your whisk moving to avoid separation). Add the lemon juice and whisk well. Remove from the heat and serve over the steamed asparagus. Garnish with a sprinkle of paprika and black sesame seeds.

Grilled Portobello Mushrooms with Béarnaise Sauce

As with hollandaise, béarnaise sauce is a staple sauce used in French haute cuisine, traditionally made with clarified butter and egg yolks. Its creation is attributed to Chef Collinet, whose other claim to fame is the puffed potato. This version receives its yellow color from turmeric, used in Indian curries. Serve as a side dish with Quiche Monet (page 85) or Seitan Bourguignon (page 84). The sauce is glorious served with grilled tofu or tempeh (see page 252).

SERVES 4

1 tablespoon wheat-free tamari or
    other soy sauce
1 tablespoon olive oil
2 teaspoons red wine vinegar
4 portobello mushrooms (see note)

BÉARNAISE SAUCE

Makes about 1 cup sauce

1 teaspoon olive oil
¼ cup diced shallot
½ cup vegan mayonnaise (Vegenaise
    or homemade; see page 261)
1 tablespoon vegan butter
¼ cup unsweetened soy milk
½ teaspoon ground turmeric
Pinch of sea salt
Pinch of freshly ground black pepper
1 teaspoon finely chopped fresh
    tarragon
1 teaspoon finely chopped fresh
    chervil (optional)
1 teaspoon white wine vinegar

1. Preheat a grill. Place the tamari, olive oil, and vinegar in a casserole dish and mix well. Add the portobello mushrooms and allow to sit for 10 minutes, flipping occasionally.
2. Prepare the béarnaise sauce. Place a small sauté pan over medium-high heat. Place the oil and shallot in the pan and cook for 2 minutes, stirring constantly. Lower the heat to medium, add the remaining ingredients, and cook for 5 minutes, stirring occasionally.
3. Grill the mushrooms until char marks appear and the mushrooms become just tender, about 7 minutes on each side. Drizzle with the sauce before serving.

Variations
- Roast the mushrooms for 10 minutes at 400°F.
- Replace the mushrooms with tofu or tempeh cutlets (see pages 250 and 251).
- Add 2 teaspoons of capers to the sauce.

Chef's Tips and Tricks

If you wish, you can remove the gills with a spoon, which helps with the texture. Also, carefully peel off the skin of the mushrooms; this allows them to absorb the marinade.

Roasted Squash with Truffle Cream Sauce

Truffles are a highly prized edible fungus. When I say "highly prized," I mean that if you wanted to purchase the most expensive variety, you would have to sell the condo on the ocean to purchase it, as a recent purchase of a 2-pound truffle went for over $300,000! Fortunately, truffle oil is available to impart some of the flavor of the ingredient. A little goes a long way in the cashew-based cream sauce, which goes well with steamed vegetables or tofu or tempeh cutlets (see pages 250 and 251). Enjoy this dish as a side with Tofu "Scallops" with Saffron Herb Butter (page 82) or Braised Tempeh with Herbes de Provence (page 80).

SERVES 2 TO 4

1 medium-size butternut squash (about 2 pounds), seeded and cut into ½-inch slices

Olive oil

Pinch of sea salt

Pinch of freshly ground black pepper

Finely chopped fresh tarragon

CARAMELIZED ONION

1 tablespoon olive oil

1 large yellow onion, sliced thinly (1¾ cups)

1 teaspoon sugar (optional)

2 teaspoons red wine vinegar

A few drops of truffle oil (optional)

⅛ teaspoon sea salt, or to taste

SAUCE

½ cup raw cashews

1¼ cups unsweetened soy, rice, or other nondairy milk

¼ teaspoon truffle oil, or to taste (see page xxxviii)

¼ teaspoon sea salt

⅛ teaspoon ground white pepper

1 teaspoon finely chopped fresh tarragon or dill

1. Preheat the oven to 450°F. Place the squash slices in a bowl and toss with a drizzle of olive oil and a sprinkle of salt and pepper. Transfer to a rimmed baking sheet or casserole dish filled with about ½ inch of water. Bake until a knife can easily pass through the squash, about 20 minutes.

2. Meanwhile, soak the cashews in about 2 cups of water for 15 minutes while you prepare the onion: Place a sauté pan over medium-high heat. Place the oil and onion in the pan and cook for 3 minutes, stirring constantly. Add the remaining ingredients for the onion mixture and cook for 15 minutes, stirring occasionally.

3. When the cashews are done soaking, drain and rinse well. Transfer to a strong blender with the remaining sauce ingredients, except the tarragon, and blend well. Transfer to a small pan, add the tarragon, and keep over low heat until ready to serve.

4. To serve, drizzle the sauce on each piece of squash, top with the caramelized onion, and garnish with tarragon before serving.

continues

continued

Variations

- Replace the butternut squash with buttercup, acorn, or delicata squash or pumpkin.
- Replace the squash with yams or sweet potatoes.
- Top the squash with a smear of vegan butter before adding the onion.
- If you have more time, the onion will become more caramelized if cooked for up to 45 minutes over low heat, stirring frequently.

Chef's Tips and Tricks

I tell my students that if they want to impress their guests with their cooking abilities, they merely need to sauté onions. Within minutes, you will have people approaching the kitchen, letting you know how good it smells and what a great cook you are!

Buckwheat Galettes with Tarragon Cream

Galettes are a popular dish from the Brittany region of France, where buckwheat fields grace the landscape. If you don't have access to buckwheat flour, you can grind your own using kasha, or toasted buckwheat. In this version, we will be creating small galettes that are rolled to contain the filling. And there is no limit to the fillings to enjoy, both sweet and savory. See below for some suggestions. This savory version is a perfect accompaniment to soups and stews such as French Onion Soup (page 60), Vegan Bouillabaisse (page 65), or Creamy Roasted Chestnut Soup (page 62).

MAKES 9 GALETTES

GALETTES

1 cup buckwheat flour

½ cup white spelt flour

½ teaspoon sea salt

¼ teaspoon baking soda

1¾ cups water

1 tablespoon ground flaxseeds
mixed with 3 tablespoons water

2 tablespoons oil

½ teaspoon freshly squeezed lemon
juice or apple cider vinegar

Oil for cooking

TARRAGON CREAM

½ cup vegan mayonnaise (Vegenaise
or homemade; see page 261)

1 garlic clove, pressed or minced

Pinch of sea salt

Pinch of freshly ground black pepper

Pinch of crushed red pepper flakes

2 tablespoons finely chopped
tarragon

Drop of truffle oil (optional)

1 tablespoon finely chopped fresh
chives (optional)

1. Prepare the galette batter: Place the buckwheat flour, spelt flour, salt, and baking soda in a bowl and whisk well. Place the water, flaxseed mixture, oil, and the lemon juice in another bowl and mix well. Add the wet mixture to the dry and mix well. Set aside.

2. Heat a large skillet over high heat. Pour a small amount of oil into the pan. Pour in ¼ cup of batter, spread thinly with a spatula to create a 6-inch galette, and cook until bubbles begin to form, about 2 minutes. Carefully flip the galette and cook until both sides are golden brown, another minute, depending upon the heat of your pan.

3. While you are making the galettes, prepare the tarragon cream by placing all of its ingredients in a small bowl and mixing well.

4. To serve, spread each galette with 2 tablespoons of the tarragon cream and gently roll to form a galette about 2 inches in diameter.

continues

continued

Variations

- Add spinach, sliced red onion, and sliced tomato to the filling.
- See the Chocolate Hazelnut Crepes variations (page 87) for more suggestions.
- For a sweet galette, add the chocolate hazelnut spread (page 87) or blintz filling (page 235) and top with confectioners' sugar.
- Try with vegan cream cheese and jam or vegan cream cheese, chutney, and avocado.
- Add the Grilled Portobello Mushrooms with Béarnaise Sauce (page 73).
- Blend the tarragon cream with Pesto Magnifico (page 31) and add sliced tomatoes.

Rice Pilaf with Fennel and Saffron

Transform your rice from ordinary to extraordinary! Using saffron, the world's most precious spice, will add color and a distinct flavor (see page xxx). White basmati rice is used to fit this dish in the 30-minute timeline. Feel free to replace with any other grain and add your favorite vegetables to create the pilaf worthy of Louis XIV. Serve as part of a Fusion meal with Tempeh Sauerbraten (page 198), Grilled Tofu with Horseradish Sauce (page 141), or Lemon Tempeh with Creamy Asparagus Sauce (page 40).

SERVES 6 TO 8

1 tablespoon olive oil

2 tablespoons minced shallots

½ cup thinly sliced fennel

2 cups uncooked white basmati rice

3½ cups vegetable stock (see page 253) or water (see note)

1 teaspoon sea salt, or to taste

¼ to ½ teaspoon saffron threads

⅛ teaspoon freshly ground black pepper

2 tablespoons freshly squeezed lemon juice

2 to 3 tablespoons vegan butter (optional)

¼ cup diced chives

½ teaspoon crushed red pepper flakes (optional)

1. Place a medium-size stockpot over medium-high heat. Place the olive oil, shallots, and fennel in the pot and cook for 3 minutes, stirring frequently.
2. Add the rice and stir for 1 minute. Add the vegetable stock, salt, and saffron threads, and bring to a boil. Lower the heat to a simmer, cover, and cook until all the liquid is absorbed, about 15 minutes. Remove from the heat. Let stand covered for an additional 5 minutes.
3. Add the remaining ingredients, and gently fluff with a fork before serving.

continues

continued

Variations

- Many are possible!
- Add 2 teaspoons of fennel seeds along with the shallots.
- Add 1 tablespoon of minced garlic or fresh ginger along with the shallots.
- Add 1 cup of thinly sliced mushrooms, such as shiitake or cremini, along with the shallots.
- Add ½ cup of thinly sliced green onion after the rice has cooked.
- Replace the saffron with 1 teaspoon of ground turmeric and add along with the shallots.
- Replace the chives with 3 tablespoons of any fresh herb, such as basil, flat-leaf parsley, or cilantro.
- Add additional herbs, such as 1 tablespoon of Herbes de Provence (page 94), marjoram, rosemary, or thyme.
- Replace the white basmati with brown basmati, other varieties of brown rice, or quinoa. See page 254 for cooking instructions.

Braised Tempeh with Herbes de Provence

The famous herbes de Provence make yet another dazzling performance and impart their savory flavor into the tempeh, which is seared and left to simmer in a tomato-based broth. This is the dish to impress the partygoers on the Côte d'Azur who are looking for an alternative to a seafood entrée. Serve with Rice Pilaf with Fennel and Saffron (page 78) and Green Beans with Beurre Blanc (page 69).

SERVES 4 TO 6

MARINADE

3 tablespoons olive oil

2 tablespoons wheat-free tamari or other soy sauce

16 ounces tempeh

1 small yellow onion, chopped (1 cup)

2 tablespoons Herbes de Provence (page 94)

1½ cups heated vegetable stock (see page 253) or water

2 tablespoons red wine vinegar

6 ounces tomato paste

3 tomatoes, seeded and chopped into ½-inch chunks (3½ cups)

½ teaspoon sea salt, or to taste

¼ teaspoon freshly ground black pepper

¼ cup thinly sliced kalamata, black, or green olives

3 tablespoons finely chopped fresh flat-leaf parsley

1. Prepare the marinade: Place 2 tablespoons of olive oil and the soy sauce in a 9 by 13-inch casserole dish and mix well. Slice the tempeh into eight ¼-inch-thick cutlets and place in the marinade. Allow to sit for 5 minutes, flipping occasionally to ensure an even coating.

2. Meanwhile, place the remaining 1 tablespoon of olive oil in a large sauté pan over medium-high heat. Add the onion and herbes de Provence and cook for 3 minutes, stirring frequently. Add the tempeh and contents of the casserole dish and cook for 5 minutes, gently flipping the tempeh with a spatula.

3. Lower the heat to medium, add the vegetable stock, vinegar, tomato paste, tomatoes, salt, and pepper, and cook for 10 minutes, gently stirring and flipping the tempeh cutlets occasionally. Garnish with the olives and parsley before serving.

Variations

- For a crisper tempeh, and if you have more time, you can add it to the sauté pan before adding the onion in step 2. Cook for 3 minutes on each side and remove from the pan. Add another tablespoon of oil, add the onion, and proceed with the recipe.
- Replace the tempeh with extra-firm or super-firm tofu.
- Add 3 pressed or minced garlic cloves, along with the onion.
- Add 1 cup of seeded and chopped red bell pepper or chopped mushrooms, along with the onion.

Rainbow Steamed Vegetables with Spicy Béchamel Sauce

Béchamel is a traditional French white sauce made with milk and thickened with butter and flour. It is considered one of the "mother sauces" of French cuisine, as it forms the base of many other sauces, including the variation below—Mornay sauce. There will be plenty of sauce to use for additional steamed veggies or as a topping for grilled tofu or tempeh cutlets (see pages 250 and 251). Serve this colorful dish as part of a Fusion meal with Baked Vegan Schnitzel (page 196) and Saffron Quinoa Pilaf (page 231).

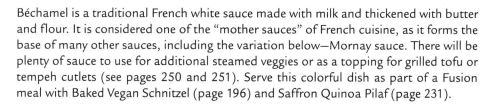

SERVES 4

2 cups small broccoli florets

2 cups small cauliflower florets

1 cup thinly sliced carrot

½ cup julienned purple cabbage

1 cup seeded and diced red bell pepper

3 tablespoons finely chopped fresh flat-leaf parsley

SPICY BÉCHAMEL SAUCE

2 tablespoons melted vegan butter

2 tablespoons spelt flour

1 tablespoon olive oil

¼ cup diced shallot

2 cloves garlic, pressed or minced

1 teaspoon seeded and diced hot chile pepper, or crushed red pepper flakes to taste

2 cups unsweetened soy milk

¼ teaspoon sea salt, or to taste

⅛ teaspoon ground white pepper

⅛ teaspoon smoked paprika (optional)

1. Place a steamer basket in a medium-size pot with 1 inch of water in the pot. Place over medium-high heat and bring to a simmer. Add the broccoli, cauliflower, and carrot and cook covered until just tender, about 5 minutes. Remove from the heat, add the purple cabbage, and allow to sit, covered, while you prepare the sauce.

2. Meanwhile, prepare the béchamel sauce. Place the butter and flour in a small bowl and mix well. Place the olive oil in a small sauté pan over medium-high heat. Add the shallot, garlic, and chile pepper, and cook for 3 minutes, stirring frequently. Add the soy milk, salt, white pepper, and smoked paprika, if using, and cook for 3 minutes, or until the milk begins to boil. Lower the heat to medium, add the flour mixture, and whisk well. Cook until the sauce thickens, about 3 minutes.

3. To serve, decoratively arrange the veggies on a serving platter or individual plates. Top with sauce and garnish with the red bell pepper and parsley.

Variation

- Create a **Mornay Sauce** by adding ½ cup of grated vegan mozzarella- or Cheddar-style cheese to the béchamel sauce once it thickens.

81

Tofu "Scallops" with Saffron Herb Butter

Going with tofu instead of fish in this dish is sure to put the ooh in your ooh-la-la. Break out your oval cookie cutters to create a scallop shape. Saffron, the crown jewel of the spice kingdom, imparts its magic to this rich vegan butter sauce, giving it a golden color and sublime flavor. Serve with Spinach Leek Rice (page 169) and Beer-Braised Greens (page 189).

SERVES 4

¼ teaspoon saffron threads (see page xxx)

2 tablespoons hot water

¼ cup freshly squeezed lemon juice

1 tablespoon olive oil

¼ teaspoon sea salt

⅛ teaspoon freshly ground black pepper

⅛ teaspoon cayenne pepper

14 ounces extra-firm or super-firm tofu

4 tablespoons vegan butter

3 tablespoons white wine (see box; optional)

1 to 2 cloves garlic, pressed or minced

1 tablespoon minced fresh marjoram

½ teaspoon dried thyme

Black sesame seeds

Fresh dill or flat-leaf parsley leaves

Chef Patrick Recommends:
French Sauvignon Blanc

1. Preheat the oven to 375°F. Place the saffron in a small bowl with the hot water and allow to steep while preparing the rest of the dish. Place 3 tablespoons of lemon juice and the olive oil, salt, pepper, and cayenne in a 9 by 13-inch casserole dish and mix well.

2. Slice the tofu lengthwise into three cutlets. If you have a small oval cookie cutter, cut out as many pieces as possible and place them in the casserole dish. Allow to sit for 5 minutes, flipping once to ensure even coating. If you do not have the cookie cutter, slice each cutlet into twelve pieces and place in the casserole dish. Bake for 20 minutes.

3. Meanwhile, place the vegan butter in a small sauté pan over medium heat. Once the butter melts, add the wine, if using, the garlic, the remaining tablespoon of lemon juice, and the marjoram, and thyme, and stir well. Add the saffron and its soaking water, being sure to use every last one of the precious threads. Stir well and lower the heat to low until the tofu is ready.

4. To serve, place a small amount of the butter sauce on each plate, top with the tofu, drizzle with more butter sauce, and garnish with a few black sesame seeds and dill or parsley leaves.

Variations

- Replace the marjoram with fresh oregano or dill.
- If no saffron is available, you can add ½ teaspoon of ground turmeric to the sauce when the butter is melted.
- Replace the tofu with tempeh or cubes of portobello mushrooms.

Kermit's Relief (Faux Frog's Legs)
with Shallots and Garlic

This was the last recipe I developed for the book. It's my commentary on the fact that, as with the escargot, at some point in human history, someone thought it was a good idea to eat the legs of a frog. It's the third dish in what I call "The Relief Series," which also includes Daffy's Relief Peking Duck included in *The 30 Minute Vegan's Taste of the East,* and Charlie's Relief Tuna-Free Salad in *Vegan Fusion World Cuisine.* You can guess why Kermit is relieved that we are using tofu instead of his legs! Enjoy as part of a meal that includes Celeriac with Morel Mushroom Sauce (page 70) and Saffron Quinoa Pilaf (page 231).

SERVES 6

MARINADE

3 tablespoons freshly squeezed lemon juice

3 tablespoons nutritional yeast

2 teaspoons olive oil

½ teaspoon sea salt

¼ teaspoon freshly ground black pepper

A few drops of liquid smoke (optional)

A few drops of truffle oil (optional)

14 ounces extra-firm tofu

SHALLOT GARLIC TOPPING

2 teaspoons olive oil

½ cup diced shallot

3 cloves garlic, pressed or minced

½ teaspoon seeded and diced hot chile pepper

¼ cup white wine (see box)

1 tablespoon vegan butter

¼ teaspoon sea salt, or to taste

1 tablespoon freshly squeezed lemon juice

2 tablespoons finely chopped fresh flat-leaf parsley

2 teaspoons finely chopped fresh tarragon

1. Preheat the oven to HIGH BROIL. Place all of the marinade ingredients, except the tofu, in a casserole dish and mix well. Slice the tofu into three cutlets. Slice each cutlet into five long strips. Place the tofu in the marinade, being sure to leave space between each piece of tofu so they will get crispy. Flip onto each side to ensure an even coating. Broil for 20 minutes, flipping the cutlets after 10 minutes.

2. Meanwhile, place a small sauté pan over medium-high heat. Place the oil, shallot, garlic, and chile pepper in the pan and cook for 3 minutes, stirring constantly. Lower the heat to low and cook for 5 minutes, stirring occasionally. Add the remaining topping ingredients and cook for 5 minutes, stirring occasionally.

3. To serve, place the tofu on a platter or individual plates and top with the shallot mixture.

Chef Patrick Recommends:
French, dry Chardonnay or Chablis

Seitan Bourguignon

Bourguignon is a classic French stew made with red Burgundy wine. Talk about social mobility: originating as a peasant dish, it is now served in the finest French restaurants around the world. This version is bursting with flavor and uses seitan, a vegan meat analogue made from wheat. If you have more time, allow this dish to cook longer at a lower temperature. Serve as part of a French feast with Roasted Squash with Truffle Cream Sauce (page 74) and Provençal Vegetable Salad (page 67).

SERVES 6 TO 8

2 tablespoons olive oil

1 yellow onion, sliced into half-moons (1¼ cups)

3 garlic cloves, minced or pressed

1 teaspoon dried thyme

16 ounces seitan, chopped into ¾-inch pieces

1 cup cremini mushrooms quartered or halved

2 cups heated vegetable stock (see page 253) or water

2½ cups Burgundy wine (see box)

2 bay leaves

1 tablespoon wheat-free tamari or other soy sauce

1 cup pearl onions

1 carrot, chopped small (1 cup)

3 tablespoons tomato paste

¼ cup chopped fresh flat-leaf parsley

1 teaspoon sea salt, or to taste

¼ teaspoon freshly ground black pepper

1. Place the olive oil in a large pot over medium-high heat. Add the onion, garlic, and thyme and cook for 3 minutes, stirring frequently.
2. Add the seitan and mushrooms and cook for 2 minutes, stirring frequently. Lower the heat to medium, add the vegetable stock, wine, bay leaves, tamari, and pearl onions, and cook for 10 minutes uncovered, stirring occasionally. Add the carrot and tomato paste and cook for 10 minutes, stirring occasionally.
3. Add the remaining ingredients and stir well. Remove the bay leaves before serving. Enjoy!

Variations
- Add ¼ teaspoon of liquid smoke along with the salt and pepper.
- Top each serving with chopped Fakin' Bacon or Tempeh Bacon (see page 251).
- For gluten-free, replace the seitan with cubed tempeh or extra-firm or super-firm tofu.

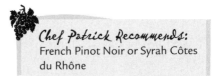

Chef Patrick Recommends:
French Pinot Noir or Syrah Côtes du Rhône

Quiche Monet

An offshoot of the famous quiche Lorraine, which typically contains bacon and eggs, this heart-healthy quiche was inspired by a trip to Monet's gardens at Giverny and uses silken tofu to create the body of the dish. This makes a delightful light lunch when served with Provençal Vegetable Salad (page 67) and Green Beans with Beurre Blanc (page 69).

SERVES 4 TO 6

1 (9-inch) vegan piecrust (go for spelt if you can)

1 tablespoon oil

1¼ cups sliced leek, rinsed and drained very well

3 garlic cloves, pressed or minced

½ cup diced chanterelle, shiitake, or cremini mushrooms

4 ounces Fakin' Bacon or Tempeh Bacon (see page 251) (¾ cup diced)

1 (12.3-ounce) package silken firm tofu

8 ounces extra-firm tofu, crumbled or grated

2 tablespoons unsweetened soy, rice, or almond milk

2 tablespoons nutritional yeast

2 tablespoons tahini

1 tablespoon freshly squeezed lemon juice

¾ teaspoon sea salt, or to taste

½ teaspoon ground tumeric

⅛ teaspoon freshly ground black pepper

¼ teaspoon cayenne pepper

1 tablespoon finely chopped fresh tarragon

2 teaspoons dried marjoram, or 1 tablespoon minced fresh

½ cup grated vegan Cheddar- or mozzarella-style cheese (optional)

1. Preheat the oven to 450°F. Poke a few holes in the pie shell with a fork and bake for 10 minutes. Remove from the oven.

2. Meanwhile, place a large sauté pan over medium-high heat. Place the oil, leeks, and garlic in the pan and cook for 2 minutes, stirring constantly. Add the mushrooms and Fakin' Bacon and cook for 3 minutes, stirring frequently.

3. Place the tofu, soy milk, nutritional yeast, tahini, lemon juice, salt, pepper, and cayenne in a food processor and process until creamy. Transfer to the sauté pan with the remaining ingredients and mix well.

4. Pour into the pie shell and bake for 10 minutes. Lower the heat to 425°F and bake for an additional 10 minutes. Serve warm or cold.

Variations

- For a creamier, less firm quiche, replace the extra-firm tofu with an additional 12.3-ounce package of silken tofu.
- Replace the chanterelle mushrooms with shiitake, oyster, or cremini mushrooms.
- Add 1 tablespoon of Herbes de Provence (page 94).
- Add 1 cup of chopped fresh spinach along with the mushrooms.

Scrambled Tofu with Chives and Wild Mushrooms

Get your scramble on with this herbes de Provence–flavored variation of this popular dish. While wild mushrooms add a deep, woodsy flavor, you can replace them with whatever exotic mushroom you can find. Serve as part of a French brunch with Pommes Frites (page 68) and Asparagus Hollandaise (page 72).

SERVES 2 TO 4

2 tablespoons olive oil

¼ cup minced shallot

1 medium-size leek, sliced thinly and cleaned well

¾ cup thinly sliced wild mushrooms (see page xxxv)

2 garlic cloves, pressed or minced

2 teaspoons Herbes de Provence (page 94)

14 ounces extra-firm tofu, crumbled

3 tablespoons nutritional yeast

2 tablespoons tahini (optional)

1 tablespoon wheat-free tamari or other soy sauce

1 tablespoon freshly squeezed lemon juice

¼ teaspoon freshly ground black pepper

¼ teaspoon sea salt, or to taste

3 tablespoons finely chopped fresh chives

1 tablespoon minced fresh tarragon

1. Place the oil in a large sauté pan over medium-high heat. Add the shallot, leek, mushrooms, garlic, and herbes de Provence, and cook for 3 minutes, stirring frequently.
2. Add the tofu and cook for 5 minutes, stirring frequently. Add the remaining ingredients, except the chives and tarragon, and cook for 5 minutes, stirring frequently. Depending upon the brand of tofu used, you may need to add 2 to 3 tablespoons of water to create a moist texture.
3. Add the chives and tarragon and stir well before serving.

Variations
- So many are possible!
- Replace the mushrooms with such veggies as seeded and diced bell pepper, seeded and chopped Roma tomatoes, or grated carrots.
- Change the herbs to create different ethnic flavors:
- For an Italian flair: replace the herbes de Provence with 1 tablespoon of Italian Spice Mix (page 51).
- For Sun-Dried Tomato Basil Scramble:, Replace the mushrooms with ¼ cup of soaked and thinly sliced sun-dried tomatoes. Replace the chives, herbes de Provence, and tarragon with 2 tablespoons of minced fresh basil and 1 teaspoon of fresh oregano.
- For a Greek taste—kalamata rosemary: add ¼ to ½ cup of thinly sliced kalamata olives. Replace the herbes de Provence and tarragon with 1 tablespoon of minced fresh rosemary.

Chocolate Hazelnut Crepes

For some, the crepe is the national dish of France. On my first trips to Paris, before my vegan days, *crêpes chocolat* was one of my four basic food groups. As with the Buckwheat Galette, there are countless fillings, both sweet and savory, that can create the crepe of your dreams. Go all out and have a *fête des crêpes* (a crepe party), and see who can come up with the most innovative filling. I list several suggestions below. If you do not have a crepe pan, you can use a large skillet or sauté pan.

MAKES 6 CREPES

CREPES: DRY

1 cup white spelt flour

⅛ teaspoon sea salt

2 tablespoons sugar (see page 261)

¼ teaspoon baking soda

CREPES: WET

1 cup soy milk

¼ cup water

2 tablespoons melted vegan butter

½ teaspoon freshly squeezed lemon juice or apple cider vinegar

½ teaspoon vanilla extract (or another flavored extract)

Oil for the crepes

Strawberries, sliced (optional)

Confectioner's sugar (optional)

CHOCOLATE HAZELNUT SPREAD

½ cup plus 2 tablespoons hazelnut butter

3 tablespoons unsweetened cocoa powder

3 tablespoons pure maple syrup or sweetener of choice

¼ teaspoon hazelnut extract

½ cup soy milk, rice milk, or almond milk (see page 259)

1. Make the crepe batter: Place the dry ingredients in a bowl and whisk well. Place the wet ingredients in another bowl and mix well. Add the wet to the dry and mix well. The consistency you are looking for is thinner than a pancake batter but thick enough to coat the back of a spoon.

2. Prepare the chocolate hazelnut spread: Place the nut butter and cocoa powder in a bowl and mix well. Place the maple syrup, hazelnut extract, and soy milk in another bowl and mix well. Slowly add the maple mixture to the nut butter mixture and mix well, adding additional soy milk if necessary to reach a spreadable consistency. Set aside.

3. Place a crepe pan over high heat and oil lightly. Pour a rounded ¼ cup of batter onto the pan and spread as thinly as possible. Cook until bubbles form over the entire surface, about 3 minutes, depending on the heat of the pan. Carefully flip and cook for an additional 3 minutes. Repeat until all the batter is used. Mix the batter in between crepes to maintain a uniform consistency.

4. To serve, spread about 2 tablespoons of the chocolate mixture in the center of each crepe. Add the strawberries if using, and fold over two opposite sides of the crepe toward the center. Then flip it over so the seam is on the bottom. Top with confectioners' sugar, if using, before serving.

continues

Chocolate Hazelnut Crepes *continued*

Variations

- You can replace the hazelnut butter with almond butter, peanut butter, cashew butter, or tahini.
- Replace the hazelnut extract with orange, coffee, or mint extract.
- Sweet filling suggestion:
  - Cashew Cream (page 90) with fresh sliced strawberries
- Some savory Fusion filling suggestions:
  - Italian: arugula and pesto
  - German: very well drained Beer-Braised Greens (page 189) with sliced Notwurst (page 197)
  - British: thinly sliced Grilled Tofu with Horseradish Sauce (page 141)
  - Romanian: Transylvanian Roasted Eggplant (page 221) with sliced tomatoes
  - Spanish: use the filling from the Empanadas (page 107)
  - Feel free to use any of the fillings from the Buckwheat Galettes (page 76) as well.

Lavender-Infused Cocoa-Dusted Truffles

Yes, the relaxation-inducing herb of spas and wellness centers has innovative applications in the culinary world. Here it is used to infuse flavor to these ambrosial and heavenly chocolate delights (for more information on cooking with lavender, see page xxix). Adjust the sweetener to taste, as some chocolate chips have more sugar than others.

MAKES ABOUT 20 TRUFFLES

½ cup regular (not light) coconut milk

2 tablespoons culinary-grade lavender flowers

1 tablespoon pure maple syrup, agave nectar, or coconut nectar (see page 261), or to taste

1 teaspoon vanilla extract

⅛ teaspoon ground cardamom (optional)

2 tablespoons unsweetened cocoa powder

1¼ cups vegan dark chocolate chips

Lavender flowers, for garnish

1. Place the coconut milk in a small pan over very low heat. Add the lavender flowers and allow to simmer for 15 minutes, stirring occasionally. Strain out the flowers and discard. Set aside the milk in a small bowl. Add the maple syrup, vanilla, and cardamom, if using, and stir well. Place the cocoa powder on a small plate.

2. After ten minutes of heating the coconut milk, melt the chocolate chips by heating them in a double boiler over medium heat until the consistency is smooth, lump-free, and creamy, stirring only once or twice. (If you don't have a double boiler, you can place a glass or stainless-steel bowl on top of a pot with 1 to 2 inches of boiling water in it.)

3. When the chocolate is melted, add the coconut milk mixture and stir well. Place in the refrigerator until firm enough to scoop, about 5 minutes.

4. Using a small scoop or a rounded tablespoon, form small balls. Place on the plate with the cocoa powder and cover each ball entirely with a light dusting. Sprinkle each truffle with a few lavender flowers. Place on a parchment paper–lined or lightly oiled baking sheet. Refrigerate until cool, about 10 minutes.

Variations
- Place a pitted cherry or a ½-inch piece of candied ginger, vegan marshmallow, or dried fruit such as papaya, fig, or apricot in the center of the chocolate ball before dusting with cocoa.
- Dust with vegan confectioners' sugar instead of cocoa.
- Add ½ teaspoon of chipotle chile powder to the melted chocolate.

Raw Pear Tart with Cashew Cream and Fresh Berries ♥

Gracing the tables of French nobility since the times of Marie Antoinette, the pear tart makes a perfect finale to any gourmet feast. With a walnut date crust and a cashew cream topping, this raw recipe demonstrates how living foods can be strikingly delicious as well as vibrantly healthful. If you want to let loose the full joie de vivre, spread a layer of Chocolate Mousse (page 92) over the crust before adding the pears and cashew cream.

MAKES ONE 9-INCH TART

CRUST

1 cup finely chopped pitted dates (try Medjool)

1¼ cups chopped pecans

Pinch of ground cinnamon

Pinch of ground cardamom

CASHEW CREAM

1 cup raw cashews

½ to ¾ cup water

2 tablespoons agave nectar, coconut nectar (see page 261), or pure maple syrup, or to taste

Pinch of sea salt

1. Place the cashews in a small bowl with 2 cups of water. Prepare the topping: Place the lemon juice, maple syrup, cinnamon, and nutmeg in a large shallow dish and mix well. Add the sliced pears and gently coat well.

2. Prepare the crust: Oil a 9-inch tart pan. Place the pecans in a food processor and process until finely ground. Add the dates, cinnamon, and cardamom and pulse-process until the ingredients are just ground up. Do not over-process or your crust will be too gummy.

3. Transfer to the tart pan and press down firmly to create the crust. The mixture should be holding together. If not, return to the processor and process a bit further. Depending upon the moisture of the dates, you may need to add a small amount of water or liquid from the topping to help hold the crust together.

4. Prepare the cashew cream: Drain and rinse the cashews well. Place them in a strong blender along with the ½ to ¾ cup of water and agave nectar. Blend until creamy. The amount of water you will need will depend on the strength of your blender.

continues

continued

TOPPING

2 tablespoons freshly squeezed
    lemon juice

3 tablespoons pure maple syrup or
    agave or coconut nectar

Pinch of ground cinnamon

Pinch of ground nutmeg, or ground
    cardamom or allspice

2 large ripe pears, sliced into ½-inch
    strips

1 pint fresh berries, rinsed and
    drained well

Mint leaves

5. Spread an even layer of the cream over the crust. Creatively place the pear slices on top of the cream. Try forming a spiral where each pear slice slightly overlaps the one next to it.

6. Decorate with fresh berries and mint leaves. If you have more time, chill for 15 minutes or more before serving.

Variations

- Add 2 tablespoons of raw almond butter to the crust.
- Add 2 tablespoons of raw cacao nibs to the crust.
- Replace the pecans with almonds or walnuts and replace the dates with dried figs.
- Replace the cashews in the cream with macadamia nuts.
- Create a multicolored cream: Reserve half of the cashew cream and blend with ½ cup of fresh blueberries or strawberries to create an additional colored cream. Creatively decorate with both creams. Think swirls!
- Experiment with different types of pears, such as Anjou, Bartlett, and Comice.
- Replace the pears with apples, peaches, or nectarines.
- Create a Lavender Cashew Cream: Soak 2 tablespoons of lavender flowers in 3 tablespoons of boiling hot water for 20 minutes. Strain the lavender flowers through a strainer, adding the liquid to the blender along with the cashews. Discard the flowers. When the tart is finished, you can garnish with a sprinkle of fresh lavender flowers.

Chocolate Mousse

Another essential dish in your French culinary repertoire, the chocolate mousse is a guaranteed crowd-pleaser. Once again, a cooked and raw version of the dish is provided so you may compare the flavors and textures. The cooked version uses melted chocolate chips as well as coconut milk, while the raw version uses avocados and raw cocoa powder to create the creamy base. Serve with Cashew Cream (page 90) and top with fresh berries and mint leaf for the perfect ending to your French feast.

COOKED VERSION: SERVES 4 TO 6

1½ cups vegan dark chocolate chips

½ cup plus 2 tablespoons regular (not light) coconut milk

½ cup soy creamer or soy milk

2 tablespoons coconut oil (optional)

3 tablespoons pure maple syrup, or to taste, depending on the sweetness of chips and soy creamer

2 teaspoons ground flaxseeds mixed with 1 tablespoon water

½ teaspoon vanilla extract

⅛ teaspoon ground cinnamon

Pinch of ground cardamom

Pinch of ground nutmeg

Pinch of sea salt

4 strawberries, sliced

8 mint leaves

1. Melt the chocolate chips in a double boiler according to the method discussed on page 89. Add the remaining ingredients, except the strawberries and mint leaves, and stir well.
2. Pour into a small bowl and place in the freezer for 20 minutes, or until just firm.
3. Mix with a hand mixer, or transfer to a food processor and process until fluffy. Top with strawberries and mint leaves before serving.

continues

continued

RAW VERSION ♥: SERVES 2 TO 4

4 to 6 large Medjool dates, pitted (¼ cup)

¼ cup water, or raw almond or macadamia milk (see page 259)

1 large avocado, pitted and mashed (1 cup)

3 tablespoons unsweetened cocoa powder

1 teaspoon ground flaxseeds mixed with 1 tablespoon water

2 tablespoons coconut oil

Pinch of sea salt

Pinch of ground cinnamon

Pinch of ground cardamom

Pinch of ground nutmeg

½ teaspoon vanilla extract, or seeds from 1 vanilla bean (optional)

2 tablespoons agave nectar or pure maple syrup, or to taste

2 tablespoons dried coconut

1. Place the dates in a small bowl with ¼ cup of water and allow to sit for 15 minutes.
2. Transfer the dates and their soaking water to a food processor with all of the remaining ingredients, except the coconut flakes, and process until smooth. Give it a taste at this point. Depending on the flavor of the avocados, you may need to add more sweetener. If so, process again.
3. Pour into individual serving bowls or one main serving dish and top with coconut flakes.

Variations
- Add 1 teaspoon of different flavored extracts, such as orange, hazelnut, coffee, or raspberry.
- For a hint of heat, add ¼ teaspoon of cayenne pepper or ½ teaspoon of chili powder.

Quicker and Easier France

Herbes de Provence

Create your own blend of this classic French herb combination. Feel free to leave out an ingredient or two (or three) if necessary. You can even experiment with different quantities of the same ingredients based upon your personal preference.

MAKES ABOUT ¾ CUP

2 tablespoons dried thyme
2 tablespoons dried summer savory
2 tablespoons dried marjoram
1 tablespoon dried rosemary
1 tablespoon dried tarragon
1 tablespoon dried oregano
1 tablespoon dried basil
1 tablespoon dried sage
2 teaspoons crushed culinary-grade lavender flowers
2 teaspoons dried fennel seeds

▶ Combine all the ingredients in a bowl and mix well. Store in a glass jar in a cool, dark place.

Credits: Mark Reinfeld

Garlic Herb Aioli

A traditional Provençal sauce that is made from garlic, olive oil, and eggs. This egg-free version is bursting with flavor and is spectacular as a spread in sandwiches and wraps. Try it on a fresh baguette, Bruschetta (page 4), or Babe's Bocadillos (page 106).

MAKES 1 CUP OF DRESSING

1 cup vegan mayonnaise (Vegenaise or homemade; see page 261)
1 to 2 garlic cloves, pressed or minced
1 tablespoon minced fresh flat-leaf parsley
¾ teaspoon minced fresh rosemary
½ teaspoon fresh thyme
½ teaspoon vegan Dijon mustard (optional)

▶ Stir together all the ingredients and store in an airtight container in the refrigerator for up to one week.

▶ For best results, store in a glass container in the refrigerator and use within a week.

Variations

- For Chipotle Aioli, add 1 to 2 chipotle chiles, soaked until soft, then seeded and minced.
- Add 2 teaspoons of dehydrated onions and ½ teaspoon of onion powder for a French Onion Dip.
- Try roasting several garlic cloves and then blending them together with the vegan mayonnaise in a mini-food processor.

Crème Fraîche

For a quick and easy vegan Crème Fraîche to garnish your dishes, use the Vegan Sour Cream (page 226), minus the dill. For a raw variety, use the Cashew Cream recipe (see page 90), minus the sweetener and vanilla, and plus 1 tablespoon of freshly squeezed lemon juice and ¼ teaspoon of sea salt, or to taste.

Quick and Easy French recipes courtesy of chef Deborah Brown Pivain, of the Gentle Gourmet in Paris, France

Here's an absolutely typical Summer French Salad from the upper half of France. Enjoy slices of steamed baby potatoes with lightly steamed and refreshed French green beans, thin radish slices, and lightly steamed refreshed carrots cut on a severe diagonal. Toss with a French vinaigrette made with 1 tablespoon of red wine vinegar for each 3 tablespoons of olive oil, 1 teaspoon of grainy mustard, and a combination of finely chopped fresh herbs (chervil and chives would be great and borage or nasturtium flowers would make it perfect). This could be served on a plate of mixed salad greens.

Salade Rubis ❤

This is my favorite French winter salad because it is all of dark red ingredients. Combine two beets (one raw and spiraled and one roasted and sliced), dried cranberries, radicchio, red endive, and unpeeled, extremely finely sliced red apple. Top with Primavera Dressing (see page 25).

Try my famous Raw Melon Cocktail ❤

Chill one ripe Charentais melon (French cantaloupe) until very cold. Cut and peel it, and put four-fifths of the pieces in a blender with a teaspoon of fruity olive oil, 1 teaspoon or more of chopped fresh tarragon, and a bit of fresh ground pepper. Blend till very smooth. Pour into glasses or soup plates and sprinkle with extremely finely sliced radishes, chopped tarragon, the leftover melon pieces cut into small dice, and a borage flower.

Credit: Mark Reinfeld

PART THREE

SPAIN AND PORTUGAL

Knowledge of what is possible is the beginning of happiness.
—George Santayana

There is something about Spain that conjures images of romance. Is it the sun-kissed red tile roofs, the flamenco dancers, or perhaps it's the steaming pots of paella? Admittedly, the culinary scene in Spain and Portugal is, shall we say, less than vegan friendly. There are, however, some popular traditional dishes, such as Gazpacho and Romesco Sauce, which are vegan by nature. Vegetarian travelers will find more of a refuge in the southern regions, where the Mediterranean (as well as North African) influences can be felt. The western and northern regions are more influenced by the cuisine of France and are more animal centered.

In the world of foodies, Spain is probably most well known for its tapas, the small portions of food, larger than an appetizer and smaller than a main dish, that are an integral part of dining in Spain. Please see below for a suggestion of a 30-Minute Vegan Tapas Fiesta.

Spanish cuisine has recently experienced a global renaissance, especially with the appearance of Ferran Adrià's El Bulli restaurant in the province of Girona. He is a pioneer of what is known as molecular gastronomy, where food science has a

99

strong role in the creation and presentation of dishes. The use of dry ice for quick freezes and the use of foaming devices to create unique textures are two of the many fascinating techniques in this emerging trend. I had the opportunity to attend a demonstration of Mr. Adrià in Amsterdam and was stunned at the level of creativity that is possible with molecular gastronomy. While most home cooks will not be breaking out their foamer or liquid nitrogen for their next cocktail party just yet, it will be exciting to see how this trend plays out in the vegan culinary world.

As far as your Spanish and Portuguese pantry, popular vegetables include artichokes, onions, mushrooms, cabbage, chile peppers, potatoes, olives, and garlic. Fruits include apples, pomegranates, figs, cherries, pears, avocados, and tomatoes. For legumes, we have lentils, fava beans, and chickpeas. Spain is one of the top producers of almonds, walnuts, and hazelnuts. Stock up on herbs and spices, including parsley, coriander, saffron, and paprika. Smoked paprika is a particularly flavorful ingredient to use. It is available in both hot and mild (or sweet) varieties.

While the focus of this section is Spanish cuisine, I've also added some Portuguese dishes including Feijoada (hearty bean soup) and Portuguese Sweet Rice. The adventurous can explore the vast world of the empanada, which is bread stuffed with a multitude of fillings, both savory and sweet. Two cold soups are featured including the famous Gazpacho and the lesser-known, though equally flavorful, Ajo Blanco, which is almond based.

Other dishes include a veganized bocadillo, the ham and cheese sandwich of Spain, as well as a simple Apple Hazelnut Salad and Paprika Tofu. Of course, no section on Spanish cuisine would be complete without including a vegan version of paella, originating in Valencia and making its way around the world culinary scene. Finish your fiesta with a dessert sampler platter of Chocolate-Stuffed Figs, Almond Brittle, and Vegan Flan and a glass of Horchata or Virgin Sangria.

Stuffed Mushrooms with Corn and Saffron

These mushrooms will be the talk of your next tapas party. Saffron blesses everything it comes in contact with, including these stuffed treats. (For more on saffron, see page xxx.) The stuffing can be used in a multitude of dishes. Serve as an appetizer before any of your Spanish feasts.

MAKES 12 STUFFED MUSHROOMS

MUSHROOM MARINADE

1 tablespoon olive oil

2 teaspoons red wine vinegar

1 tablespoon wheat-free tamari or other soy sauce

2 tablespoons freshly squeezed lemon juice

12 large cremini mushrooms, stems removed and discarded

STUFFING

1 tablespoon olive oil

2 tablespoons finely diced yellow onion

3 tablespoons diced celery

2 garlic cloves, minced or pressed

⅛ teaspoon saffron threads in ¼ cup hot water or vegetable stock

¼ cup plus 1 tablespoon bread crumbs

¼ cup corn

¼ teaspoon sea salt, or to taste

Pinch of freshly ground black pepper

Pinch of crushed red pepper flakes

2 teaspoons nutritional yeast (optional)

1 teaspoon minced fresh tarragon

¼ cup grated vegan Cheddar- or mozzarella-style cheese (optional but recommended)

1. Preheat the oven to 400°F. Prepare the mushrooms: Place the marinade ingredients in an 8-inch casserole dish and mix well. Clean the mushrooms with a mushroom brush or a slightly damp cloth. Add the mushrooms to the casserole dish and allow them to sit in the marinade while you prepare the stuffing. Flip periodically to ensure an even coating.

2. Prepare the stuffing: Place the olive oil in a small sauté pan over medium-high heat. Add the onion, celery, and garlic, and cook for 3 minutes, stirring frequently. Add the remaining ingredients, except the tarragon and the vegan cheese but including the saffron and its soaking water, and cook for 3 minutes, stirring frequently. Add the tarragon and mix well.

3. Fill the mushrooms with the stuffing mixture. You can form a small mound of stuffing on each mushroom. Top with the vegan cheese, if using, and bake for 20 minutes before serving.

Variations

- Replace the tarragon with 1 tablespoon of finely chopped fresh flat-leaf parsley or basil.
- Replace the corn with chopped walnuts, pecans, or hazelnuts.
- Replace the red wine vinegar in the marinade with balsamic vinegar and add 1 teaspoon of pure maple syrup and 1 teaspoon of vegan Dijon mustard.
- For gluten-free, use gluten-free bread crumbs.

Gazpacho ♥

Originating in the southern Andalusia region of Spain, and popular throughout Spain, as well as Portugal (and Latin America for that matter), this cold raw soup is a veritable fiesta in a bowl. Seek out the best tomatoes you can find and your efforts will be greatly rewarded. I recommend using local, organic heirloom tomatoes if you can find them. A high-quality olive oil will also really increase the flavor. Serve with Stuffed Mushrooms with Corn and Saffron (page 110) and Spanish Rice (page 111).

SERVES 6

4 cups diced tomatoes, with juice, pressed firmly

½ cup diced red onion

2 garlic cloves, pressed or minced

2 tablespoons freshly squeezed lime juice

1 small green bell pepper, seeded and diced (¾ cup)

2 tablespoons red wine vinegar

2 tablespoons olive oil

1½ teaspoons ground cumin (optionally toasted; see page 249)

½ teaspoon sea salt, or to taste

⅛ teaspoon freshly ground black pepper

⅛ teaspoon cayenne pepper

½ cup seeded and diced cucumber

1 tablespoon minced fresh mint

½ avocado, peeled, pitted, and cut into ½-inch cubes

1. Combine all the ingredients, except ¼ cup of the red onion, and the cucumber, mint, and avocado, in a strong blender and blend well. For a chunkier gazpacho, you can pulse chop some of the soup in a food processor instead of blending. Transfer to a large bowl.

2. Add the remaining onion, cucumber, and mint and mix well. For best results, refrigerate for 20 minutes or longer. Top with the avocado cubes before serving.

Variations

- Try topping with a dollop of Vegan Sour Cream (page 226) and a fresh cilantro leaf garnish.
- Add 1 teaspoon of smoked paprika along with the cumin.
- Add 1 slice of toasted bread before blending.
- Add 1 teaspoon of seeded and diced jalapeño before blending.
- Add 2 tablespoons of finely chopped fresh basil, cilantro, or flat-leaf parsley after blending.
- Add 1 cup of corn after blending.

Ajo Blanco

The stepsister of gazpacho and also originating in the Andalusian region of Spain, *ajo blanco* is a refreshing almond-based soup that is enjoyed chilled. Do as the Granadians do and enjoy with a baked potato, or partake during your siesta with Babe's Bocadillos (page 106) and Apple Hazelnut Salad with Shaved Fennel (page 105).

SERVES 4 TO 6

1¾ cups slivered almonds

2 large garlic cloves

4 cups water

2 tablespoons olive oil

2 teaspoons sherry vinegar, or
  1 teaspoon red wine vinegar

1½ cups cubed plain (not multigrain
  or rye) bread

½ teaspoon sea salt, or to taste

½ teaspoon hot chile pepper, seeded
  and diced

¼ cup diced red onion (optional)

12 to 18 green grapes, sliced in half

1. Combine all the ingredients, except the grapes, in a strong blender and blend until smooth.
2. Place in the freezer to chill for 10 to 15 minutes.
3. Garnish with grapes and enjoy!

Variations
- Add ¼ teaspoon of saffron threads soaked in water for 10 minutes.
- Replace the almonds with macadamia nuts or cashews.

If You Have More Time

For best results, allow to chill in the refrigerator (instead of the freezer) for 30 minutes or longer before serving.

Portuguese Feijoada

The bean stew of Portugal, this hearty dish is traditionally made with pork. Use a few drops of liquid smoke instead and you can make Miss Piggy a happy camper. Serve with Spanish Rice (page 111) and Radicchio and Endive with Shaved Fennel and Italian Vinaigrette (page 13) for an absolutely lovely meal.

SERVES 6 TO 8

1 tablespoon olive oil

1 yellow onion, chopped small (1½ cups)

3 garlic cloves, pressed or minced

8 ounces seitan strips or tofu ham (see page 106)

4 cups heated vegetable stock (see page 253) or water

2 bay leaves

1 large carrot, sliced (1 cup)

¾ teaspoon liquid smoke

1 (15-ounce) can black beans, drained and rinsed, or 1¾ cups cooked (see page 257)

1 (15-ounce) can pinto beans, drained and rinsed, or 1¾ cups cooked (see page 257)

2 tablespoons wheat-free tamari or other soy sauce

2 cups chopped collard, chard, or kale

1 tablespoon finely chopped fresh cilantro

2 teaspoons ground coriander

½ teaspoon sea salt, or to taste

¼ teaspoon freshly ground black pepper

¼ teaspoon crushed red pepper flakes

1. Place a large pot over medium-high heat. Place the oil, onion, and garlic in the pot and cook for 2 minutes, stirring constantly. Add the seitan and stir well.
2. Add the vegetable stock, bay leaves, carrot, and liquid smoke and cook for 10 minutes, stirring occasionally.
3. Add the remaining ingredients, lower the heat to medium, and cook for 10 minutes, stirring occasionally. Remove the bay leaves before serving.

Variations

- For a thicker soup, just before serving, place 1 to 2 cups of the contents of the pot into a blender and blend until just pureed. Return to the pot and mix well before serving.
- Add 7 ounces of sliced vegan sausage or Field Roast.
- For a gluten-free version, replace the seitan with liquid smoke–marinated and roasted tofu or tempeh (see page 252).
- Replace the beans with your favorite, such as black-eye peas, cannellini beans, or chickpeas.
- Replace the cilantro with fresh dill or your favorite fresh herbs.

Apple Hazelnut Salad with Shaved Fennel ♥

There are lots of flavors going on in this simple and refreshing raw dish. Soaking the walnuts gives them an almost buttery sweet flavor. Be sure to zest the lime before you juice it. Serve on its own as a light fruit salad.

SERVES 4 TO 6

1 large apple, cored and cut into ½-inch cubes (2 cups); try Honey Crisp, Red Delicious, Granny Smith, or Gala

¾ cup roughly chopped hazelnuts

½ cup diced celery

½ cup shaved fennel (see note on page 13)

¼ teaspoon lime zest

2 tablespoons freshly squeezed lime juice

1 tablespoon chiffonaded fresh mint

Pinch of chile powder, smoked paprika, or chipotle chile powder

Pinch of ground cinnamon

1 teaspoon pure maple syrup or agave nectar, or to taste, depending upon the sweetness of the apples

1. Combine all the ingredients in a bowl and mix well. For best results, allow to chill in the refrigerator for 10 minutes or longer before serving.

Variations

- Replace the hazelnuts with slivered almonds, walnuts, chopped pecans, or pistachio nuts.
- For a richer flavor, you can toast the hazelnuts (see page 188).

Babe's Bocadillos

The ham and cheese sandwich of the Iberian Peninsula, this version uses a marinated and roasted tofu to create our vegan ham. Create a Barcelonean soup and sandwich combo and enjoy your *bocadillo* with Gazpacho (page 102) or Ajo Blanco (page 103). You can also serve the tofu on its own as a bacon replacement along with your Spanish Omelet (page 116) and Pommes Frites (page 68).

SERVES 4 TO 6

TOFU HAM

2 tablespoons wheat-free tamari or other soy sauce

1 tablespoon olive oil

1 teaspoon smoked paprika, or ½ teaspoon liquid smoke

1 tablespoon fresh oregano, or 1 teaspoon dried

1 teaspoon pure maple syrup

14 ounces extra-firm tofu

FIXINGS

Stone-ground mustard (optional)

¼ to ½ cup vegan mayonnaise (Vegenaise or homemade; see page 261), Garlic Herb Aioli (page 95), or Pesto Magnifico (page 31)

8 to 12 slices of bread or baguette

6 to 8 ounces vegan Cheddar- or mozzarella-style cheese

4 to 6 slices tomato

4 to 6 slices red onion

1. Preheat the oven to 400°F. Place all of the tofu ham ingredients, except the tofu, on a baking sheet and mix well. Slice the tofu in half, then cut each half into six thin slices to yield twelve thin cutlets.

2. Place the tofu on the baking sheet and allow to sit for a few minutes. Flip after 1 minute to ensure an even coating. Bake for 20 minutes, flipping the cutlets after 10 minutes.

3. Meanwhile, prepare the fixings. Create each *bocadillo* by placing the mustard, if using, and the mayonnaise or other spread on both slices of bread and topping with the vegan ham, cheese, tomato, and onion.

Variation

- Replace the tofu with thinly sliced tempeh.

Empanadas

Ode to the stuffed bread! With origins in medieval Spain and Portugal, courtesy of the Moorish invasions, and even gracing the pages of a Catalan cookbook from the 1500s, the empanada sensation has gone worldwide. So many fillings are possible; a few are listed in the variations. Serve on their own with some Vegan Sour Cream (page 226) or go World Fusion and serve with Pesto Magnifico (page 95), Welsh Rarebit Cheese Sauce (page 140), or Roasted Tomato and Garlic Sauce (page 35).

SERVES 6

DOUGH: DRY

2 cups white spelt flour

¼ teaspoon baking soda

⅛ teaspoon sea salt

DOUGH: WET

¼ cup plus 1 tablespoon water

4 tablespoons melted vegan butter or coconut oil

1 teaspoon ground flaxseeds mixed with 1 tablespoon water

¼ teaspoon freshly squeezed lemon juice or apple cider vinegar

FILLING

1 tablespoon oil

½ cup diced yellow onion

½ cup thinly sliced and chopped leek

2 garlic cloves, pressed or minced

1 cup finely chopped vegan sausage or Field Roast (about 7 ounces)

½ teaspoon paprika (try smoked)

1½ tablespoons tomato paste

3 tablespoons water

2 teaspoons wheat-free tamari or other soy sauce

1 teaspoon red wine vinegar

2 teaspoons freshly squeezed lime or lemon juice (optional)

Sea salt and freshly ground black pepper

1. Preheat the oven to 425°F and oil a baking sheet. Prepare the empanada dough: Place the dry ingredients in a large bowl and whisk well. Place the wet ingredients in another bowl and mix well. Add the wet to dry and mix well. Form into a ball.
2. Prepare the filling: Place a sauté pan over medium-high heat. Add the oil, onion, leek, and garlic and cook for 2 minutes, stirring constantly. Add the vegan sausage and cook for 3 minutes, stirring frequently. Add the remaining ingredients, seasoning to taste, mix well, and cook for 3 minutes, stirring frequently.
3. Place the dough on a clean, dry cutting board and roll into a log. Slice into four equal-size pieces. Using a rolling pin or your hands, form each piece of dough into a 4-inch circle. Place 2 to 3 tablespoons of filling in the center of each circle, fold in half, and seal by pinching tightly together the bottom and top edges of the empanada. You can also use a fork to score the seal.
4. Place on the prepared baking sheet and bake for 15 minutes. If you wish, you can baste the top of each empanada with vegan butter after 10 minutes of baking. Enjoy warm with Vegan Sour Cream (page 226).

Variation

- Replace the vegan sausage with tofu, tempeh, seitan, or Tofu Ham (page 106).
- For a sweet empanada, use the apple filling from Apple Strudel (see page 203) and dust with confectioners' sugar.

Escalavida Grilled Vegetables

Originating in Catalan Spain, *escalavida* is made with assorted grilled vegetables, frequently including eggplant and peppers as key ingredients. It translates literally as "to cook in hot ashes." For the most authentic flavor, use a wood grill. Gas or charcoal grills and even roasting in the oven produces a most excellent result. Serve along with Artichoke Heart and Saffron Paella (page 112), Moussaka (page 175), or Braised Tempeh with Herbes de Provence (page 80).

SERVES 4

3 tablespoons olive oil

1 tablespoon red wine vinegar

2 garlic cloves, pressed or minced

1 teaspoon sea salt, or to taste

½ teaspoon freshly ground black pepper

½ cup port or vegetable stock

1 medium-size eggplant or zucchini, sliced thickly

1 red bell pepper, sliced in half and seeded

1 green bell pepper, sliced in half and seeded

3 medium-size Roma tomatoes

1 leek, sliced in half and well rinsed

¼ cup sliced green or kalamata olives

2 tablespoons finely chopped fresh flat-leaf parsley

¼ cup sliced green onion

1. Preheat a grill (see notes below for cooking variations). Create a marinade by placing the olive oil, vinegar, garlic, salt, pepper, paprika, and port in a 9 by 13-inch casserole dish and stir well. Dip the eggplant, peppers, tomatoes, and leek into the marinade, flipping to coat well, before placing on the grill.
2. Grill the vegetables until just soft and char marks appear, about 10 minutes, flipping occasionally and basting with the marinade.
3. Chop the vegetables into 1-inch pieces and place in a large bowl with the remaining ingredients and remaining marinade. Stir well before serving warm.

Variations

- Try adding one portobello mushroom and one or two mild chile peppers for grilling.
- Add 1 tablespoon paprika to the marinade.
- If roasting instead of grilling the vegetables, preheat the oven to 400°F. Place all the ingredients except the olives, parsley, and green onion in a casserole dish and add ¼ teaspoon of liquid smoke or 1 tablespoon smoked paprika to give it that smoky flavor. Roast until the vegetables are soft, about 20 minutes, stirring occasionally. Chop the vegetables into 1-inch pieces and place in a large bowl with the remaining ingredients. Stir well before serving.

White Beans with Mushrooms and Sherry

Here we have the "bean" portion of the Spanish bean and rice combo of worldwide acclaim. Many variations are possible on this theme. See below for a few suggestions. Serve with, you guessed it, Spanish Rice (page 111). Add Escalivada Grilled Vegetables (page 108) and you have a complete meal.

SERVES 2 TO 4

2 teaspoons oil

¾ cup diced yellow onion

4 garlic cloves, pressed or minced

½ teaspoon seeded and diced hot chile pepper

1¼ cups diced shiitake mushrooms

1 (14-ounce can) white beans, drained and rinsed, or 1¾ cups cooked (see page 257)

1 (14.5-ounce) can fire-roasted chopped tomatoes, or 1¾ cups diced tomatoes with juice

½ cup dry sherry

½ teaspoon vegan Dijon mustard

1 teaspoon dried thyme

2 teaspoons red wine vinegar

½ teaspoon smoked paprika

2 teaspoons freshly squeezed lime juice

¾ teaspoon sea salt, or to taste

⅛ teaspoon freshly ground black pepper

1 tablespoon wheat-free tamari or other soy sauce, or to taste

2 tablespoons finely chopped fresh flat-leaf parsley

¼ teaspoon crushed red pepper flakes or cayenne pepper

1. Place a pot over medium-high heat. Place the oil, onion, garlic, chile pepper, and mushrooms in the pot and cook for 3 minutes, stirring constantly.
2. Add the beans and tomatoes, lower the heat to medium and cook for 5 minutes, stirring frequently.
3. Add the remaining ingredients and cook for 5 minutes, gently stirring occasionally.

Variations
- Replace the parsley with fresh cilantro.
- Replace the white beans with great northern beans, cannellini beans, black-eyed peas, fava beans, or black beans.
- Replace the mushrooms with bell peppers or zucchini.

Chickpeas and Roasted Garlic

One of the earliest cultivated crops, the chickpea (or garbanzo bean) has been enjoyed by humans since Neolithic and possibly earlier times. For the modern-day garlic lovers among us, this is a simple dish that can be made with many other legumes. Serve as a side with Spanish Rice (page 111) and Brussels Sprouts and Red Cabbage (page 190).

SERVES 4

15 to 20 garlic cloves

2 tablespoons olive oil

1 cup diced yellow onion

¾ cup thinly sliced celery

1 small red bell pepper, seeded and diced (about 1 cup)

1 (15-ounce) can chickpeas, drained and rinsed, or 1¾ cups cooked (see page 257)

1 teaspoon paprika

¼ teaspoon chile powder or chipotle chile powder

2 tablespoons freshly squeezed lemon juice

2 teaspoons red wine vinegar

¼ cup thinly sliced Spanish olives

¼ cup thinly sliced green onion

¼ teaspoon sea salt

⅛ teaspoon freshly ground black pepper

2 tablespoons finely chopped fresh flat-leaf parsley or basil

⅛ teaspoon liquid smoke (optional)

1. Preheat the oven to 400°F. Place the garlic cloves and 1 tablespoon of olive oil in a small casserole dish and mix well. Bake for 10 minutes.
2. Meanwhile, place the remaining tablespoon of olive oil in a large sauté pan over medium-high heat. Add the onion, celery, and red bell pepper, and cook for 3 minutes, stirring frequently. Add the chickpeas, paprika, and chile powder, and cook for 7 minutes, stirring frequently.
3. Add the remaining ingredients, including the roasted garlic, and stir well before serving.

Variations
- Replace the chickpeas with other legumes, such as black beans, black-eyed peas, or pinto beans.
- Add 1 cup of finely chopped zucchini or mushrooms along with the red peppers.
- Add 1 cup of corn along with the garbanzo beans.
- Add ¼ cup diced fennel to the garlic before roasting.
- Replace the Spanish olives with your olive of choice.
- Replace the paprika with smoked paprika and leave out the liquid smoke.

Spanish Rice

Popular throughout the Spanish-speaking world from Madrid to Tijuana, Spanish rice is simple to prepare and a fantastic way to enhance the flavor of a humble bowl of rice. Serve as a side with any of your fiestas including Tempeh Romesco (page 114) or Paprika Tofu (page 113), and Chickpeas and Roasted Garlic (page 110).

MAKES 6 CUPS RICE

2 teaspoons olive oil

½ cup diced yellow onion

2 garlic cloves, pressed or minced

½ teaspoon seeded and diced hot chile pepper

1 teaspoon paprika, preferably smoked

¾ teaspoon sea salt

1½ cups uncooked white basmati rice

2 cups vegetable stock (see page 253) or water

1 (14.5-ounce) can fire-roasted tomatoes, undrained, or 1¾ cup diced tomatoes with juice

½ cup thinly sliced Spanish olives (optional)

2 tablespoons capers (optional)

1. Place a pot over medium-high heat. Place the oil, onion, garlic, chile pepper, if using, and the paprika and salt in the pot and stir well. Cook for 2 minutes, stirring constantly. Add the rice and cook for 1 minute, stirring constantly.
2. Add the stock and tomatoes, and the olives and capers, if using, and bring to a boil, stirring occasionally. Cover, lower the heat to low, and cook until all the liquid is absorbed, about 20 minutes.
3. Remove from the heat and allow to sit for 5 minutes before gently stirring well and serving.

Variations

- Add ¼ to ½ teaspoon of saffron threads along with stock (see page xxx for more info about saffron).
- Add ¼ cup of seeded and diced bell pepper and diced mushrooms along with the onion.
- Add ½ cup slivered almonds after the rice has cooked.

Artichoke Heart and Saffron Paella

The crown jewel of Spanish cuisine, and originating in Valencia, paella is typically seafood based. This dish uses artichoke hearts, chickpeas, and saffron. For even more of the flavor of the sea, use the *arame* and shiitake mushrooms mentioned below. This close-to-30-minute version is baked in a high-temperature oven, instead of over an open flame. We also use quick-cooking basmati rice instead of short-grain brown rice. If you want to impress your guests, serve in a paella pan (a two-handled pan with shallow and sloping sides) with fresh lemon wedges as a garnish. Create the Spanish meal of your dreams by serving with Stuffed Mushrooms with Corn and Saffron (page 101), Paprika Tofu (page 113), and if there is any room left . . . Vegan Flan (page 121).

SERVES 6

1¼ cups uncooked white basmati rice

2 cups heated vegetable stock (see page 253) or water

¼ cup red wine (optional; see box)

1 teaspoon sea salt, or to taste

1 cup chopped brine-preserved artichoke hearts

1 (14.5-ounce) can diced fire-roasted tomatoes, or 1¾ cups tomatoes with juice

3 tablespoons freshly squeezed lemon juice

2 tablespoons finely chopped fresh flat-leaf parsley

1 (15-ounce) can chickpeas, drained and rinsed, or 1¾ cups cooked (see page 257)

¼ teaspoon freshly ground black pepper

¼ teaspoon crushed red pepper flakes or cayenne pepper, or ½ teaspoon seeded and diced hot chile pepper

¼ teaspoon saffron threads soaked in 2 tablespoons hot water (see page xxx for more info on saffron)

1. Preheat the oven to 450°F.
2. Place all of the ingredients except the saffron in a 9 by 13-inch casserole dish and mix well. Add the saffron and its soaking water, making sure to get every last strand, and mix well.
3. Cover the casserole dish and bake for 25 minutes. Serve hot.

Variations

- Try adding ¼ cup of *arame* soaked in 1 cup hot water. Use the *arame* soaking water to replace an equal amount of stock.
- Replace the chickpeas with cooked fava beans.
- Add ½ cup of diced shiitake mushrooms.
- Replace the basmati with brown rice and use 3½ cups of water or vegetable stock.

Chef Patrick Recommends:
Spanish, Tempranillo varietal

Paprika Tofu

Grown abundantly in Spain as well as Hungary, paprika is made from ground bell peppers or chile peppers. It adds a red color to dishes as well as a unique flavor. If you can get to an ethnic or spice market, you can experiment with different varieties of Spanish paprika, including mild, moderate, or spicy. There are also smoked varieties. Serve with Spanish Rice (page 111) and Gazpacho (page 102).

SERVES 4

3 tablespoons olive oil

2 tablespoons wheat-free tamari or other soy sauce

1 tablespoon pure maple syrup or sweetener of choice

4 garlic cloves, minced or pressed

14 ounces extra-firm or super-firm tofu

1 yellow onion, sliced thinly

1 red bell pepper, seeded and sliced thinly

1 zucchini, sliced thinly

2 tablespoons vegetable stock (see page 253) or water

1 tablespoon freshly squeezed lemon juice

1 tablespoon balsamic vinegar

1 tablespoon paprika (try smoked)

¾ teaspoon sea salt

¼ teaspoon chile powder

¼ teaspoon freshly ground black pepper

1. Preheat the oven to 425°F. Place 1 tablespoon of the olive oil and the soy sauce and maple syrup in a 9 by 13-inch casserole dish and mix well. Slice the tofu lengthwise into four cutlets and allow to sit in the dish for 5 minutes, flipping occasionally.

2. Meanwhile, place the remaining ingredients, including the remaining 2 tablespoons of olive oil, in a large bowl and mix well, ensuring that all the veggies are well coated. Transfer to the casserole dish on top of the tofu cutlets and cover with a lid.

3. Bake until just tender, about 20 minutes, before serving. For additional flavor, and if you have more time, allow to cook for an additional 10 minutes.

Variations

- You can also bake the tofu and vegetables in separate well-oiled casserole dishes and combine at the end.
- Try topping with a mixture of 2 tablespoons of finely chopped fresh flat-leaf parsley, 1 tablespoon of minced fresh marjoram, and 2 teaspoons minced fresh tarragon after removing from the oven.
- Replace the tofu with tempeh, portobello mushrooms, or ½-inch-thick slices of eggplant.
- Replace the balsamic vinegar with red wine vinegar.

Tempeh Romesco

You can tell by the sound of its name that you are in for a bold, richly flavored sauce when Romesco is on the menu. Originating in a town called Tarragona in Catalonia Spain, Romesco is a thick tomato and red bell pepper–based sauce thickened with blended nuts. Serve this hearty dish with Spanish Rice (page 111) and mixed wild greens with Toasted Hazelnut Vinaigrette (page 188).

SERVES 6 TO 8

16 ounces tempeh

TEMPEH MARINADE

3 tablespoons wheat-free tamari or other soy sauce

1½ tablespoons olive oil

1 tablespoon red wine vinegar

ROMESCO SAUCE

¾ cup almonds

3 tablespoons olive oil

1 small yellow onion, chopped small (1¼ cups)

6 garlic cloves

½ cup sliced fennel, leaves reserved

1 medium-size red bell pepper, seeded and chopped

3 to 4 tomatoes, chopped into ½-inch chunks (4 cups)

1 ancho chile, soaked in hot water until soft, then seeded and chopped

½ cup red wine (optional; see box)

1 tablespoon red wine vinegar

2 teaspoons paprika

¼ teaspoon crushed red pepper flakes

1½ teaspoons sea salt, or to taste

½ teaspoon freshly ground black pepper

1. Preheat the oven to 425°F. Place the almonds on a small baking sheet and toast for 5 minutes. Transfer to a small bowl.

2. Reset the oven to 375°F. Slice the tempeh into eight cutlets. Place a steamer basket in a pot filled with ½ inch of water. Place over medium-high heat and bring to a simmer. Place the tempeh in the steamer basket and cook, covered, for 10 minutes.

3. Place all of the marinade ingredients, except the tempeh, in a 9 by 13-inch casserole dish and stir well. Add the tempeh to the casserole dish. Allow to sit for 5 minutes, flipping occasionally. Bake for 10 minutes.

4. Meanwhile, place the olive oil in a large sauté pan over medium-high heat. Add the onion, garlic, fennel, and bell pepper and cook for 5 minutes, stirring frequently. Add the remaining Romesco sauce ingredients, except the almonds and fennel leaves, and cook for 5 minutes, stirring frequently.

5. Transfer to a strong blender, along with the almonds, and blend until creamy. Return the mixture to the sauté pan over low heat.

6. To serve, liberally coat each cutlet with sauce and garnish with fennel leaves.

continues

Chef Patrick Recommends:
Spanish Rosé or Rioja varietal

continued

Variations
- Replace the tempeh with tofu, portobello mushrooms, or ½-inch-thick slices of eggplant.
- Replace the red pepper with *noras*—small, heart-shaped, dried sweet peppers used extensively in Spanish cuisine.
- Add two slices of toast to the blender.
- You can also garnish with toasted slivered almonds (see page 249).

Spanish Omelet

Vegans beware! A tortilla in Spain is not the same as a tortilla in the rest of the world. Order one in Spain, and much to your chagrin, you will get an egg and potato omelet. This 30-Minute Vegan version uses tofu to replace the eggs. I recommend using an ovenproof pan, such as cast iron, if you have one. Serve on its own with some whole-grain toast for breakfast, or make a meal of it with Spanish Rice (page 111) or Pommes Frites (page 68) and Heirloom Tomato Salad (page 4).

SERVES 6 TO 8

1 tablespoon oil

1 cup thinly sliced (half-moons) yellow onion

2 garlic cloves, pressed or minced

2 small potatoes, sliced thinly (1½ cups) (try Yukon Gold or Red Bliss)

12.3 ounces silken firm tofu

8 ounces extra-firm tofu, crumbled or grated

2 tablespoons nutritional yeast

2 tablespoons unsweetened soy milk

1 tablespoon freshly squeezed lemon juice

¾ teaspoon ground turmeric

1 teaspoon sea salt, or to taste

¼ teaspoon freshly ground black pepper, or to taste

2 teaspoons paprika

1. Preheat the oven to 400°F. Place a large sauté pan over medium-high heat. Place the oil, onion, and garlic in the pan and cook for 2 minutes, stirring constantly.

2. Add the potatoes and cook until they are just soft, about 7 minutes, adding small amounts of water or vegetable stock (page 253) when necessary to prevent sticking.

3. Combine the remaining ingredients in a blender or food processor and blend until smooth. Transfer to the sauté pan and stir well. Give it a taste and add additional salt and pepper if necessary. If you are using an ovenproof pan, you can now place it in the oven. If not, transfer the contents to an 8-inch baking dish. Bake for 20 minutes. If you have more time, allow to cool for 10 minutes before serving.

Variations

- Make the most of your omelet experience by adding any or all of the following: 1 teaspoon of seeded and diced chile pepper, 4 ounces of thinly sliced vegan ham, and ½ cup of thinly sliced bell pepper and/or mushrooms.
- For *zarangollo* (a popular dish similar to the Spanish tortilla, but one that uses zucchini), replace the potato with sliced zucchini.

Raw Ravioli with Sun-Dried Tomato Sauce • page 16

Tempeh Neatballs • page 34

French Onion Soup • page 60

Chocolate Hazelnut Crepes • page 87

Raw Pear Tart with Cashew Cream
and Fresh Berries • page 90

Borscht • page 217

Provençal Vegetable Salad • page 67

Stuffed Mushrooms with Corn and Saffron • page 101

Almond Brittle • page 118

Chocolate-Stuffed Figs • page 117

Vegan Flan • page 121

Horchata • page 123
Amsterdam Mintade • page 241
Six-Herb Botanical Juice • page 207

Grilled Tofu with Horseradish Sauce • page 141
Raw Kale Salad with Cranberries and Walnuts • page 132
Glazed Roasted Root Vegetables • page 133

Irish Soda Bread • page 139

Currant Scones • page 150

Spanikopita Triangles • page 173

Moussaka • page 175

Brussels Sprouts and Red Cabbage • page 190
Baked Vegan Schnitzel • 196

Baked Potato Latkes • page 213
Vegan Sour Cream • page 226

Black Forest Parfait • page 205

Blueberry Blintzes • page 235

Mediterranean Pistachio-Crusted Tofu • page 229
Saffron Quinoa Pilaf • page 231

Chocolate-Stuffed Figs

Prepare for an ambrosial feast with this simple yet exotic dessert. Experiment with different figs, such as Black Mission, Calimyrna, and Kadota. For a delightfully divine dish, serve with Cashew Cream (page 90).

MAKES 12 STUFFED FIGS

¼ cup vegan dark chocolate chips

¼ cup chopped raw almonds

Zest of 1 orange

½ teaspoon vanilla extract

¼ cup freshly squeezed orange juice

Pinch of salt

Pinch of ground cinnamon

Pinch of ground cardamom

12 fresh figs

12 whole almonds (optionally toasted; see page 249)

Fresh mint leaves

SAUCE

¼ cup freshly squeezed orange juice

3 tablespoons date syrup (see page 264)

Pinch of ground cinnamon

1. Preheat the oven to 400°F. Place the chocolate chips, almonds, vanilla, orange juice, orange zest, salt, cinnamon, and cardamom in a food processor and pulse-chop for a minute, or until the almonds and chocolate chips are well chopped. Do not process into a paste. Transfer to a small bowl.

2. Slice off the very top of the figs, and using a ½-teaspoon measuring spoon, fill each fig with the filling and top with a whole almond. Place in a small casserole dish.

3. Prepare the sauce by blending all of its ingredients well. Pour the sauce into the casserole dish. Bake for 10 minutes. Garnish with mint leaves and serve warm.

Variations

- For an extra kick, add a pinch of cayenne or chile powder to the stuffing.
- Replace the chocolate chips with dried fruit, such as raisins, currants, or chopped apricots, papaya, or mango.
- Replace the almonds with hazelnuts, pecans, or walnuts—raw or toasted (see page 249).
- You can also replace the almonds with seeds, such as sunflower, hemp, or pumpkin.
- ♥ For a raw variation, replace the chocolate chips with cacao nibs and leave out the cooking.
- You can replace the fresh figs with dried Calimyrna figs and bake for an additional 5 minutes.

Almond Brittle

How can so few ingredients taste so good? The sugar and vegan butter combo can provide a clue. The sugar creates a syrup that holds the toasted almonds together. Serve at your next flamenco party, along with Horchata (page 123).

SERVES 12

2 cups light brown sugar

½ cup water

½ cup brown rice syrup (optional)

8 tablespoons vegan butter

1 teaspoon vanilla extract

⅛ teaspoon sea salt

1½ cups slivered almonds, toasted

½ teaspoon baking soda

1 to 2 tablespoons coarse sea salt (optional)

1. Line a baking sheet or 9 by 13-inch casserole dish with parchment paper.
2. Place all the ingredients, except the almonds, baking soda, and salt, in a large, heavy-bottomed pan over medium-high heat. Stir well. Using a candy thermometer, cook until the temperature reaches 300°F, about 10 minutes. Do not stir the mixture. If you do not cook it long enough, it will not reach the brittle stage. If you cook it for too long, it may burn, so keep a close eye on it.
3. Add the almonds and baking soda, mix well, and pour the mixture onto the lined baking sheet or casserole dish. Spread with a spatula to create about a ¼-inch depth. At this point, you can sprinkle evenly with the coarse salt, if using.
4. Chill in the refrigerator until the brittle hardens, about 10 minutes. Break apart with your hands to create twelve pieces of brittle and enjoy!

Variations
- Add 1 cup of vegan chocolate chips when adding the almonds.
- Add 1 teaspoon of smoked paprika along with the salt.

Portuguese Sweet Rice (Arroz Doce)

Sweet rice is a dish that has made its way into so many different ethnic cuisines, and for good reason. The rice, sugar, and in this case, rich soy creamer is a combo that is sure to please. Experiment with different nondairy milks, flavor extracts, sweeteners, nuts, and fruit, and you will find an infinite array of variations are possible. Serve as part of a dessert sampler with Chocolate-Stuffed Figs (page 117) and Almond Brittle (page 118), or even try it as a decadent breakfast with fresh fruit!

SERVES 4 TO 6

1 cup uncooked white basmati rice

1½ cups water

1½ cups soy creamer or soy, hemp, rice, coconut, or almond milk (see page 259)

Pinch of sea salt

¼ teaspoon ground cinnamon

⅛ teaspoon ground allspice or nutmeg

½ teaspoon lightly packed orange zest

¼ teaspoon lightly packed lemon zest

½ teaspoon vanilla extract

¼ teaspoon almond extract, or ½ teaspoon hazelnut extract (optional)

¼ cup plus 2 tablespoons sugar (see page 261)

2 tablespoons pure maple syrup, or more sugar to taste

¼ cup raisins, currants, sultanas, or other chopped dried fruit . . . or vegan chocolate chips (optional)

½ cup chopped pistachio nuts

¼ cup hazelnut-flavored soy creamer (optional)

1. Place a pot over high heat. Place all of the ingredients except the raisins, if using, pistachio nuts, and hazelnut creamer, if using, in the pot, stir well, and bring to a boil. Cover, lower the heat to low, and cook for 20 minutes.
2. Add the raisins, if using, mix well, and cook for 5 minutes, stirring occasionally.
3. Before serving, top with pistachio nuts and the hazelnut-flavored soy creamer, if using. Serve warm.

Variations

- Replace the basmati rice with brown rice and add an extra ½ cup of water.
- If you wish to vary the flavor, you can combine milks, such as half hemp milk and half coconut milk.
- Replace the pistachio nuts with chopped pecans, walnuts, or macadamia nuts, raw or toasted.
- Add ¼ cup of toasted coconut flakes along with the pistachio nuts.

continues

Portuguese Sweet Rice (Arroz Doce) *continued*

Chef's Tips and Tricks

Zesting Citrus

Adding the zest of lemons, limes, or oranges to your dish is a simple and effective way to add a burst of flavor. To zest, use a Microplane zester (one of my favorite kitchen gadgets) or the fine grate portion of a cheese grater and grate only the very outer portion of the fruit. If you go too deep, you will begin to grate the white pith under the skin, which will only add bitterness to your dish. You can also use a vegetable peeler to thinly peel the zest, and mince before adding.

Vegan Flan

With Roman origins and developed and perfected by the inhabitants of Spain for generations, flan is a custard dessert typically made with milk, eggs, and sugar. This version uses a vegan creamer and silken tofu as the base and is thickened with agar flakes. A sweet caramel syrup is drizzled on top of the custard to create a sublime dessert experience. Remember to prepare the syrup shortly before serving. Serve at the end of any of your Spanish feasts and you are sure to receive many a *gracias*.

SERVES 4

CUSTARD

1 cup soy or coconut creamer, or
    soy or coconut milk
2 tablespoons agar flakes (see note)
12.5 ounces silken firm tofu
¼ cup agave or coconut nectar
    (see page 261)
2 teaspoons vanilla extract
Pinch of sea salt
4 fresh mint leaves

CARAMEL SYRUP

¾ cup Sucanat or organic brown
    sugar (see page 261)
¼ cup water
1 teaspoon vanilla extract
1 teaspoon freshly squeezed
    lemon juice

1. Prepare the custard: Place the creamer and agar flakes in a saucepan over medium-high heat. Cook until the agar flakes dissolve, about 12 minutes, whisking frequently.
2. Meanwhile, place the tofu, agave nectar, vanilla extract, and salt in a blender.
3. When the agar flakes dissolve, pour the creamer mixture into the blender and blend well. Pour into four 4-ounce ramekins and place in the refrigerator. Refrigerate until firm, about 30 minutes.
4. Prepare the caramel sauce just before serving: Place all of its ingredients in a saucepan over low heat. Cook for 5 minutes, stirring frequently.
5. To serve, flip the ramekins over onto a serving plate and top each with 1 tablespoon of sauce. Garnish with mint leaves before serving. Can you say Yumalicious!?

continues

Vegan Flan *continued*

Variations

- Replace the soy creamer with rice or almond milk, though soy or coconut milk provides the creamiest dessert.
- Replace the agave with pure maple syrup or a sweetener of choice. Keep in mind that the darker the sweetener, the darker the custard will be.

Agar is a seaweed that is used to thicken desserts, sauces, and puddings. A vegan version of gelatin, agar is a key ingredient in the Japanese dessert *kanten*. Unlike other common thickeners such as cornstarch or arrowroot, agar takes several minutes of heating to be fully dissolved for thickening purposes.

Horchata

In all likelihood, your local grocery store will not be carrying *chufa,* or tiger nuts, the original nut used in this flavorful beverage that comes from Valencia, Spain. Try this version, using almonds and rice to create the creamy base. You will need a very fine strainer for optimal results. This is a tantalizing beverage to enjoy while nibbling on your Chocolate-Stuffed Figs (page 117) or Almond Brittle (page 118).

SERVES 4 TO 6

1 cup uncooked brown rice

½ cup almonds, cashews, or macadamia nuts

4 cups water

2 to 3 tablespoons agave nectar, pure maple syrup, or sweetener of choice, or to taste (see page 261)

2 cinnamon sticks

1 vanilla bean, or 2 teaspoons vanilla extract

Pinch of salt

1. Place the rice and almonds in a bowl with ample water to cover. Allow to soak for 15 minutes before draining and rinsing well.
2. Transfer to a blender with the remaining ingredients and blend until creamy. Pour into a pitcher through a fine-mesh strainer or sprout bag. Be sure to stir well before serving. Serve over ice.

Variations

- Use the *chufa* nuts if you can find them.
- If you have more time, allow the *horchata* to chill in the refrigerator for at least 30 minutes before serving.
- For Rosewater Horchata, add 2 teaspoons food-grade rose water after straining and stir well.

Quicker and Easier Spain

Herb-Marinated Olives ❤ _____

Combine 1 cup of pitted olives, 1 tablespoon of minced fresh flat-leaf parsley or cilantro, 1 teaspoon of fresh thyme, and ¼ teaspoon of smoked paprika in a small bowl and mix well. Serve as part of your tapas fiesta.

Virgin Sangria ❤ _____

Combine 2 cups of grape juice, 1 cup of apple or pear juice, ½ cup of freshly squeezed orange juice, 2 cups of sparkling water, 1 tablespoon of freshly squeezed lemon or lime juice, one sliced orange, one cored and sliced apple, one cored and sliced pear, and one sliced lime in a large pitcher and place in the freezer for 15 minutes. If you have more time, allow the sangria to sit in the refrigerator for up to overnight. Enjoy over ice. Feel free to substitute peaches, pineapple, blueberries, strawberries, or your favorite fruit.

Have Your Own Vegan Tapas Fiesta!

As mentioned earlier, tapas-style meals are extremely popular throughout Spain. This trendy form of dining is now making its way into restaurants all around the globe. Rather than ordering one large main dish per person, a tapas-style meal would consist of several dishes that are shared among the group. The main aspect of the tapas meal is the smaller size of the portion. Virtually any dish, even soups, can be included in your tapas party. Here are a few suggestions from the recipes in this section.

Stuffed Mushrooms with Corn and Saffron

Babe's Bocadillos

Empanadas

Apple Hazelnut Salad with Shaved Fennel

Chickpeas and Roasted Garlic

White Beans with Mushrooms and Sherry

Paprika Tofu (cut into small portions)

Escalavida Grilled Vegetables

Spanish Omelet

Spanish Rice

Tempeh Romesco (cut into small portions)

Herb-Marinated Olives

Gazpacho or Ajo Blanco (in small shot glasses)

PART FOUR

UNITED KINGDOM AND IRELAND

Imagination is the beginning of creation.
You imagine what you desire, you will what you imagine,
and at last you create what you will.

—GEORGE BERNARD SHAW

From leprechauns and druids to the Loch Ness Monster, the land of the United Kingdom and Ireland is infused with ancient mystery. Whether it's a journey to Stonehenge, the metropolis of London, or the Blarney Stone, adventure certainly awaits you. Each region covered here—England, Scotland, Wales, and Ireland—has its own unique cuisine. The United Kingdom is a melting pot where immigrants from India, Pakistan, Middle Eastern and Asian countries, as well as from continental Europe, have brought their culinary treasures into the mix. In this small section, I have focused on some of the more traditional dishes.

England has a long history of vegetarianism and both the Vegetarian Society and the Vegan Society were formed here. George Cheyne, a famous physician and peer of Sir Isaac Newton, was advocating a vegetarian diet in the early 1700s. My own introduction to British cuisine came during my year studying at the London School of Economics, when I was introduced to many of the unique British dining habits, including having Beanie Toast for breakfast (see page 154), and the use of Marmite, the yeast extract that is a by-product of the beer-making process. (The official motto of Marmite may give you a hint into its flavor—"Love it or hate it.")

Activism is still very strong in the current generation. Legislation for animal welfare in farming is one of the most robust in the world. And, long maligned for their nation's seemingly bland fare, chefs in England are blazing new trails— including animal-free ones. It was truly an honor to teach the first international Vegan Fusion Cuisine workshop in England on my last trip (even though my accent and my use of the word *awesome* was a constant source of amusement for the participants). The motto for the course was "Go Vegan and Live!"

Pantry items for these countries include such vegetables as carrots, potatoes, cabbage, kale, horseradish, rhubarb, broccoli, tomato, garlic, leeks, parsnips, asparagus, celery, cucumbers, peas, and turnips. Popular fruits include peaches, oranges, lemons, berries, apples, cherries, grapes, pears, and plums. For herbs and spices there are parsley, chives, coriander, marjoram, rosemary, spearmint, and ginger. Nuts include hazelnuts and popular grains are rye, oats, barley, and wheat.

Included here are hearty dishes such as shepherd's pie and vegetable potpie, as well as vegan translations of Bangers and Mash, Welsh Rarebit, and Irish Stew. Several baked goods in this section include Scottish Oatcakes, Scottish Crumpets, Yorkshire Pudding, Irish Soda Bread, and Currant Scones. Partake of an alcohol-free version of ginger beer (which originated in the United Kingdom) and an English Custard to finish off an absolutely brilliant meal.

Credit: Mark Reinfeld

Creamy Parsnip and Roasted Jerusalem Artichoke Soup

Old country meets new country with this dish. Root vegetables such as parsnips are popular in several countries in Europe, including the United Kingdom. Jerusalem artichoke, also known as sunchoke, sunroot, and earth apple, is a tuber with origins in North America. It is wonderful roasted and also grated raw in salads. For a British soup and salad meal, serve with Raw Kale Salad with Cranberries and Walnuts (page 132).

SERVES 6

3 tablespoons olive oil

2½ cups cubed (½-inch dice) Jerusalem artichoke, cleaned well

¾ teaspoon sea salt, or to taste

¼ teaspoon freshly ground black pepper

1 yellow onion, chopped small (1½ cups)

1 cup thinly sliced celery

4 cloves garlic, pressed or minced

2 parsnips, chopped small (2½ cups)

4 cups heated vegetable stock (see page 253) or water

2 cups unsweetened soy, rice, or almond milk (see page 259)

Pinch of cayenne pepper

1 teaspoon minced fresh dill, or ½ teaspoon dried

3 tablespoons nutritional yeast, or ½ cup grated vegan cheddar- or mozzarella-style cheese

1 cup corn (optional)

1. Preheat the oven to 425°F. Place 2 tablespoons of the oil, the Jerusalem artichokes, and a pinch of salt and pepper in a small casserole dish and mix well. Bake for 15 minutes.

2. Meanwhile, place the remaining tablespoon of oil in a large pot over medium-high heat. Add the onion, celery, and garlic, and cook for 3 minutes, stirring frequently. Add the parsnips, vegetable stock, soy milk, and cayenne, and cook for 12 minutes, stirring occasionally.

3. Add the nutritional yeast, if using, and mix well. Carefully transfer the contents of the pot to a strong blender, along with the Jerusalem artichokes, and blend until creamy. You may need to do this in batches, depending upon the size of your blender. Return the mixture to the pot over medium heat.

4. Add the remaining ingredients and mix well. Cook for 3 minutes before serving.

Variations

- Replace the dill with 2 tablespoons of minced fresh cilantro, flat-leaf parsley, or basil.
- Replace the corn with your vegetable of choice, such as finely chopped mushrooms, zucchini, broccoli, or cauliflower.

Irish Stew

You probably won't find this vegan version of Irish stew in the pubs around the Blarney Stone. Actually, you probably won't find it anywhere in Ireland. Seitan is used to replace the animal product in this thick, satisfying, and delectable traditional dish. The Guinness beer adds a sweet rich flavor that puts it over the top. Serve with Irish Soda Bread (page 139) and Ginger Brew (page 153).

SERVES 4

2 tablespoons olive oil

1 yellow onion, chopped small
(1½ cups)

4 cloves garlic, pressed or minced

2 teaspoons minced fresh rosemary

8 ounces beef-style seitan, chopped,
or Field Roast, chopped

1 small potato, chopped into ½-inch
chunks (1¼ cups)

1½ cups beer (see box)

¼ cup tomato paste

3 cups heated vegetable stock
(see page 253) or water

1 teaspoon sea salt, or to taste

¼ teaspoon ground black pepper

2 tablespoons finely chopped fresh
flat-leaf parsley

⅛ teaspoon cayenne pepper

1 tablespoon arrowroot powder
dissolved in 2 tablespoons
cold water

1. Place the olive oil in a 3-quart pot over medium-high heat. Add the onion, garlic, and rosemary, and cook for 3 minutes, stirring frequently. Add the seitan and cook for 3 minutes, stirring frequently.

2. Add the potato, beer, and tomato paste and cook for 3 minutes, stirring frequently. Add the vegetable stock and cook for 15 minutes, stirring occasionally. Add the remaining ingredients, except the arrowroot mixture, and stir well. For optimal flavor, and if you have more time, cook for an additional 10 minutes, stirring occasionally.

3. Add the arrowroot mixture and cook until the stew thickens slightly, about 2 minutes, stirring constantly.

Variations

- Try adding 1 cup of chopped carrot, parsnips, mushrooms, or your vegetables of choice.
- For a gluten-free version, replace the seitan with cubed tempeh or extra-firm or super-firm tofu. You can roast the tempeh or tofu cubes before adding them to the stew (see page 252).

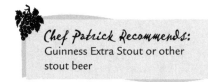

Chef Patrick Recommends:
Guinness Extra Stout or other stout beer

Watercress with Raspberry Vinaigrette ♥

Grown throughout the United Kingdom, nutrient-rich watercress is one of the oldest plants eaten by humans. Enjoy it with this tangy vinaigrette as part of a British feast of Grilled Tofu with Horseradish Sauce (page 141), Glazed Roasted Root Vegetables (page 133), and English Custard (page 151).

SERVES 4

7 ounces watercress (about 4 cups)

12 string beans, cut in half

12 cherry tomatoes

DRESSING

Makes about 1 cup dressing

1 cup raspberries

½ cup safflower oil

1 tablespoon raw apple cider vinegar

2 teaspoons pure maple syrup, or to taste

4 teaspoons freshly squeezed lime juice

1 teaspoon wheat-free tamari or other soy sauce

¼ teaspoon peeled and minced fresh ginger

Pinch of cayenne pepper or crushed red pepper flakes

⅛ teaspoon sea salt, or to taste

Pinch of freshly ground black pepper

1. Place the salad ingredients in a bowl or on individual serving plates.
2. Combine the dressing ingredients in a strong blender and blend well.
3. Drizzle over the salad and enjoy. Store the dressing in a glass jar in the refrigerator for up to 5 days.

Variations

- Replace the raspberries with strawberries.
- Replace the raspberries with an equivalent amount of roasted red peppers (see page 19).
- Replace the watercress with arugula, micro greens, and/or mixed salad greens.
- Add your favorite chopped vegetables to the salad, such as bell peppers, mushrooms, or red cabbage.

Raw Kale Salad with Cranberries and Walnuts

Kale is king of the green veggies, one of the most healthful additions to your lifestyle. Eating kale in its raw form is one of the best ways to absorb all of its nutrients. By massaging the kale with the dressing, it becomes soft and irresistible. So put on some Enya tunes and massage away! If you have more time, allow the salad to sit in the refrigerator for 20 minutes or longer before serving. Serve as a side with Shepherdess's Pie (page 145), Grilled Tofu with Horseradish Sauce (page 141), or Bangers and Mash (page 147).

SERVES 4 TO 6

½ cup walnuts

2 to 3 bunches curly kale, rinsed well, stems removed, torn into bite-size pieces (8 cups)

½ cup dried cranberries

¼ cup thinly sliced green onion

DRESSING

3 tablespoons olive oil

2 tablespoons nutritional yeast

1 tablespoon freshly squeezed lemon juice

½ teaspoon English mustard or other mustard

1 teaspoon red wine vinegar

1 teaspoon pure maple syrup or agave nectar

1 teaspoon wheat-free tamari or other soy sauce, to taste

⅛ teaspoon cayenne pepper

Pinch of sea salt

1. Place the walnuts in a small bowl with 1 to 2 cups of water. Place the kale in a large bowl.
2. Prepare the dressing by combining all of its ingredients in a small bowl and whisking well.
3. Pour onto the kale and massage the dressing into the kale, making sure you massage every piece of kale. This process can last for 5 to 10 minutes, depending on how relaxed you want the kale to be.
4. Drain the walnuts, rinse well, and add to the kale along with the cranberries and green onion. Toss well before serving.

Variations

- Countless variations are possible. Once the kale is sufficiently massaged, you can add 1 to 2 cups of mixed vegetables, such as grated carrots, parsnips, beets or, daikon radish. Other vegetables to add include corn, thinly sliced celery, thinly sliced red cabbage, or red onion. I think you get the idea.
- Add 2 tablespoons of a fresh minced herb medley including basil, thyme, oregano, and flat-leaf parsley.

Glazed Roasted Root Vegetables

This is a simple, delicious roasted vegetable medley that uses agave nectar or maple syrup instead of the honey frequently used in glazed carrot dishes. The Jerusalem artichokes add a pleasant crunch. Once you experience the roasted parsnip and Jerusalem artichoke combination, you will be converted for life. Serve as part of a Fusion meal with Tofu Scaloppine (page 37), Scrambled Tofu with Chives and Wild Mushrooms (page 86), or Babe's Bocadillos (page 106).

SERVES 2 TO 4

2 carrots, chopped small (2 cups)

2 parsnips, chopped small (2 cups)

2 Jerusalem artichokes, chopped small (1 cup)

2 tablespoons olive oil

½ teaspoon sea salt

¼ teaspoon freshly ground black pepper

¼ teaspoon crushed red pepper flakes

1½ tablespoons agave nectar, coconut nectar (see page 261), or pure maple syrup

1½ teaspoons apple cider, balsamic, or red wine vinegar

1 tablespoon vegan butter (optional)

2 tablespoons finely chopped fresh flat-leaf parsley

1. Preheat the oven to 425°F. Place the carrots, parsnips, Jerusalem artichokes, olive oil, salt, pepper, and crushed red pepper flakes in a large casserole dish and stir well. Bake for 15 minutes.

2. Add the remaining ingredients, except the parsley, stir well, and return the casserole dish to the oven. Bake for an additional 5 minutes. Add additional salt and pepper if necessary. Garnish with parsley and serve warm.

Variations

- This dish is wonderful with any combination of root vegetables you have on hand, including celeriac, beet, turnip, radish, or yam.
- Add 1 tablespoon minced fresh herbs along with or instead of the parsley, such as dill, cilantro, or basil.

Baked Onion and Tomato with Dill

Here is a simple quick and easy recipe for baked or roasted vegetables that can be served as a side dish with any of the entrées in the book. The tomatoes in particular are part of a traditional English breakfast that also includes Beanie Toast (page 154). You can replace the vegetables as you choose. See the variations for some suggestions. Serve with Grilled Tofu with Horseradish Sauce (page 141), Moussaka (page 175), or Tempeh Romesco (page 114).

SERVES 4

2 small yellow onions

2 medium-size tomatoes, halved

2 teaspoons olive oil

½ teaspoon sea salt

⅛ teaspoon freshly ground black pepper

2 cups tightly packed bite-size pieces kale

1 teaspoon balsamic vinegar

2 tablespoons vegan butter (optional)

1 to 2 teaspoons fresh dill or sorrel

1. Preheat the oven to 425°F. Peel the onions and slice in half. Place on a well-oiled baking dish along with the tomatoes, drizzle with 1 teaspoon of olive oil, and top with a pinch of salt and pepper. Bake for 15 minutes. If you have more time, and for optimal flavor, bake the onions for 10 minutes before adding the tomatoes.

2. Meanwhile, place the kale in a bowl with the remaining teaspoon of olive oil, and massage the oil into the kale for a few minutes.

3. After the onions and tomatoes have cooked for 15 minutes, add the kale to the baking dish and bake for an additional 5 minutes. Drizzle with the vinegar and top with the vegan butter, if using, and the dill and the remaining salt and pepper before serving.

Variations

- This is a template recipe for baked or roasted vegetables. Replace the onions and tomatoes with zucchini, bell peppers, cabbage, even broccoli or cauliflower.
- Replace the kale with chard or collards.
- Replace the dill with 1 tablespoon of minced fresh flat-leaf parsley, basil, or cilantro.
- Experiment with different flavors of vinegar.

Parsnip Colcannon

Easier to prepare than to pronounce, *colcannon* is an Irish word that translates as "white-headed cabbage" and is traditionally made with mashed potatoes and kale or cabbage. This version adds parsnips to the mix. You can add more or less soy milk to reach your desired creaminess. Parsnips are native to Europe; are in the carrot family; and have a sweet, creamy flavor. In addition to your enjoying them steamed, they are amazing when roasted, or even grated raw in a salad. Serve as a side with Grilled Tofu with Horseradish Sauce (page 141), Braised Tempeh with Herbes de Provence (page 80), or Tofu Cacciatore (page 32).

SERVES 4 TO 6

1 large potato, chopped small (2 cups; try russet or Yukon Gold)

2 small parsnips, chopped small (2 cups)

4 to 6 garlic cloves

1 cup soy, rice, or almond milk (optionally warmed)

2 tablespoons vegan butter (optional)

¾ teaspoon sea salt, or to taste

¼ teaspoon freshly ground black pepper

3 cups finely chopped, stemmed kale

3 tablespoons chopped fresh flat-leaf parsley

Pinch of crushed red pepper flakes

1. Place a steamer basket in a pot filled with 1 inch of water. Place over medium-high heat and bring to a simmer. Place the potato, parsnips, and garlic in the steamer basket and cook covered until the vegetables are just soft, about 15 minutes.
2. Strain well, return the vegetables to the pot (without the steamer basket), and mash well with a potato masher or sturdy whisk. Add the remaining ingredients and stir well.

Variations

- In this version, the heat from the cooked potato and parsnips will slightly cook the kale. If you wish, you can steam or sauté the kale separately before adding to the other ingredients.
- Replace the parsley with other fresh herbs. Try adding 2 teaspoons of minced fresh rosemary, oregano, dill, or marjoram.

Champ with Crispy Onions

Champ, or *poundies* to some, is an Irish dish made with potatoes, butter, milk, and green onions. Simple to veganize, the dairy is replaced by an animal-free alternative. The sautéed onions create a sublime taste sensation. Serve as the "mash" in Bangers and Mash (page 147) or as part of a Fusion meal with Grilled Portobello Mushrooms with Béarnaise Sauce (page 73) and Beer-Braised Greens (page 189).

SERVES 4 TO 6

1 tablespoon olive oil

1 yellow onion, diced (1½ cups)

2 medium-size russet potatoes, chopped into ½-inch chunks (4 cups)

½ cup thinly sliced green onion

2 tablespoons vegan butter

¾ teaspoon sea salt, or to taste

¼ teaspoon freshly ground black pepper

½ cup unsweetened soy milk

½ cup grated vegan cheddar- or mozzarella-style cheese (optional)

1. Place the olive oil in a small sauté pan over medium heat. Add the yellow onion and cook for 15 to 20 minutes, stirring frequently and adding small amounts of water if necessary to prevent sticking.

2. Meanwhile, place a steamer basket in a pot filled with 1 inch water. Place over medium-high heat and bring to a simmer. Place the potatoes in the steamer basket and cook covered until they are just soft, about 15 minutes. Transfer to a large bowl.

3. Add the onion to the potatoes, along with the remaining ingredients, and mash well before serving.

Variation

- Replace the cooked onion with ¼ cup of finely chopped dulse, ¼ cup of finely chopped chives, and 3 tablespoons of finely chopped fresh flat-leaf parsley.

Scottish Crumpets

Having heard the expression *tea and crumpets* for years, I was never quite sure what a crumpet was. You may also be interested to know that they are griddlecakes that have been part of the British culinary scene for ages. Here is a savory variation of this popular dish. Serve on its own with . . . you guessed it—tea, or as a side with a bowl of Creamy Parsnip and Roasted Jerusalem Artichoke Soup (page 129).

MAKES 8 CRUMPETS

DRY

1½ cups white spelt flour
1 teaspoon baking powder
¼ teaspoon sea salt

WET

1¼ cups unsweetened soy milk
2 tablespoons ground flaxseeds
mixed with 6 tablespoons water
1 tablespoon vegan butter, softened
1 tablespoon freshly squeezed
lemon juice
¼ cup minced green onion
1 tablespoon minced chive

Oil for sautéing
Vegan Sour Cream (page 226)
Cucumber slices
Tomato slices
Sea salt and freshly ground
black pepper

1. Place the dry ingredients in a large bowl and mix well. Place the wet ingredients in another bowl and mix well. Add the wet to the dry and mix well.
2. Place a large skillet or sauté pan over high heat. Add a small amount of oil and allow to heat for a minute. Pour ¼ cup of batter into the pan to create a 4-inch-diameter crumpet. Be careful when pouring to avoid splattering. Cook until bubbles form throughout the crumpet, about 3 minutes.
3. Flip and cook for 3 minutes, pressing down with the spatula for 5 to 10 seconds to cook the inside thoroughly. Flip again and cook for 1 minute, pressing down with the spatula for 5 to 10 seconds. Stack on a plate until ready to serve.
4. To serve, top each crumpet with some Vegan Sour Cream, a few slices of cucumber and tomato, and a pinch of salt and pepper.

Variation

- For a sweet version, add 2 tablespoons of organic sugar (see page xxi) to the dry ingredients. Leave out the green onion and chives and serve with vegan butter, jam, and almond butter or confectioners' sugar.

Yorkshire Pudding

More of a bread than what most Americans consider a pudding, this dish originated in Yorkshire, England, in the 1700s. According to tradition, it is baked underneath a pot roast so that the drippings from the roast can flavor the bread (have I got your appetite whetted yet?). Thankfully, this recipe calls for liquid smoke instead of the drippings. Serve with Vegetable Potpie (page 143) and Onion Gravy (page 147).

SERVES 6

DRY
1½ cups white spelt flour
½ teaspoon sea salt
¾ teaspoon baking soda

WET
1 cup unsweetened soy milk
2 tablespoons ground flaxseeds mixed with 6 tablespoons water
2 tablespoons vegan butter or oil
¼ teaspoon liquid smoke
¾ teaspoon apple cider vinegar

1. Preheat the oven to 450°F.
2. Place the dry ingredients in a bowl and whisk well. Place the wet ingredients in another bowl and mix well. Add the wet to the dry and mix well.
3. Well oil six compartments of a muffin tin. Pour about 6 tablespoons of batter into each compartment. Bake until the tops bounce back when you lightly touch them, about 15 minutes. Serve warm.

Irish Soda Bread

The luck of the Irish was with me when I created my first soda bread, which gets its name from the fact that it uses baking soda instead of yeast for the leavening. Traditionally made with buttermilk, we use soy milk with some fresh lemon juice instead. Scoring the bread allows the inside to cook more quickly. Serve on its own as a snack or as the perfect side to Irish Stew (page 130).

SERVES 8 TO 10

DRY

2½ cups white spelt flour

2 tablespoons cane sugar
(see page 261)

1¼ teaspoons baking soda

½ teaspoon sea salt

WET

¾ cup soy milk

2 tablespoons freshly squeezed
lemon juice

½ teaspoon apple cider vinegar

1 tablespoon ground flaxseeds
mixed with 3 tablespoons water

½ cup raisins (optional)

1. Preheat the oven to 425°F. Oil a baking sheet well or line it with parchment paper. Place the wet ingredients in a bowl and whisk well. Allow to sit for 5 minutes. Meanwhile, place the dry ingredients in another bowl and mix well. Add the wet to the dry and mix well. Add additional soy milk if necessary to create a firm and moist dough that can be rolled into a log.
2. Transfer to a well-floured cutting board, roll into a log, and slice in half. Create two round loaves and place on the prepared baking sheet. Use a knife to create an X score through the top of each loaf.
3. Bake for 15 minutes, or until golden brown. Remove from the oven. Allow to cool on the baking sheet for 5 minutes before transferring to a cooling rack or a clean serving plate. Enjoy warm with vegan butter.

Variations

- For a Stout Bread, replace the soy milk, lemon juice, and vinegar with an equivalent amount of stout beer, such as Guinness Extra Stout.
- It's an American invention, but you can add 1 tablespoon of caraway seeds to the dry ingredients.
- Replace the raisins with the dried fruit of your choosing, such as chopped dates, apricots, or figs.
- Replace half the raisins with seeds, such as sunflower or pumpkin; or finely chopped nuts, such as walnut, pecan, or macadamia.

Welsh Rarebit

When I first selected this dish, going by the name (it is also called Welsh Rabbit), I thought I would be developing a rabbit-free dish. Only later did I realize that Rarebit is the Welsh equivalent of toast and cheese, with beer thrown in for good measure. It definitely works! Enjoy on its own as a midnight or between-meal snack.

SERVES 4 TO 6

4 English muffins or 8 slices toast

CHEESE SAUCE

2 tablespoons vegan butter or oil

2 tablespoons flour (try white spelt or gluten-free)

¾ cup soy creamer or soy, rice, or other nondairy milk

½ teaspoon mustard powder, or 1 teaspoon vegan Dijon mustard

⅛ teaspoon cayenne pepper

1 tablespoon nutritional yeast

2 teaspoons vegan Worcestershire sauce (optional)

½ teaspoon paprika (try smoked)

¼ teaspoon sea salt, or to taste

⅛ teaspoon freshly ground black pepper

½ cup stout beer (see box)

1¼ cups grated vegan Cheddar-style cheese

1. Place a pot over medium-high heat. Place the vegan butter and flour in the pot and cook for 1 minute, stirring constantly. Lower the heat to medium, add the remaining sauce ingredients, except the beer and vegan cheese, and cook for 5 minutes, whisking frequently.
2. Lower the heat to low, add the beer and cheese, and cook for 5 minutes, stirring frequently.
3. Toast the English muffins until golden brown. Place on individual serving plates.
4. Top with a liberal amount of the sauce before serving.

Variation
- If you have more time, replace the toast with Irish Soda Bread (page 139) or Scottish Crumpets (page 137).

Chef Patrick Recommends:
Guinness Extra Stout or other stout beer

Grilled Tofu with Horseradish Sauce

On the culinary scene since Greek and Egyptian times, and steeped in medieval folklore, horseradish adds a spunky spice to dishes. It is part of the same family of plants as mustard, wasabi, broccoli and cabbage. The British frequently serve cutlets with a creamy horseradish and mustard sauce. There is enough sauce in this recipe for two batches of tofu. Serve with Champ with Crispy Onions (page 136) and Watercress with Raspberry Vinaigrette (page 131).

SERVES 4

TOFU MARINADE

1 tablespoon olive oil

2 tablespoons wheat-free tamari or other soy sauce

¼ teaspoon crushed red pepper flakes

14 ounces extra-firm tofu, sliced into 4 cutlets

HORSERADISH SAUCE

2 cups unsweetened soy milk

3 to 4 tablespoons horseradish (see box)

½ teaspoon mustard powder

2 tablespoons nutritional yeast

¼ teaspoon sea salt, or to taste

⅛ teaspoon ground white pepper

⅛ teaspoon cayenne pepper, or to taste

3 tablespoons flour (try white spelt, or gluten-free)

2 tablespoons vegan butter or olive oil

2 tablespoons finely chopped fresh flat-leaf parsley

Black sesame seeds

1. Preheat a grill to high heat. Place all of the marinade ingredients, except the tofu cutlets, in a small casserole dish and mix well. Add the tofu and allow to sit for 10 minutes, flipping occasionally to ensure an even coating. Place the cutlets on the grill and grill until the tofu is cooked through and char marks appear, about 5 minutes on each side.

2. Meanwhile, place the soy milk, horseradish, mustard, nutritional yeast, salt, white pepper, and cayenne in a saucepan over medium-high heat. Cook for 5 minutes, whisking frequently.

3. Place the flour and vegan butter in a small bowl and mix well to create a roux. Add to the saucepan and continue to whisk until the sauce thickens, about 5 minutes.

4. To serve, pour the sauce over cutlets and garnish with parsley and black sesame seeds.

continues

Grilled Tofu with Horseradish Sauce *continued*

Variations

- You can also roast the tofu instead of grilling it. To do so, preheat the oven to 375°F. Place all of the marinade ingredients, except the tofu cutlets, in a small casserole dish and mix well. Add the tofu and allow to sit for 5 minutes, flipping occasionally to ensure an even coating. Bake for 20 minutes.
- Replace the tofu with tempeh, portobello mushrooms, or thick slices of eggplant or zucchini.
- Replace the parsley with fresh cilantro or basil, or 1 tablespoon of minced fresh dill.

Chef's Tips and Tricks

Fresh horseradish on its own does not have much of a bite. Use the prepared varieties available at your local market for maximum flavor.

Vegetable Potpie

The quintessential pub meal, and the favorite of TV dinner fans everywhere, potpies come in many shapes and sizes. Although they are typically made with all kinds of meat, we prefer a kinder and gentler version where tofu reigns supreme. Serve with Parsnip Colcannon (page 135) and Onion Gravy (page 147).

SERVES 4 TO 6

2 unbaked premade vegan piecrusts, preferably spelt, or homemade crust (see box)

Vegan Sour Cream (page 226)

FILLING

1 tablespoon oil

1 cup diced yellow onion

2 to 3 garlic cloves, pressed or minced

½ cup diced celery

1 cup diced potatoes (try Yukon Gold)

8 ounces extra-firm tofu, grated or crumbled (see page 250)

8 ounces frozen vegetable medley of corn, peas, and beans

¼ cup tomato paste

1 cup water

1 teaspoon sea salt

¼ teaspoon freshly ground black pepper

⅛ teaspoon cayenne pepper or ¼ teaspoon crushed red pepper flakes

4 teaspoons wheat-free tamari or other soy sauce, or to taste

1 tablespoon nutritional yeast (optional)

1 tablespoon vegan Worcestershire sauce (optional)

1. Preheat the oven to 425°F. Poke a few holes in one of the piecrusts with a fork and bake for 10 minutes. Remove from the oven and set aside.
2. Meanwhile, prepare the filling: Place a large sauté pan over medium high heat. Place the oil, onion, garlic, and celery in the pan and cook for 3 minutes, stirring constantly. Add the potato and tofu and cook for 3 minutes, stirring frequently and adding small amounts of water if necessary to prevent sticking. Add the remaining filling ingredients and cook for 5 minutes, stirring occasionally. Transfer to the baked pie shell.
3. Top with the second piecrust and seal the edges.
4. Bake until golden brown, about 20 minutes. Serve with a dollop of Vegan Sour Cream (page 226).

Variations

- If you have more time, double the homemade crust recipe (see box) and use as the bottom portion of the pie shell, instead of using a premade pie shell.
- Replace the veggies with your favorites, such as mushrooms, peppers, cabbage, or zucchini.
- Replace the tofu with chopped tempeh or seitan.

continues

Vegetable Potpie *continued*

If You Have More Time

You can create your own top crust for the pie by following this recipe. To create both bottom and top crusts, double the recipe and then divide in half before rolling out.

    1 cup white spelt flour
    2 tablespoons vegan butter or coconut oil
    2 tablespoons water
    ¼ teaspoon sea salt
    1 teaspoon ground flaxseeds mixed with 1 tablespoon water

Place all the ingredients in a bowl and mix well. Knead into a ball and place on a flour-dusted dry surface, such as a cutting board. Roll with a flour-dusted rolling pin until the dough is about 9 inches in diameter. Place this dough on top of the pie and pinch-seal the dough along the rim of the lower pie shell. Poke a few holes in the top with a fork before placing in the oven.

Shepherdess's Pie

Not to be confused with shepherd's pie or even cottage pie, both of which use animal products, our shepherdess happens to be vegan, so she prefers tempeh. This is a super-hearty and filling comfort food to power you through those cold British nights. Serve with Raw Kale Salad with Cranberries and Walnuts (page 132) and finish off with a Ginger Brew (page 153).

SERVES 4

POTATO LAYER

2 potatoes, chopped small (4 cups; try russet or Yukon Gold; if you have more time, you can peel)

½ cup unsweetened soy, rice, or other nondairy milk

2 tablespoons vegan butter (optional)

½ teaspoon salt, or to taste

¼ teaspoon freshly ground black pepper

BOTTOM LAYER

1 tablespoon oil

1 cup diced yellow onion

3 garlic cloves, pressed or minced

½ cup diced celery

½ cup diced carrot

1 cup diced mushrooms (shiitake, cremini, button, or your favorite)

8 ounces tempeh, chopped small

2 tablespoons finely chopped fresh flat-leaf parsley

1 tablespoon finely chopped fresh sage

¼ teaspoon crushed red pepper (optional)

continues

1. Prepare the potatoes: Place a steamer basket in a large pot filled with about 1 inch of water. Place over high heat and bring to a simmer. Cover, bring to a boil, and add the potatoes to the steamer basket. Cover, lower the heat to medium, and cook covered until the potatoes are just soft, about 10 minutes. Transfer to a colander and drain well. Place in a bowl with the remaining potato layer ingredients and mash well with a potato masher or a strong whisk. Add salt to taste. Set aside.

2. Meanwhile, prepare the bottom layer: Set the oven to HIGH BROIL and oil an 8-inch casserole dish well. Place a large sauté pan over medium-high heat. Add the oil, onion, garlic, and celery and cook for 3 minutes, stirring constantly. Add the carrot, mushrooms, and tempeh and cook for 8 minutes, stirring frequently and adding small amounts of water if necessary to prevent sticking. Add the remaining ingredients and cook for 5 minutes, stirring frequently. Transfer to the prepared casserole dish.

3. Place the potato layer on top of the filling and spread evenly with a spatula. If you wish, score the potatoes by running a fork several times from one side of the dish to the other. Sprinkle with paprika before baking for 5 to 10 minutes.

4. Serve hot with a dollop of Vegan Sour Cream and a sprig of fresh parsley.

continues

Shepherdess's Pie *continued*

Bottom Layer *continued*

3 tablespoons nutritional yeast
(optional)

1 tablespoon agave nectar, pure
maple syrup, or sweetener of
choice (optional)

2 teaspoons vegan Worcestershire
sauce (optional)

2 tablespoons wheat-free tamari or
other soy sauce, or to taste

1½ cups water

2 tablespoons white spelt flour
mixed with 2 tablespoons
olive oil

TOPPINGS

Paprika (try smoked)

Vegan Sour Cream (page 226)

Fresh parsley

Variations

- Experiment with different vegetables, such as a frozen corn, pea, and bean medley.
- Replace the potatoes with sweet potatoes.
- For a reduced-oil version, replace the spelt flour and water with 2 tablespoons of arrowroot powder mixed with ¼ cup of cold water.

Bangers and Mash

Not the name of the latest British punk band, this is a popular meal throughout England that includes sausages placed over mashed potatoes and topped with gravy. The *bang* is said to refer to the sound of the sausages while cooking, *mash* being the potatoes. You will have three pans going at once for this dish: one for the potatoes, one for the gravy, then a third for the vegan sausage, all coming together in a final crescendo for your dining pleasure. Make a meal out of it and serve with Baked Onion and Tomato with Dill (page 134).

SERVES 4 TO 6

1 recipe mashed potatoes
   (see page 145)

1 tablespoon oil

1 cup thinly sliced yellow onion

14 ounces vegan sausage or
   Field Roast

Sea salt and freshly ground black
   pepper

ONION GRAVY

Makes about 2½ cups gravy

2 tablespoons oil (try safflower,
   coconut, or olive)

¾ cup thinly sliced yellow onion

3 garlic cloves, pressed or minced

3 tablespoons white spelt flour

2 cups vegetable stock (see page
   253) or water

2 tablespoons wheat-free tamari or
   other soy sauce, or to taste

2 tablespoons nutritional yeast

¼ teaspoon sea salt, or to taste

⅛ teaspoon freshly ground black
   pepper

Pinch of crushed red pepper flakes

A few drops of liquid smoke
   (optional), or ½ teaspoon
   smoked paprika

1 tablespoon minced fresh parsley
   or finely chopped fresh sage

1. Prepare the mashed potatoes and place over low heat to keep warm.

2. Meanwhile, prepare the gravy: Place a pot over medium-high heat. Place the oil, onion, and garlic in the pan and cook for 3 minutes, stirring constantly. If you have more time, you can cook for an additional 5 minutes, stirring frequently and adding small amounts of water if necessary to prevent sticking. Add the flour and cook for 1 minute, stirring constantly. Whisk in the remaining ingredients, except the parsley, and cook for 5 minutes, stirring occasionally. Add the parsley, stir well, and cook over low heat until ready to serve. Give it a taste and add additional tamari if necessary.

3. Meanwhile, place a sauté pan over medium-high heat. Place the tablespoon of oil and the sliced onion in the pan and cook for 3 minutes, stirring constantly. Add the vegan sausage and cook for 10 minutes, gently stirring and flipping the sausage with tongs.

4. To serve, place the mashed potatoes on a plate. Top with the sausage, and a liberal serving of gravy.

continues

Bangers and Mash *continued*

Variations

- Add ½ cup of sliced shiitake mushrooms or seeded and sliced bell peppers along with the onion in the gravy.
- Replace the sausage with roasted tempeh or tofu (see page 252).
- Replace the sausage with Tempeh Bacon (page 251) or Tofu Ham (see page 106).

Scottish Oatcakes

The things you learn when writing a cookbook! Apparently, oatcakes are the breakfast of choice for Queen Elizabeth II and have been a staple of the Scottish diet for centuries. Enjoy as part of an Elizabethan-style breakfast, served warm with jam and vegan butter or almond butter. Long live the Queen!

SERVES 8

DRY

2 cups rolled oats

1 cup white spelt flour

¼ cup Sucanat or organic brown sugar (see page 261)

¼ teaspoon sea salt

1 teaspoon baking soda

¼ cup dried fruit: raisins, chopped dates, figs, apricots, or crystallized ginger

¼ teaspoon ground cinnamon

⅛ teaspoon ground nutmeg

WET

¾ cup soy milk

4 tablespoons melted vegan butter

3 tablespoons pure maple syrup

1 tablespoon freshly squeezed lemon juice

1 teaspoon vanilla extract

1. Preheat the oven to 425°F. Oil an 8-inch casserole dish well. Place the dry ingredients in a large bowl and mix well.
2. Place the wet ingredients in another bowl and mix well. Add the wet to the dry and mix well.
3. Transfer immediately to a the prepared casserole dish and bake for 20 minutes.
4. Slice into eight pieces before serving.

Variation
- Bring a hint of the tropics to your Scottish treat by adding 2 tablespoons of dried coconut to the dry ingredients.

Currant Scones

The sun never sets on Britain's culinary empire. Originating in Scotland in the fifteenth century, scones are the poster child for British teatime that has taken the world by storm. Have fun creating many variations using this recipe as a base. Serve on their own with tea or as part of a Fusion breakfast alongside a Spanish Omelet (page 116).

MAKES 8 SCONES

DRY

2½ cups white spelt flour

¾ cup cane sugar (see page 261)

1 teaspoon baking powder

½ teaspoon ground cinnamon

¼ teaspoon ground nutmeg

⅛ teaspoon sea salt

¼ cup dried currants

¼ cup chopped walnuts

WET

4 tablespoons melted vegan butter

½ cup soy milk

2 tablespoons ground flaxseeds mixed with 6 tablespoons water

1 teaspoon vanilla extract

1. Preheat the oven to 425°F. Oil a baking sheet well or line with parchment paper. Place the dry ingredients in a bowl and whisk well. Place the wet ingredients in another bowl and mix well. Add the wet to the dry and mix well.
2. Scoop out about ¾ cup batter for each scone onto the prepared baking sheet.
3. Bake for 15 minutes, or until golden brown. Remove from the oven. Allow to cool on the baking sheet for 5 minutes before transferring to a cooling rack or a serving plate. Serve warm with vegan butter and jam or tahini.

Variations

- Replace the walnuts with pistachios, almonds, macadamia nuts, or hazelnuts. Replace the currants with raisins or chopped dried fruit, such as apricots, dates, or papaya.
- For a Welsh Cake: pour the batter onto a well-oiled griddle pan, then cook for about 4 minutes on each side, pressing down with the spatula to help cook the inside.
- For Vanilla Peach: replace the walnuts and currants with chopped peaches and add another 2 teaspoons of vanilla extract or the seeds of one vanilla bean (page 152).
- For Cacao Goji: replace the walnuts with cacao nibs or vegan chocolate chips, and replace the currants with goji berries.
- For a savory scone: add ¼ cup of grated vegan Cheddar- or mozzarella-style cheese, 1 tablespoon of minced fresh chives, and 2 teaspoons of minced fresh dill.
- Other savory variations include adding ¼ cup of chopped sundried tomatoes and 1 tablespoon of minced fresh rosemary, or ¼ cup of diced olives and ¼ cup of thinly sliced green onions.

English Custard

Passed down from generation to generation since the Middle Ages, custard desserts are traditionally made with egg yolks and milk or cream. This recipe uses a soy creamer for the base and is thickened with kudzu root, a starchy tuber that is available in your local natural foods store. We turn once again to the trusty turmeric to create a lovely yellow hue. Serve as a light dessert after Shepherdess's Pie (page 145).

SERVES 4

2 cups soy creamer or soy milk

¼ cup plus 3 tablespoons sugar, or to taste, depending on the soy creamer

¼ teaspoon ground turmeric

¼ teaspoon ground cinnamon

Pinch of ground nutmeg

Pinch of sea salt

2 teaspoons vanilla extract

2 tablespoons kudzu root dissolved in ¼ cup cold water (see note)

Strawberries

Fresh mint leaves

1. Place a small pot over medium-high heat. Place the soy milk, sugar, turmeric, cinnamon, nutmeg, and sea salt in the pot and cook for 5 minutes, whisking frequently. Lower the heat if it begins to boil.

2. Add the vanilla and the kudzu root mixture and whisk well. Cook for 15 minutes, or until the custard thickens. Pour into four individual ramekins and chill in the freezer for 10 minutes, or until firm. If you have more time, you can place in the refrigerator for 30 minutes or until firm.

3. Garnish with strawberries and mint leaves before serving.

Variations

- Replace the vanilla extract with the seeds of one vanilla bean (see box).
- Replace the creamer with rice, hemp, or almond milk, or a combination.
- Add a pinch of ground cardamom or allspice.
- Add ½ cup of vegan chocolate chips.

continues

English Custard *continued*

Chef's Tips and Tricks

Seeding a Vanilla Bean

Carefully run a knife through the length of the vanilla bean. Using a spoon or a paring knife, scoop out all the seeds. You can place the rest of the bean in a jar of agave nectar for a couple of weeks, to have vanilla-flavored agave.

Chef's Tips and Tricks

What Is Kudzu?

Kudzu is a trailing vine, native to Japan and southeast China, which now grows in great abundance in the southern United States. The starchy root is used to thicken soups, sauces, and puddings.

Ginger Brew

This is a nonalcoholic take on ginger beer, one of England's claims to fame in the 1800s. Ginger is one of the more healthful ingredients in our pantry and is revered as an effective tonic and digestive aid. You can actually make two or three 10-ounce servings, depending upon how spicy you like your brew. Enjoy this effervescent beverage along with any of your meals or to wash down your Welsh Rarebit (page 140).

MAKES TWO 10-OUNCE GLASSES

¼ cup plus 2 tablespoons peeled and thinly sliced fresh ginger

2 tablespoons freshly squeezed lime juice

1 cup water

¼ cup organic sugar or sweetener of choice

16 ounces sparkling water

1. Place the ginger and water in a blender and blend until smooth. Pour through a fine strainer, extracting as much of the liquid as possible.
2. Transfer to a small pot over medium heat, add the sugar, and cook until the liquid is reduced by half, about 10 minutes. Add the lime juice and stir well.
3. Pour into two ice-filled glasses. Add sparkling water and stir well.

Variations

- ♥ For a raw and more strongly spiced beverage, do not cook down the ginger. This will yield more syrup—enough for four 10-ounce servings.
- Add ¼ cup of fresh mint to the blender along with the ginger, and blend well.

Quicker and Easier
United Kingdom and Ireland

Beanie Toast

Heat up one 15-ounce can, drained and rinsed, or 1¾ cups of cooked pinto beans in a small pot over low heat. Add 2 tablespoons of tomato paste and ¾ cup of water. Add salt and pepper to taste. Serve over toast. You can also serve with baked tomato (see page 134).

Pea Puree

This is a quick alternative to mushy peas, a popular British dish that involves soaking fresh peas overnight and cooking them in boiling water and baking soda for a couple of hours before serving. For this version, bring a few cups of water to a boil. Add one 10-ounce bag of frozen peas and cook for 5 minutes. Drain well and place in a food processor with 2 tablespoons of finely chopped fresh flat-leaf parsley, 1 tablespoon of finely chopped fresh marjoram, and 2 tablespoons of finely chopped fresh mint. Process until smooth. Add sea salt and freshly ground black pepper to taste. You can optionally add ¼ cup of unsweetened soy, rice, or almond milk. Serve warm with Bangers and Mash (page 147) or as a side with Shepherdess's Pie (page 145).

Credit: Mark Reinfeld

Jacket Potatoes

Standard fare at pubs and cafés across the United Kingdom, these are baked potatoes with all manner of fillings, virtually anything you can think of. Here are a few jacket potato filling suggestions: Vegan Sour Cream (page 226) with fresh chives; beans from Beanie Toast (page 154) topped with grated vegan Cheddar- or mozzarella-style cheese; steamed vegetables tossed with Pesto Magnifico (page 31) or Italian Vinaigrette (page 14); or Mediterranean Steamed Greens (page 181), with the addition of sautéed mushrooms topped with Vegan Sour Cream (page 226).

Credits: Mark Reinfeld

Credit: Mark Reinfeld

PART FIVE

GREECE

At the touch of love, everyone becomes a poet.

—PLATO

A s with most creative endeavors, The 30-Minute Vegan books rest on the shoulders of those who have come before us. The person with the most cookbook authors standing on his shoulders is the Greek Archestratus, who wrote the first known cookbook in 330 BC. As you can imagine, a lot has happened since, and a lot of plates have been smashed during Greece's four-thousand-year-old culinary history. In fact, we may even be able to trace the fast-food movement back to ancient Greece, where the likes of Aristotle and Socrates dined on souvlaki, gyros, and *spanikopita* as fast-food treats.

In addition to being the birthplace of democracy, Greece may also claim to be the birthplace of the modern-day vegetarian movement in Europe. As mentioned in the introduction to this book, it is reputed that Pythagoras, the famous Greek philosopher and mathematician (a.k.a. the triangle guy) traveled to India and learned the veggie ways from the sages he met on his journey. The rest, as they say, is history.

The past certainly comes to life and is palpable as you explore Greece. As a vegan traveler, I was delighted to be able to enjoy salads, stuffed peppers, fava beans in tomato sauce, and steamed greens with lemon juice, to name a few of my go-to dishes. As Greece is part of the Mediterranean region, it has a history of plant-based cuisine. Also, many dishes are influenced by Italian and French cooking;

some trace back to the Ottoman Empire, with Turkish, Arabic, or Persian origins, including two of those included here: Moussaka and Tzatziki.

Popular Greek vegetables include tomatoes, potatoes, green beans, spinach, eggplant, okra, onions, garlic, and green bell peppers. Fruits include olives and the citrus family of lemons, oranges, and bitter oranges. For herbs and spices, there are thyme, oregano, basil, fennel seeds, dill, mint, bay leaves, cinnamon, and cloves. Indigenous grains include wheat and barley. Pita bread is very popular and served at many meals. Legumes frequently seen are fava beans, lentils, lima beans, and black-eyed peas. Wine is the most popular beverage and was allegedly invented on the Greek island of Icaria.

Similar to Spanish tapas, the Greek meze is a style of meal preparation that includes a variety of appetizer portion-size dishes. Please see page 180 for some suggestions for a Vegan Meze using the recipes in this section.

In this Greek exploration, you will also find a veganized version of the popular Gyros; a vegan feta is used in our Spanikopita Triangles and tops the Cucumber "Feta" Salad. Ambrosial desserts such as baklava and halvah are included and are suitable for Aphrodite herself. You can toast to her with your glass of Louisa Tea!

Stuffed Grape Leaves (Dolmas)

The dainty of choice of the Ottoman Empire, stuffed grape leaves are a hallmark of Greek cuisine and are popular throughout the region from Russia to Crete. Most of your time will be spent rolling the dolmas, so to fit this more into a 30-minute time frame, use only half of the filling for the dolmas and serve the rest of the filling as a nice stand-alone dish. Serve warm or cold as part of your meze meal with a side of Tzatziki (page 162).

MAKES 24 DOLMAS

48 grape leaves

FILLING

Makes 1¾ cups filling

¾ cup white basmati rice

1½ cups vegetable stock (page 253) or water

1 garlic clove, pressed or minced

1 teaspoon sea salt

3 tablespoons finely diced kalamata olives

¼ cup diced red onion

2 tablespoons tomato paste

2 tablespoons pine nuts (optionally toasted, see page 249)

1 tablespoon chiffonaded fresh mint

1 tablespoon finely chopped fresh flat-leaf parsley

1 teaspoon minced fresh dill

½ teaspoon ground coriander

⅛ teaspoon freshly ground black pepper

1 tablespoon freshly squeezed lemon juice

1 teaspoon balsamic vinegar

1. Rinse the grape leaves and set aside.
2. Place the rice, vegetable stock, garlic, and salt in a pot over high heat. Bring to a boil. Cover, lower the heat to a simmer, and cook until all the liquid is absorbed, about 10 minutes. Allow to sit for 5 minutes. Gently fluff with a fork.
3. Meanwhile, place the remaining ingredients in a small mixing bowl and stir well. Add to the pot with the rice and mix well.
4. Place one grape leaf on a clean, dry surface. Place a second leaf below the first with a slight overlap of the edges. Place about 1 rounded tablespoon of the rice mixture on the center of the bottom grape leaf, toward the bottom of the leaf. Fold in the sides and carefully roll up the leaf, continuing to roll with the top leaf as well. Create as tight a roll as possible. You are looking to create a roll about 1½ inches tall and 3 inches long. Repeat with the remaining leaves. Serve warm or cold.

Variations
- Add ½ teaspoon of ground cinnamon and 2 tablespoons of dried currants.
- If you have more time, replace the basmati rice with brown rice, quinoa, or millet (see page 255).
- Feel free to replace the grape leaves with lightly steamed collard greens, chard, or kale.

Creamy Chickpea Soup (Revithia)

Satisfying snack cravings since Neolithic times, and popular in Mediterranean as well as Middle Eastern cuisine, the humble chickpea (a.k.a. garbanzo bean) is one of the oldest cultivated crops. This unforgettable soup is simply divine when served with warm pita bread and a side of mixed olives.

SERVES 6

1 tablespoon olive oil

1 yellow onion, diced (1½ cups)

4 to 6 whole garlic cloves

1 cup thinly sliced celery

1 teaspoon minced fresh rosemary

2 teaspoons finely chopped fresh oregano

½ teaspoon dried thyme

½ teaspoon seeded and diced chile pepper, or ¼ teaspoon cayenne pepper or crushed red pepper flakes

1 carrot, chopped small (1 cup)

3 cups heated vegetable stock (page 253) or water

1½ cups unsweetened soy, rice, or almond milk

2 (15-ounce) cans chickpeas, drained and rinsed, or 3½ cups cooked (see page 257)

2 tablespoons freshly squeezed lemon juice

2 tablespoons nutritional yeast (optional)

1 tablespoon wheat-free tamari or other soy sauce

2 teaspoons balsamic vinegar

1½ teaspoons sea salt, or to taste

¼ to ½ teaspoon crushed red pepper flakes

2 tablespoons finely chopped fresh flat-leaf parsley

1 cup finely chopped tomatoes

Fresh dill or additional rosemary

Black sesame seeds

1. Place the oil in a large pot over medium-high heat. Add the onion, garlic, celery, rosemary, oregano, and thyme, and stir well. Cook for 3 minutes, stirring frequently. Add the carrot, vegetable stock, soy milk, and one can of the chickpeas and cook for 10 minutes, stirring occasionally.

2. Carefully transfer the contents of the pot to a blender and blend until creamy. Return to the pot. Add the remaining ingredients (including the remaining chickpeas), except the tomatoes, and cook for 5 minutes, stirring occasionally.

3. Add the tomatoes and gently stir well before serving. Garnish with fresh herbs and black sesame seeds.

Variations

- Replace the chickpeas with white beans.
- Replace the parsley with cilantro or basil.

Red Lentil Soup (Fakes)

When Socrates was reasoning with Plato, there was likely a bowl of lentil soup on the menu. A staple in homes throughout Greece, don't let its name (actually pronounced "fah-kehs") deceive you—this soup is the real deal. Pulses such as lentils have been known for their health-giving effects since biblical times. While the dish is traditionally made with tomatoes, lots of variations are possible. Be sure to wait until the lentils are completely cooked before adding any salt, to ensure a tender bean. For an Athenian Soup and Salad extraordinaire, serve with Cucumber "Feta" Salad (page 163).

SERVES 6

2 tablespoons olive oil

1 yellow onion, chopped small (1½ cups)

1 cup sliced celery

1 large carrot, sliced (1 cup)

3 garlic cloves, minced or pressed

2 tablespoons fresh oregano, or 4 teaspoons dried

2 teaspoons dried thyme

1 bay leaf

1¼ cups dried red lentils

6 cups heated vegetable stock (page 253) or water

1 (14.5-ounce) can chopped fire-roasted tomatoes, undrained, or 1¾ cups tomatoes, seeded and diced with juice

6 ounces tomato paste (optional, though recommended if using fresh tomatoes instead of canned)

1 tablespoon balsamic vinegar

¼ cup finely chopped fresh flat-leaf parsley

2 tablespoons fresh marjoram, or 4 teaspoons dried (optional)

2 teaspoons minced fresh rosemary (optional)

1 tablespoon wheat-free tamari or other soy sauce (optional)

½ teaspoon sea salt, or to taste

½ teaspoon freshly ground black pepper, or to taste

½ teaspoon crushed red pepper flakes

1. Place the olive oil in a large pot over medium-high heat. Add the onion, celery, carrot, garlic, oregano, thyme, and bay leaf, and cook for 3 minutes, stirring frequently. Add the lentils and vegetable stock and cook for 10 minutes, stirring occasionally.

2. Add the tomatoes, and tomato paste, if using, and cook until the lentils are just soft, 5 to 10 minutes.

3. Add the remaining ingredients, remove the bay leaf, and stir well before serving. If you have more time, and for optimal flavor, allow to simmer over low heat for an additional 10 minutes before serving.

Variations

- Top with 1 cup of chopped Tempeh Bacon (page 251).
- Add 1 cup of sliced shiitake or cremini mushrooms and/or ½ cup of sliced fennel, along with the onion.
- Top the soup with some crumbled Tofu Feta (page 163).
- If you have more time, replace the red lentils with green lentils.

Tzatziki

Try saying that five times fast! A cold yogurt and cucumber dish that is popular throughout the region, this delicacy is served in Turkey, Cyprus, Bulgaria, and the Caucus states. It is even popular in Iraq and Iran. Sometimes served as an appetizer, enjoy it as a side dish with Gyros (page 172); Gemista (page 170); or Fava Beans with Parsley, Oregano, and Thyme (page 165).

MAKES 2 CUPS SAUCE

1 medium-size cucumber, peeled, sliced in half, and seeded

2 cups vegan mayonnaise (Vegenaise or homemade; see page 261)

2 tablespoons chiffonaded fresh mint

¼ cup freshly squeezed lemon juice

4 to 6 garlic cloves, pressed or minced

1 tablespoon minced fresh dill, or 1 teaspoon dried

⅛ teaspoon sea salt, or to taste

⅛ teaspoon freshly ground black pepper

Pinch of cayenne pepper

1. Grate the cucumber on the large holes of a cheese grater. You should have ½ to ¾ cup.

2. Combine with the remaining ingredients in a large bowl and mix well. Add additional lemon juice if you wish for a tarter *tzatziki*.

Cucumber "Feta" Salad

Feta cheese, with its unique tangy flavor, is a traditional ingredient in Greek salads and numerous other popular Greek dishes. This version is tofu based and gets its tang from miso paste and lemon juice. If you have the time, prepare the tofu feta the day before and allow to marinate in the refrigerator overnight before using in this salad. This multicultural salad can be served as a side with Moussaka (page 175), Manicotti (page 27), or Shepherdess's Pie (page 145).

SERVES 4

TOFU FETA

14 ounces extra-firm or super-firm tofu, quartered

¼ cup freshly squeezed lemon juice

1 tablespoon light miso paste (see page xxii)

1 teaspoon minced fresh oregano

1 tablespoon minced fresh flat-leaf parsley

½ teaspoon sea salt

¼ teaspoon freshly ground black pepper

DRESSING

2 tablespoons olive oil

2 teaspoons red wine vinegar

¼ teaspoon crushed red pepper

½ teaspoon sea salt

¼ teaspoon freshly ground black pepper

1 teaspoon agave or coconut nectar (see page 261) or pure maple syrup

SALAD MIX

2¼ cups seeded and diced cucumber

¼ cup diced red onion

1 tablespoon capers

2 tablespoons chiffonaded fresh mint

About 6 cups salad mix or lettuce of choice (4 ounces)

8 to 12 pitted kalamata olives

1. Place a steamer basket in a 3-quart pot filled with ½ inch of water. Place over medium-high heat and bring to a simmer. Place the tofu in the steamer basket and cook covered for 5 minutes. Remove from the heat and run under cold water.
2. Meanwhile, place the remaining tofu feta ingredients in a small bowl and whisk well. Crumble the tofu into the bowl and stir well. Allow it to sit for at least 5 minutes and up to overnight.
3. Prepare the dressing by combining all of its ingredients in a small bowl and whisking well.
4. Combine the cucumber, red onion, and mint in a small bowl and gently stir well. Add the tofu feta and stir well.
5. Place the salad mix in a large bowl and toss with half of the salad dressing. Divide among individual serving plates. Top with the feta mixture and drizzle with the remaining dressing. Top with olives before serving.

Variations

- Go wild and add chopped artichoke hearts, sun-dried tomatoes, and hearts of palm to your creation.

Lima Bean and Beet Salad

Although originating in South America, lima beans (also called butter beans for their creamy flavor) are a common ingredient in Greek and Central Asian cuisine. Lima beans have gotten a bad rap but they are actually in the "you have to try it to believe it" category of yummy foods. Serve this vibrant dish over a bed of lettuce and as side along with Gyros (page 172) and Gemista (page 170).

SERVES 6

2 beets, well cleaned or peeled, chopped into ¼-inch chunks (2½ cups)

16 ounces frozen lima beans

½ teaspoon salt, plus ½ teaspoon sea salt, or to taste

2 tablespoons olive oil

2 garlic cloves, minced or pressed

3 tablespoons chopped kalamata olives

2 tablespoons freshly squeezed lemon juice

1 tablespoon minced fresh dill

¼ teaspoon freshly ground black pepper

Pinch of cayenne pepper

2 tablespoons vegan mayonnaise (Vegenaise or homemade; see page 261) and/or 1 tablespoon vegan butter (optional)

1. Place a steamer basket in a large pot filled with about 1 inch of water. Place over high heat and bring to a simmer. Place the beets in the steamer basket and cook covered over low heat until the beets are just soft, about 15 minutes. Drain well and transfer to a large bowl.

2. Meanwhile, bring 2 quarts of water to a boil in another pot. Lower the heat to a simmer, add the lima beans and ½ teaspoon of salt, and cook for 10 to 12 minutes, stirring occasionally. Drain well.

3. Add to the beets with the remaining ingredients. Mix well before serving.

Variations

- You can also roast the beets. To do so, preheat the oven to 400°F. Combine the beets, olive oil, and a pinch of salt and pepper in a casserole dish and mix well. Bake until the beets are just tender, 20 to 25 minutes. Place in a large bowl.
- Replace the beets with carrots or parsnips.
- Replace the dill with other minced fresh herbs such as thyme, oregano, chervil, or tarragon.
- Replace the lima beans with legumes of your choosing, such as black-eyed peas, pinto beans, or cannellini beans.

Fava Beans with Parsley, Oregano, and Thyme

Not quite the new kid on the block, fava beans (or broad beans) have been part of the Mediterranean diet along with lentils, peas, and chickpeas since 6000 BC. This popular bean is frequently served in a simple tomato-based sauce. Serve as part of a Bacchanalian feast along with Gemista (page 170), Cucumber "Feta" Salad (page 163), and Bulgur Pilaf with Currants (page 167).

SERVES 6

2 (15-ounce) cans fava beans, drained and rinsed, or 3½ cups cooked (see box)

¼ cup tomato paste

¾ cup water

2 tablespoons finely chopped fresh flat-leaf parsley

1 tablespoon finely chopped fresh oregano

1 teaspoon fresh thyme

2 teaspoons red wine vinegar

½ teaspoon seeded and diced hot chile pepper, or ¼ teaspoon crushed red pepper flakes

1 teaspoon sea salt, or to taste

¼ teaspoon freshly ground black pepper

2 teaspoons wheat-free tamari or other soy sauce (optional)

1. Heat the fava beans in a small pan over low heat.
2. Add the remaining ingredients and stir well.
3. Cook for 5 minutes, gently stirring occasionally. Serve warm or at room temperature.

Variations

- Sauté ½ cup of diced onion and 2 cloves of pressed or minced garlic in 2 teaspoons of oil for a few minutes, stirring frequently, before adding the beans.
- Replace the fava beans with black-eyed peas, lima beans, or another bean of choice.
- Replace the beans with sautéed okra to create a dish called *Bamies*
- Create a fava bean spread by placing all the ingredients in a food processor and processing until smooth. Add additional water to reach desired consistency. Season with additional salt and pepper to taste.

continues

Fava Beans with Parsley, Oregano, and Thyme *continued*

Chef's Tips and Tricks

To cook fava beans, use unsalted boiling water. Fresh fava beans take about 20 minutes to cook; whole, unsoaked dried beans take about 2½ hours. For best results, quickly blanch the dried beans to remove their outer skin. Soak the skinned dried beans overnight and cook for about 1½ hours. As a caveat, using fresh fava beans will greatly test your culinary patience. What looks like a lot of pods will actually yield a small amount of beans. If you are up for the effort, you will be greatly rewarded! (Note: It's exceedingly rare, but some people can have a serious allergic reaction to fava beans. Consult with a qualified health-care practitioner if you have any concerns.)

Bulgur Pilaf with Currants

Popular throughout the Ottoman Empire and part of the cuisines of Turkey, Armenia, and the Middle East, bulgur is parboiled wheat that has been dried and had some of its bran removed. (The gluten-free among us can easily substitute quinoa for the bulgur.) Dried currants are small seedless raisins grown throughout the Mediterranean. To fit this dish into a 30-minute time frame, prep your ingredients while the bulgur is soaking. There are countless variations possible for this dish. Serve as part of a light meal with Fava Beans with Parsley, Oregano, and Thyme (page 165) and Creamy Chickpea Soup (page 160).

SERVES 6

3 cups boiling water or vegetable stock (page 253)

2 tablespoons vegan butter or olive oil

1 teaspoon sea salt, or to taste

1½ cups uncooked bulgur wheat (4½ cups cooked; see note)

¼ teaspoon freshly ground black pepper, or to taste

2 tablespoons finely chopped fresh flat-leaf parsley

¼ cup thinly sliced green onion

½ cup dried currants or golden raisins

¼ cup diced kalamata olives

1 tablespoon chiffonaded fresh mint

2 teaspoons freshly squeezed lemon juice

½ teaspoon loosely packed lemon zest

¼ teaspoon crushed red pepper flakes, or to taste

¼ cup slivered almonds or chopped pistachio nuts (optional)

1. Bring the water, vegan butter, and salt to a boil.

2. Place the bulgur wheat in a large bowl. Pour the water into the bowl, stir well, and cover. Allow to sit until all the grain is tender, about 25 minutes. Drain any excess liquid and fluff with a fork.

3. Add the remaining ingredients and gently stir well.

continues

167

Bulgur Pilaf with Currants *continued*

Variations

- For a gluten-free version, replace the bulgur with quinoa. See the cooking chart on page 255 for cooking instructions.
- Add 2 cloves of minced garlic to the boiling water.
- You can sauté 1 cup of vegetables, such as mushrooms, bell peppers, or red cabbage, and add to the pilaf when the bulgur is cooked.
- Try adding 1 cup of grated carrot or beet.
- Replace the parsley with basil or cilantro.
- Replace the mint with 2 teaspoons chopped fresh dill.

Chef's Tips and Tricks

A few varieties of bulgur wheat are available. Use a medium or coarse grain, if you can find it, for this dish. You can also use the fine grain. If so, you may not need to drain any excess water.

Spinach Leek Rice (Prassorizo)

Spinach leek is a classic combo popular in many culinary traditions and for good reason! This dish is a simple way to take your rice experience to the next level of culinary magnificence. Feel free to change up the basmati with your favorite grain. Using the basmati rice allows the dish to fit into a 30-minute meal. Serve as part of a Fusion meal with Tempeh Romesco (page 114), Hungarian Goulash (page 225), or Tofu Scaloppine (page 37).

SERVES 6 TO 8

1 tablespoon olive oil

1 large leek, sliced thinly, rinsed, and drained well (1 cup)

3 to 4 garlic cloves, pressed or minced

2 cups uncooked white basmati rice

1 teaspoon dried oregano

½ teaspoon dried thyme

3½ cups vegetable stock (page 253) or water

1½ teaspoons sea salt, or to taste

2 tablespoons vegan butter (optional)

1 cup thinly sliced and tightly packed spinach, rinsed and drained well, or 5 ounces of frozen spinach, thawed and drained well

2 tablespoons freshly squeezed lemon juice

½ teaspoon lemon zest

1. Place the olive oil in a pot over medium-high heat. Add the leek, garlic, rice, oregano, and thyme and cook for 3 minutes, stirring frequently.
2. Add the vegetable stock, salt, and vegan butter, if using, and bring to a boil. Lower the heat to a simmer, cover, and cook until all the liquid is absorbed, about 15 minutes. Remove from the heat, and allow to sit for 5 minutes.
3. Add the spinach, lemon juice, and lemon zest, and gently stir well before serving.

Variations

- Replace the dried herbs with 1 tablespoon of dried oregano and 1½ teaspoons of dried thyme. You can also replace them with 3 tablespoons of fresh herbs such as cilantro, basil, or flat-leaf parsley gently stirred in at the end.
- Try replacing the herbs with 1 teaspoon dried or 1 tablespoon fresh finely chopped dill.
- You can add several whole cloves of garlic along with the vegetable stock.
- Replace the rice with quinoa or millet and adjust liquid accordingly (see page 255).
- If you have more time, replace the white basmati rice with brown basmati rice or other variety of brown rice. See page 256 for cooking instructions.

Rice-Stuffed Vegetables (Gemista)

As a vegan traveling through Greece, I always breathed a sigh of relief when I saw *gemista* on the menu. The rice and herb–stuffed vegetables, typically peppers, were a welcome sight amid the many animal product dishes that composed most of the menu. Serve warm with Cucumber "Feta" Salad (page 163) and Lima Bean and Beet Salad (page 164).

SERVES 4

1 cup uncooked white basmati rice

1¾ cups vegetable stock (page 253) or water

¼ teaspoon sea salt

4 bell peppers

1 tablespoon olive oil

¾ cup diced yellow onion

3 large garlic cloves, pressed or minced

1 (14.5-ounce) can diced fire-roasted tomatoes, undrained, or 1¾ cups tomatoes with juice

2 tablespoons tomato paste

2 tablespoons freshly squeezed lemon juice

2 tablespoons finely chopped fresh flat-leaf parsley

1 tablespoon chopped fresh oregano

1 tablespoon chiffonaded fresh mint

½ teaspoon sea salt

¼ teaspoon freshly ground black pepper

¼ teaspoon crushed red pepper flakes

1. Preheat the oven to 400°F. Place the rice, vegetable stock, and salt in a pot over high heat. Bring to a boil. Cover, lower the heat to a simmer, and cook until all the liquid is absorbed, about 10 minutes. Allow to sit for 5 minutes. Gently fluff with a fork.

2. Meanwhile, slice about ¼ inch of the top off the bell peppers. Finely chop the tops and set aside. Remove the membrane and seeds from inside and place the peppers in a small casserole dish with about ¼ inch of water. Place in the oven while you prepare the filling.

3. Place a sauté pan over medium-high heat. Place the oil, onion, and garlic in the pan and cook for 2 minutes, stirring constantly. Add the pepper tops and cook for 2 minutes, stirring frequently. Add the remaining ingredients, stir well, and cook for 3 minutes, stirring frequently. Transfer to a bowl along with the cooked rice and mix well. (If either the sauté pan or the pot in which the rice was cooked is large enough, you can combine and mix all ingredients in it.)

4. Remove the peppers from the oven. Carefully place the mixture into the peppers (try using a baking mitt to hold the peppers) and bake for 10 minutes before serving. If your casserole dish has a lid, feel free to use it. You can also cover with foil before baking.

continues

continued

Variations

- You can replace the peppers with large tomatoes, sliced in half and with the insides removed. You only need to bake them for 10 minutes total.
- Add ½ cup of finely chopped vegan sausage, tempeh, or extra-firm tofu to the sauté pan along with the pepper tops.
- Stuff the peppers with the Spanikopita Triangles filling (page 173).
- Replace the parsley with chiffonaded fresh basil or 2 teaspoons of minced fresh dill.
- Add 1 cup of diced mushrooms or zucchini along with the onion.

Gyros

You have probably seen it—that slab of unidentifiable meat in the shape of an inverted triangle on a rotisserie in front of a Greek or Middle Eastern restaurant. Carved-off pieces are then added to a pita with other ingredients and the gyro is born. This version uses seitan; enjoy in a pita with all the fixings. If you want the full experience, take the time to prepare the Pommes Frites (page 68) and Tzatziki (page 162).

SERVES 2 TO 4

SEITAN

1 tablespoon olive oil

1 yellow onion, sliced thinly (1¼ cups)

1 small bell pepper, sliced thinly

2 to 3 large garlic cloves, pressed or minced

8 ounces seitan strips

¼ teaspoon liquid smoke

1 tablespoon finely chopped fresh oregano

1 teaspoon minced fresh rosemary

⅛ teaspoon freshly ground black pepper

2 tablespoons freshly squeezed lemon juice

2 teaspoons wheat-free tamari or other soy sauce

FIXINGS

2 to 4 pita breads

Tomato, sliced thinly

Red onion, sliced thinly

Lettuce, sliced thinly

Vegan mayonnaise (Vegenaise or homemade; see page 261) or Tzatziki (page 162)

Pommes Frites (optional, page 68)

Mediterranean Hot Sauce (page 243)

1. Prepare the seitan: Place a sauté pan over medium-high heat. Place the oil, onion, pepper, and garlic in the pan and cook for 2 minutes, stirring constantly. Add the seitan and cook for 2 minutes, stirring frequently. Lower the heat to low, add the remaining ingredients, and cook for 15 minutes, stirring occasionally.

2. Meanwhile, prepare the fixings. Warm the pita breads on a skillet or in the oven.

3. To assemble, stuff your pita with the fixings, add the seitan, and enjoy. For an authentic Greek experience, smash your plate when finished.

Variations

- Replace the seitan with sliced Field Roast, vegan sausage, or Gardein chicken products (see page xxii).
- For a gluten-free version, replace the seitan with extra firm tofu or tempeh.

Spanikopita Triangles

Even though this dish goes over the 30 minutes, what section on Greek cuisine would be complete without *spanikopita*, the spinach and feta pastry of world fame? This version includes a combination of tofu, tahini, and nutritional yeast for a vegan cheese that fills the phyllo pastry. Remember to place the phyllo dough in the refrigerator the day before to begin the thawing process. Serve as part of a meze with Stuffed Grape Leaves (page 159), Tzatziki (page 162), and Herb-Marinated Olives (page 124).

MAKES 12 TRIANGLES

8 sheets phyllo dough, preferably organic spelt, defrosted according to the package directions

Olive oil for the baking sheet and basting

TOFU-SPINACH FILLING

2 tablespoons olive oil

½ cup diced yellow onion

3 large garlic cloves, pressed or minced

14 ounces extra-firm tofu, well drained and crumbled

2 tablespoons nutritional yeast

¼ cup tahini (see note)

10 ounces thawed and well-drained frozen chopped spinach

3 tablespoons chiffonaded fresh basil

2 tablespoons freshly squeezed lemon juice

1 tablespoon wheat-free tamari or other soy sauce

2 teaspoons dried oregano

1 teaspoon dried thyme

½ teaspoon sea salt, or to taste

¼ teaspoon freshly ground black pepper

¼ teaspoon crushed red pepper flakes

½ cup grated vegan mozzarella-style cheese (optional)

1. Set out the thawed phyllo in its package at room temperature. Preheat the oven to 425°F. Oil a baking sheet.

2. Make the filling: Place the olive oil in a sauté pan over medium-high heat. Add the onion and garlic and cook for 3 minutes, stirring frequently. Add the tofu and cook for 3 minutes, stirring frequently. Add the remaining filling ingredients and cook for 2 minutes, stirring well to make sure the spinach is evenly distributed. Remove from the heat.

3. Place a sheet of phyllo dough on a clean, dry surface. Place a second sheet of phyllo on top of this sheet. You can optionally baste the first sheet with oil. Slice into thirds. Cover the remaining sheets with a slightly damp cloth to prevent them from drying out. Place ¼ cup of filling at the bottom of the sheet. Begin to fold the dough in triangles, as you would fold a flag. Lightly baste with oil. Repeat with remaining sheets. Place on the prepared baking sheet and bake until crisp, about 20 minutes.

continues

Spanikopita Triangles *continued*

Chef's Tips and Tricks

Be sure to use a creamy variety of tahini (sesame paste) if you can find it. If not, mix the tahini in a small bowl with a bit of olive or sesame oil to thin it out.

Variations

- You can replace the frozen spinach with fresh spinach, chard, or beet greens. To do so, clean the greens well, chop finely, and steam for 5 minutes. Drain well before using in the recipe. Ten ounces of frozen spinach is about 1 cup steamed and drained fresh greens. You can also double this amount for a more spinachy *spanikopita*.

- If you have more time (and highly recommended!), add ¼ cup of sliced sun-dried tomatoes and ¼ cup of sliced kalamata olives to the sauté pan along with the spinach.

- Use the filling in stuffed mushrooms (try with the Grilled Portobello Mushrooms with Béarnaise Sauce, page 73) or tomatoes. If using mushrooms (try cremini or portobello), remove the stems before stuffing. If using tomatoes, slice off the top and scoop out the inside. Roast in a 350°F oven for 15 minutes.

- You can also use the filling to create zucchini or eggplant roulades. Slice one medium-size zucchini into ¼-inch-thick strips. Place on a well-oiled baking sheet, lightly brush with olive oil, and sprinkle with sea salt and pepper. Roast in a preheated 375°F oven until just soft, about 10 minutes. Place a large spoonful of filling at the bottom of each slice and roll it up. Return the roulades to the oven for 5 minutes before serving.

Moussaka 🕐

The mother of all Greek dishes and traditionally made with eggplant and tomatoes, versions of this dish are popular in many countries and regions including Turkey, Hungary, Slavic countries, and the Middle East. The Greek version typically includes minced meat and is made with a béchamel sauce. This is a rich and decadent, close to a 30-minute version of a dish that can take hours to prepare. Served warm as well as hot, it's wonderful with a side of Horta (page 181) and a salad such as Cucumber "Feta" Salad (page 163) or mixed wild greens with Toasted Hazelnut Vinaigrette (page 188).

SERVES 6 TO 8

2 tablespoons olive oil

1 small yellow onion, diced (1¼ cups)

4 garlic cloves, pressed or minced

1 small eggplant, cut into ½-inch cubes (3 cups) (see note)

8 ounces tempeh, diced

¾ cup red wine (see box) or vegetable stock (page 253) or water

1 (14.5-ounce) can fire-roasted tomatoes, or 1¾ cups diced and pressed firm tomatoes with juice

2 tablespoons tomato paste

¼ teaspoon ground cinnamon

¼ teaspoon ground allspice

¼ teaspoon crushed red pepper flakes

1 teaspoon sea salt, or to taste

¼ teaspoon freshly ground black pepper

½ cup bread crumbs

1 cup grated vegan cheese

BÉCHAMEL SAUCE

1¼ cups unsweetened soy milk

¼ teaspoon sea salt

3 tablespoons spelt flour

2 tablespoons softened vegan butter or olive oil

1. Preheat the oven to 425°F. Place the olive oil in a large sauté pan over medium-high heat. Add the onion and garlic and cook for 3 minutes, stirring frequently. Add the eggplant, tempeh, wine, tomatoes, tomato paste, cinnamon, allspice, and crushed red pepper flakes, and cook until the eggplant is just soft, about 18 minutes, stirring frequently. You may need to add a small amount of water to prevent sticking. Add the salt and pepper to taste.

2. Meanwhile, prepare the béchamel sauce: Place the soy milk and salt in a small saucepan over medium-high heat. Heat until the milk is just about to boil, about 3 minutes. Lower the heat to low. Create a roux by combining the flour and vegan butter in a small bowl and mixing well. Add this to the soy milk and whisk well until the sauce thickens, about 3 minutes.

3. Transfer the eggplant mixture to a well-oiled 8-inch casserole dish. Evenly sprinkle the bread crumbs on top. Pour the béchamel sauce on top of the bread crumbs and top with the grated vegan cheese.

4. Bake until the cheese melts, about 10 minutes. Congratulate yourself for making moussaka before serving it warm.

continues

Moussaka *continued*

Variation

- If you have more time, you can slice the eggplant into ¼-inch strips and grill it according to the method on page 252. Instead of mixing in the eggplant with the tempeh layer, you can create a layer of eggplant slices on the bottom of the casserole, which is how the dish is traditionally made.
- Replace the tempeh with an equal amount of chopped seitan or crumbled extra-firm or super-firm tofu.
- For a gluten-free version, be sure to use gluten-free bread crumbs.

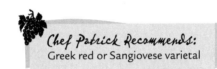

Chef Patrick Recommends:
Greek red or Sangiovese varietal

If You Have More Time

You can sweat the eggplant before using in this dish (see note on page 8). Slice the eggplant into ½-inch cutlets, then slice the cutlets into ½-inch cubes. Arrange in a single layer on a baking sheet or casserole dish and sprinkle liberally with salt. Allow to sit for 20 to 30 minutes before rinsing with water and draining well.

Greek Halvah

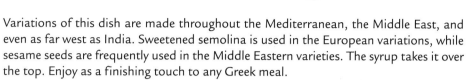

Variations of this dish are made throughout the Mediterranean, the Middle East, and even as far west as India. Sweetened semolina is used in the European variations, while sesame seeds are frequently used in the Middle Eastern varieties. The syrup takes it over the top. Enjoy as a finishing touch to any Greek meal.

MAKES 16 SMALL TREATS

2 cups soy or coconut creamer or soy, rice, almond, or macadamia milk (see page 259)

¾ cup water

½ cup organic sugar, or sweetener of choice to taste

4 tablespoons vegan butter

2 tablespoons olive oil

2 teaspoons rose water (optional but recommended)

½ teaspoon ground cinnamon

⅛ teaspoon sea salt

1 cup semolina flour

¼ cup slivered or chopped almonds, plus 16 whole raw or roasted almonds

¼ cup raisins

Edible rose petals

Small mint leaves

SYRUP

1 tablespoon freshly squeezed lemon juice

½ cup organic sugar (see page xxi)

Lemon peel from 1 lemon (see box)

1 cup water

1 teaspoon vanilla extract

1 cinnamon stick

½ teaspoon whole cloves

1. Oil an 8-inch casserole dish well.
2. Place the creamer and water in a saucepan over medium-high heat. Add the sugar, vegan butter, olive oil, rose water, if using, cinnamon, and salt, and whisk well. Cook for 3 minutes, stirring frequently.
3. Lower the heat to medium, slowly add the semolina flour, and cook for 5 minutes, stirring frequently. Add the slivered almonds and raisins and cook for 3 minutes, stirring frequently.
4. Pour the mixture into the prepared casserole dish and spread evenly. Top with four rows of four almonds evenly spaced. Place in the refrigerator and cool until firm, about 20 minutes.
5. Meanwhile, prepare the syrup by combining all of its ingredients, including the lemon peel, in a small saucepan over medium heat. Cook for 5 minutes, stirring frequently. Lower the heat to low. Allow to sit until the halvah is ready to serve. Pour through a strainer into a small bowl.
6. To serve, slice the halvah into sixteen squares. Top with the syrup, rose petals, and mint leaves.

continues

Greek Halvah *continued*

Variations
- Replace the almonds with pistachios, walnuts, or pecans.
- Replace the raisins with dried currants or chopped dried apricots or figs.

Chef's Tips and Tricks

Step 5 involves steeping lemon peel in the syrup. It's a wonderfully effective way to infuse a liquid with lemon flavor. To remove the peel from the lemon, use a paring knife or a vegetable peeler. Be careful not to remove too much of the white pith, which has a bitter flavor.

Baklava Roulade

Traditionally drenched in honey, this phyllo pastry dessert is another delicacy from the Ottoman Empire and is popular throughout Central and Southwest Asia. No Greek meal would be complete without this decadent treat. Enjoy it after the Moussaka (page 175) and before the plate-smashing ritual. A word of advice: remember to follow the package instructions on thawing the phyllo dough (I speak from experience on this one!).

3 sheets phyllo dough, preferably organic spelt, thawed according to the package directions

4 tablespoons vegan butter or coconut oil

FILLING

1 cup chopped pistachio nuts

¼ teaspoon ground cinnamon

⅛ teaspoon ground cardamom

3 tablespoons agave nectar

2 tablespoons pure maple syrup

1 tablespoon freshly squeezed lemon juice

½ teaspoon lemon zest

1 tablespoon freshly squeezed orange juice

½ teaspoon rose water (optional)

Pinch of sea salt

1. Preheat the oven to 450°F. Place the thawed phyllo sheets on a clean, dry surface, covered with a slightly damp cloth. Place the butter in a small pan and heat over low heat until melted.

2. Meanwhile, combine the filling ingredients in a food processor and process until the nuts are finely ground. Make sure not to overprocess or the filling will be too pasty.

3. Place a phyllo sheet in an 8-inch casserole dish, allowing half of the sheet to drape over the side of the dish. Brush the portion in the dish with melted vegan butter. Fold the sheet back over itself and brush with butter. Repeat with the remaining phyllo sheets, ensuring that each layer has a brushing of butter.

4. Spread the filling equally over the phyllo sheet, leaving an inch on either side and 2 inches on the bottom and top. Carefully roll, creating as tight a roulade as possible. Brush with the remaining vegan butter. Bake until golden brown, about 15 minutes. Slice into 1-inch pieces and serve warm or chilled.

continues

Baklava Roulade *continued*

Variations

- Add ½ cup of pomegranate seeds to the filling.
- For a gluten-free version that would be a total stretch to still call baklava, you can place some of the filling inside a slightly moistened rice paper wrapper used in spring rolls and summer rolls. Place a small amount of filling in the center toward the bottom. Fold in the sides and roll tightly away from you. Serve as is, or pan-sear on both sides in a bit of oil until crispy, about 3 minutes.

Vegan Meze Party

Inherited from the Ottoman Empire, meze is a selection of small dishes served as part of or at the beginning of a large meal. The portions are generally slightly larger than an appetizer. This custom is popular throughout the Mediterranean and Middle Eastern regions. For a traditional Greek (though not an environmentally-friendly) finish, smash the plates when done.

Enjoy a vegan meze with Stuffed Grape Leaves, Cucumber "Feta" Salad, Spanikopita Triangles, Bulgur Pilaf with Currants, Gemista, Tzatziki, Herb-Marinated Olives, and/or Fava Beans with Parsley, and Thyme. Small portions of Halvah and Baklava can seal the deal!

Quicker and Easier Greece

Mediterranean Steamed Greens (Horta) _____

This is a go-to recipe for steamed greens with a Mediterranean flair. Place a steamer basket in a large pot filled with 1 inch of water. Place over high heat, cover, and bring to a boil. Place two bunches of very well rinsed, drained, and chopped spinach in the steamer basket and cook covered until the spinach is just soft, about 3 minutes. Drain well and place in a large bowl with the juice of 1 lemon. Drizzle with olive oil, and add salt and pepper to taste. Gently toss well. Options are to replace the spinach with other greens, such as kale, chard and collards. Other variations include adding a clove of minced or pressed garlic plus a dash of balsamic vinegar, and garnishing with toasted pine nuts. Of course, you can also use this recipe for asparagus, zucchini, broccoli, or a medley of your favorite veggies.

Credit: Mark Reinfeld

181

Cabbage Salad (Lachanosalata) _____

Here's another delicious and amazingly simple dish. Finely shred cabbage and mix it with fresh minced parsley, oregano, and thyme. Toss the mixture with freshly squeezed lemon juice, olive oil, red wine vinegar, and sea salt, and add freshly ground black pepper to taste.

Yiaourti me Meli _____

For a vegan version of a classic Greek dessert, enjoy vegan yogurt mixed with a pinch each of cinnamon and cloves, and sweetened to taste with agave nectar.

Louisa Tea _____

For a Greek-inspired tea, steep 2 tablespoons of lemon verbena in 4 cups of hot water for 10 minutes. Strain and sweeten to taste if desired. Serve warm or iced.

Credit: Mark Reinfeld

Credits: Mark Reinfeld

183

Credit: Mark Reinfeld

PART SIX

GERMANY

Constant kindness can accomplish much. As the sun makes ice melt, kindness causes misunderstanding, mistrust, and hostility to evaporate.

—ALBERT SCHWEITZER

From the streets of Berlin to the heights of the Alps, Germany is vibrant with the energy of a new generation, infused with the legacy of the past. One of the greatest moments I have experienced was standing at Checkpoint Charlie in Berlin when the wall was opened, especially after having participated in demonstrations in East Germany and writing "Love Thy Neighbor" on the wall the day before. Since the reunification, there has been more of a merging of the culture and cuisine of the country.

German cuisine has a rich, albeit predominantly meat-based history. In addition to its own unique evolution, it has also been influenced by its bordering countries, particularly France. Many popular French sauces such as tartar, hollandaise, and béarnaise are common on German menus. The beloved *Pfannkuchen*, a thin pancake served with jam, is the German equivalent of a French crepe. In addition to French, there are Eastern European influences in Eastern Germany and Italian influences to the South. Many of the dishes and ingredients abundant in Germany, including schnitzel and strudel, are likewise popular in Austria.

Veganizing German cuisine is no easy matter. It's the world capital of sausage and cold cuts (aptly named *Wurst*), with over 1,500 varieties (That's a lot of *Wurst!*).

185

Fortunately for sausage aficionados inclined to kick the habit, vegan sausages are now becoming available. Please enjoy them when you have your *Wurst* craving.

Popular foods gracing the German tables include potato (Germany has one of the highest per capita potato consumptions anywhere), many types of cabbage (and its fermented form of sauerkraut), asparagus, carrots, beans, turnips, peas, spinach, cucumbers, onions, tomatoes, and horseradish. For fruit, we have apples, cherries, plums, and strawberries. Popular grains include wheat, barley, oats, and rye.

Herbs and spices include caraway, anise seed, cinnamon, parsley, thyme, laurel, chives, juniper berries, cardamom, mustard, bay leaves, dill, marjoram, parsley, white pepper, chamomile, rose hips, and peppermint.

Beer of course is the national beverage of Germany. I enjoyed using it in the Beer-Braised Greens, Brussels Sprouts and Red Cabbage, and Beer Soup. Also presented here for your German exploration is a German Potato Salad inspired by my brother-in-law Bill's grandmother. Veganized versions of sauerbraten, schnitzel, and Bratwurst, along with traditional side dishes of spaetzle and white asparagus, can now grace your next vegan potluck.

And with no disrespect to JFK, who uttered the famous words, *"Ich bin ein Berliner,"* there are no jelly doughnut recipes here. Instead, you can feast on Apple Strudel, Bread Pudding with Chocolate Sauce, or Black Forest Parfait. For an über-trendy finish to your meal, you can savor a botanical juice.

I would like to thank former Blossoming Lotus chef Surdham Daniele Goeb for his guidance with this section, for contributing the Quick and Easy Section, and for being my rocking guide in Munich.

Beer Soup

While beer has been brewed and imbibed in Europe since Neolithic times, many would agree that the Germans have come close to perfecting it. Traditionally made with cheese, this version of beer soup is just as creamy and rich. As you can imagine, the flavor of the beer is going to be the main determinant in the flavor of the soup, so choose one that you love, or follow the recommendations below. Go for the soup and salad combo and enjoy with mixed wild greens with Toasted Hazelnut Vinaigrette (page 188) and a few slices of pumpernickel bread.

SERVES 4 TO 6

1 tablespoon grapeseed, safflower, sunflower, coconut, or olive oil

1 yellow onion, diced (1½ cups)

¼ cup thinly sliced celery

3 garlic cloves

2 cups chopped potato, such as Yukon Gold or new potatoes

1¼ cups vegetable stock (page 253) or water

2 cups German beer (see box)

1½ teaspoons sea salt

¼ teaspoon freshly ground black pepper

3 tablespoons nutritional yeast

1 tablespoon freshly squeezed lemon juice

1 teaspoon stone-ground mustard

1 teaspoon minced fresh dill, or ½ teaspoon dried

½ cup grated vegan Cheddar-style cheese

2 teaspoons wheat-free tamari or other soy sauce (optional)

1. Place a large pot over medium-high heat. Place the oil, onion, celery, and garlic in the pot and cook for 3 minutes, stirring frequently. Add the potatoes, vegetable stock, and beer and cook for 10 minutes, or until the potatoes are just soft, stirring occasionally.

2. Remove from the heat, and add the salt, pepper, nutritional yeast, lemon juice, and mustard and stir well. Carefully transfer to a blender and blend until just creamy.

3. Return to the pot. Add the remaining ingredients and cook over low heat for 5 minutes, stirring occasionally.

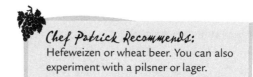

Chef Patrick Recommends:
Hefeweizen or wheat beer. You can also experiment with a pilsner or lager.

Toasted Hazelnut Vinaigrette

Hazelnuts, or filberts to those in the know, are one of the more popular nuts in European cuisine, especially in Central European countries such as Germany. This is an exceedingly versatile dressing that lends itself to many different variations. Serve with mixed wild greens or baby arugula and your fixings of choice. May also be used as a sauce for sautéed greens or Broccoli Rabe with Garlic and Red Pepperv (page 19).

MAKES 1¾ CUPS DRESSING

3 tablespoons finely chopped, toasted hazelnuts (see note)

1¼ cups safflower oil

¼ cup water

3 tablespoons raw apple cider vinegar

1 tablespoon pure maple syrup

1 tablespoon freshly squeezed lemon juice

¼ teaspoon sea salt

⅛ teaspoon freshly ground black pepper

1 small garlic clove

Pinch of cayenne pepper

2½ teaspoons wheat-free tamari or other soy sauce, or extra salt to taste

2 teaspoons minced shallot

2 teaspoons minced fresh ginger

1. Toast the hazelnuts and remove the skins according to the method in the note below.
2. Place them in a blender with the remaining ingredients and blend well. If using a strong blender such as a Vitamix, its best to blend on low speed. The higher speeds will emulsify the dressing.
3. Store in a glass jar in the refrigerator for 4 or 5 days.

Variations

- For a raw version, replace the hazelnuts with pecans, sunflower seeds, macadamia nuts, or your favorite raw seeds or nuts. ♥
- For a toasted variation, feel free to experiment with toasting nuts or seeds and using them in place of the hazelnuts.

Chef's Tips and Tricks

To toast hazelnuts: Preheat the oven or toaster oven to 350°F. Place the hazelnuts on a baking sheet and bake for 10 to12 minutes, or until the skins darken and the nuts become fragrant. Transfer the nuts to the center of a clean dish towel placed on a dry surface. Fold the towel over to cover the nuts. Apply pressure to the top of the towel and rub vigorously. The friction created will remove the majority of the skins.

Beer-Braised Greens

This simple and healthful dish is imbued with the flavor of beer, the alcohol content of which is cooked away in the braising process. Experiment with different greens to experience the subtle flavor combinations. Serve as a side dish with any entrée such as Tempeh Sauerbraten (page 198), Notwurst (page 197), or Baked Vegan Schnitzel (page 196).

SERVES 4 TO 6

2 tablespoons olive oil

1 tablespoon minced garlic or fresh ginger

2 teaspoon caraway seeds (optional)

½ teaspoon seeded and diced hot chile pepper, or ¼ teaspoon crushed red pepper flakes

8 cups chopped, rinsed, and tightly packed kale or other green leafy vegetable such as chard, collards, or a combination

½ cup German beer (see box)

1 teaspoon freshly squeezed lemon juice

2 teaspoons red wine vinegar

Pinch of sea salt

Freshly ground black pepper

1. Place a large sauté pan over medium-high heat. Place the oil, garlic, caraway seeds if using, and chile pepper in the pan, and cook for 1 minute, stirring constantly. Add the kale and beer, and cook until the kale is just tender, about 5 minutes, stirring frequently with tongs and adding small amounts of water if necessary to prevent sticking.
2. Just before serving, toss with the lemon juice and red wine vinegar. Season with salt and pepper to taste, and serve immediately.

Chef Patrick Recommends:
pilsner or amber ale

Variations

- Add 1 tablespoon of finely chopped fresh marjoram after the greens are cooked.
- Add a few tablespoons of toasted and chopped hazelnuts.
- You can leave out the beer and replace the red wine vinegar with 1 tablespoon of balsamic vinegar.
- Add a few tablespoons each of toasted pine nuts and kalamata olives.
- For an oil-free version, add ¼ cup of water or vegetable stock to the pan before adding the garlic.

Brussels Sprouts and Red Cabbage

One of the nutritional powerhouses of the plant kingdom and a member of the wild cabbage family, the forefathers of what we now call Brussels sprouts have been cultivated since ancient Roman times. The modern-day veggie takes its name from the town where, rumor has it, the festivities began in the 1300s. Here, beer imparts a sweet and tangy touch to the dish. For the most vibrant color, be sure to add the vinegar right before serving. Serve as a side with Baked Vegan Schnitzel (page 196), Notwurst (page 197) or Tempeh Sauerbraten (page 198).

SERVES 4 TO 6

2 tablespoons olive oil

1 pound Brussels sprouts, trimmed and halved or quartered (about 4 cups), rinsed and drained well

1 cup German beer (see box)

1 cup thinly sliced red cabbage

2 teaspoons raw apple cider vinegar or red wine vinegar

2 teaspoons wheat-free tamari or other soy sauce (optional)

1 tablespoon ground mustard

1 teaspoon sea salt, or to taste

¼ teaspoon freshly ground black pepper

¼ teaspoon crushed red pepper

Black and white sesame seeds

1. Place the oil in a large sauté pan over medium-high heat. Add the Brussels sprouts and cook for 5 minutes, stirring frequently.
2. Lower the heat to medium, add the beer, and cook for 5 minutes, stirring frequently. Add the red cabbage and cook for 8 minutes, or until the Brussels sprouts are just tender, stirring occasionally.
3. Add the remaining ingredients, stir well, and garnish with white and black sesame seeds before serving.

Variation
- Add ½ cup of toasted and chopped hazelnuts (see page 188).

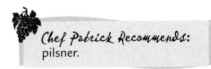

Chef Patrick Recommends: pilsner.

continues

continued

Chef's Tips and Tricks

The Great Brussels Sprouts Secret Recipe

Thanks to recipe tester Suzanne Rudolph of Rudymademeals.com for the inspiration of this dish. She made a variation of the Krispy Kale recipe in *The 30-Minute Vegan*, using Brussels sprout leaves instead of kale leaves.

    1 pound Brussels sprouts, washed and trimmed
    3 tablespoons olive oil
    2 tablespoons nutritional yeast
    ¾ teaspoon sea salt
    ⅛ teaspoon freshly ground black pepper

1. Preheat the oven to 375°F. Separate the Brussels sprout leaves and place them on a well-oiled baking sheet. Bake until the leaves are crispy, about 15 minutes.
2. Place in a large bowl with remaining ingredients and gently toss well. Warning: This is a highly addictive dish!

Roasted White Asparagus
with Nutmeg Cream Sauce

Asparagus is so beloved in Germany that it is often referred to as the king's vegetable. The white asparagus is exceptionally revered, especially during the main harvest season of mid-May to mid-June, where entire menus are sometimes devoted to this one veggie. Feel free to use green asparagus, or live on the edge and replace with broccoli rabe. The dairy-free cream sauce is a magical addition to any steamed, roasted, or grilled vegetable. Serve the asparagus along with Baked Vegan Schnitzel (page 196) or Tempeh Sauerbraten (page 198).

SERVES 2 TO 4

2 teaspoons olive oil

2 teaspoons freshly squeezed lemon juice

Pinch of sea salt

Pinch of freshly ground black pepper

1 large bunch white asparagus, bottom stems removed

¼ cup seeded and diced red bell pepper

1 teaspoon minced fresh dill, or 1 tablespoon finely chopped fresh flat-leaf parsley

SAUCE

1¼ cups soy, rice, or almond milk (page 259)

½ teaspoon sea salt

¼ teaspoon ground nutmeg

⅛ teaspoon ground white pepper

Pinch of cayenne pepper

1 tablespoon softened vegan butter or oil

5 teaspoons white spelt flour

2 ounces vegan ham, chopped (about ¼ cup; optional)

1. Preheat the oven to 400°F. Place the olive oil, lemon juice, salt, and pepper in a casserole dish or baking sheet. Add the asparagus and toss until well coated. Bake until just tender, about 10 minutes. Carefully turn the asparagus midway through to ensure even cooking.

2. Meanwhile, prepare the sauce. Place the soy milk in a small pot or sauté pan over medium-high heat. Add the salt, nutmeg, pepper, and cayenne, if using, and whisk well.

3. Combine the vegan butter and flour in a small bowl and mix well. Add to the pot and whisk until the sauce thickens, about 2 minutes.

4. Add the vegan ham and mix well. Cook for 2 minutes, stirring occasionally. To serve, remove the asparagus from the oven and top liberally with the sauce. Garnish with the bell pepper and dill before serving.

continues

continued

Variations

- Replace the white asparagus with green asparagus, or broccoli rabe, broccoli, or cauliflower.
- For a crispier asparagus, allow to bake until slightly caramelized, about 5 minutes longer.
- If you do not have the vegan ham, you can add ¼ teaspoon of liquid smoke.
- You can also steam the asparagus before roasting: Place a steamer basket in a large pot containing about 1 inch of water. Bring to a simmer over high heat. Place the asparagus in the steamer basket and cook covered for 5 minutes.

German Potato Salad

This is not the typical potato salad you will find at your neighborhood block party, unless of course you live in Hamburg. The German version of potato salad is traditionally prepared with bacon and served hot. This vegan version is made with tempeh and a warm oil and vinegar-based sauce. Enjoy with Beer Soup (page 187) and mixed wild greens with Toasted Hazelnut Vinaigrette (page 188) as part of an authentic German soup and salad combo.

SERVES 4 TO 6

1½ pounds potatoes, cut into ½-inch cubes (4 cups)

2 tablespoons olive oil

1 cup diced yellow or white onion

2 garlic cloves, pressed or minced

1 cup seeded and diced red bell pepper

6 ounces (9 strips) Fakin' Bacon or Tempeh Bacon (page 251), diced

¼ cup raw apple cider vinegar, or 3 tablespoons red wine vinegar

1 tablespoon stone-ground mustard

1½ teaspoons sea salt, or to taste

¼ teaspoon freshly ground black pepper

2 tablespoons fresh flat-leaf parsley

1 teaspoon paprika (try smoked; optional)

1. Place a steamer basket in a medium-size pot with 1 inch of water. Bring to a simmer over high heat. Place the potatoes in the steamer basket and cook covered until the potatoes are just soft, about 12 minutes.

2. Meanwhile, place the oil in a large sauté pan over medium-high heat. Add the onion and garlic and cook for 3 minutes, stirring frequently. Lower the heat to medium, add the bell pepper and Fakin' Bacon, and cook for 5 minutes, gently stirring occasionally.

3. When the potatoes are done cooking and are still hot, transfer them to a large bowl with the onion mixture plus the remaining ingredients, and gently stir well.

Spaetzle Noodles

If you have a spaetzle maker, now is the time to use it! Popular in German and Austrian cuisine, spaetzle is an egg-and-flour noodle that is created by pouring the dough through a graterlike device and into boiling water, resulting in thin noodles. This version uses ground flaxseeds instead of eggs as the binder. If you lack a spaetzle maker, you can pour the dough through a colander with large holes, which will require the addition of more liquid (see below), or cut long thin strips of the dough with a knife and drop them into the boiling water. Serve at your Oktoberfest celebration along with Tempeh Sauerbraten (page 198) and Brussels Sprouts and Red Cabbage (page 190).

SERVES 4 TO 6

1½ cups white spelt flour

2½ teaspoons sea salt, or to taste

½ teaspoon ground allspice or nutmeg

1 tablespoon ground flaxseeds mixed with 3 tablespoons water

½ cup unsweetened soy, rice, or almond milk (see page 259)

1 tablespoon softened vegan butter or oil

1 tablespoon minced fresh chives, flat-leaf parsley, or dill

Freshly ground black pepper

1. Place a large pot of water with an optional 2 teaspoons of sea salt over high heat and bring to a boil. Meanwhile, combine the flour, remaining ½ teaspoon of sea salt, and allspice in a large bowl and whisk well.
2. Combine the ground flaxseeds and water in a small bowl and mix well. Add the soy milk and vegan butter and mix well. Add the wet ingredients to the dry and mix well.
3. Pour through a spaetzle maker and cook until the dough rises to the surface, 3 to 5 minutes. You can also slice the batter into eight long, thin strips on a clean, dry cutting board. Flatten each strip slightly and cut into ¾-inch pieces. Carefully drop into the water.
4. Remove with a mesh strainer or slotted spoon. Serve with vegan butter, topped with the chives and salt and pepper to taste.

Variation
- If you do not have a spaetzle maker, you can increase the soy milk to 1 cup and press the batter with a spatula through a large-holed colander into the boiling water.
- For optimal flavor, once the spaetzle have been removed from the water, you can heat oil in a large sauté pan over medium-high heat and sauté the spaetzle for a few minutes before serving with vegan butter and chives.

Baked Vegan Schnitzel

Besides being fun to say in your best German accent, nothing conjures images of German cuisine quite like schnitzel. Of Austrian origin, schnitzel refers to a pounded cutlet. This animal-friendly version uses tofu, marinated in a bit of liquid smoke to give your cutlet more of an authentic flavor. The cornflake crust makes the dish, thanks to the suggestion from contributing chef Surdham Goeb. Serve with Beer-Braised Greens (page 189) and Spaetzle Noodles (page 195).

SERVES 4

TOFU MARINADE

1 tablespoon olive oil

2 tablespoons wheat-free tamari or other soy sauce

¼ teaspoon liquid smoke

14 ounces extra-firm tofu

TAHINI SPREAD

2 tablespoons tahini

2 teaspoons freshly squeezed lemon juice

2 to 3 tablespoons water

1 teaspoon wheat-free tamari or other soy sauce

CRUST

1½ cups cornflakes, pretzels, or bread crumbs

2 tablespoons gluten-free or spelt flour

1 teaspoon paprika (try smoked)

⅛ teaspoon sea salt

⅛ teaspoon freshly ground black pepper

1. Preheat the oven to 375°F. Prepare the marinade: Place the olive oil, soy sauce, and liquid smoke on a small baking sheet and stir well. Slice the tofu into four cutlets lengthwise and place in the marinade for 5 minutes. Flip midway through to ensure an even coating. Bake for 10 minutes, flipping once after 5 minutes.

2. Meanwhile, prepare the tahini spread by placing all the ingredients in a small bowl adding enough water to create a spreadable consistency and stirring well.

3. Prepare the crust by pulse-chopping the cornflakes in a food processor or with a mortar and pestle and transferring to a small bowl with the remaining crust ingredients.

4. Remove the tofu from oven, spread a thin coating of tahini on both sides of each cutlet, and liberally coat each side with the crust. Return the tofu to the oven and bake for an additional 10 minutes before serving.

Variations

- Replace the tofu with tempeh or portobello mushrooms.
- You can also sauté the cutlets in oil for a few minutes on each side before serving.

Notwurst (Vegan Bratwurst)

To begin with, this ain't your grandma's bratwurst. I shudder when I think of the nutritional composition of traditional bratwurst, a sausage with origins dating back to 1313 Germany. Give thanks for the evolution of vegan recipe developers who have created plant-based alternatives that allow us to savor the flavors without compromising our health. Serve with additional sauerkraut and a dollop of mustard and horseradish, along with mixed wild greens and Toasted Hazelnut Vinaigrette (page 188).

SERVES 4 TO 6

1 tablespoon oil

1 small yellow onion, sliced thinly into half-moons (1½ cups)

2 garlic cloves, minced or pressed

1½ teaspoons caraway seeds

2 ounces Fakin' Bacon or Tempeh Bacon, diced (page 251; ½ cup)

13 to 14 ounces vegan sausage (such as Tofurky or Field Roast brand)

½ cup sauerkraut

½ cup German beer (see box)

1 tablespoon white wine vinegar or raw apple cider vinegar

2 teaspoons stone-ground mustard

½ teaspoon sea salt, or to taste

Pinch of freshly ground black pepper

Fresh dill

1. Place a large sauté pan over medium-high heat. Place the oil, onion, garlic, and caraway seeds in the pan and cook for 2 minutes, stirring constantly.
2. Lower the heat to medium, add the Fakin' Bacon and vegan sausage, and cook for 10 minutes, stirring occasionally with tongs and adding small amounts of water if necessary to prevent sticking.
3. Add the remaining ingredients, except the dill, and cook for 5 minutes, gently stirring occasionally. Garnish with fresh dill before serving.

Variations

- Add ½ cup of thinly sliced green apples along with the onion.
- Replace the vegan sausage with thick slices of tofu or tempeh. Place in the marinade used in the Baked Vegan Schnitzel recipe (see page 196) before roasting for 20 minutes.

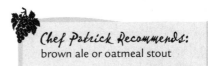

Chef Patrick Recommends:
brown ale or oatmeal stout

Tempeh Sauerbraten

Originally made from horsemeat (yum!), sauerbraten is a German pot roast and one of the signature dishes of the country. This horse-friendly version uses tempeh as the main component of the dish. The brown sauce pairs well with grilled tofu or tempeh (see page 252) or entrées such as Baked Vegan Schnitzel (page 196). Experience the sauerbraten alongside Beer-Braised Greens (page 189) and Saffron Quinoa Pilaf (page 231).

SERVES 4 TO 6

TEMPEH MARINADE

3 tablespoons red wine vinegar

2 tablespoons wheat-free tamari or other soy sauce

1 tablespoon olive oil

¼ teaspoon ground nutmeg

⅛ teaspoon ground cloves

16 ounces tempeh

1. Preheat the oven to 375°F. Place the vinegar, soy sauce, olive oil, nutmeg, and cloves on a baking sheet or casserole dish and whisk well. Slice the tempeh into eight ¼-inch cutlets and place in the marinade. Allow to sit for 5 minutes, flipping after a few minutes to ensure an even coating. Bake for 15 minutes.

continues

continued

SAUCE

1 tablespoon oil

1 cup diced yellow onion

2 garlic cloves, pressed or minced

½ teaspoon seeded and diced hot chile pepper

½ cup finely chopped carrot

½ cup finely chopped parsnip

1 cup peeled and chopped celeriac or celery

½ cup red wine (see box)

2¼ cups vegetable stock (page 253) or water

1 teaspoon sea salt

1 tablespoon wheat-free tamari or other soy sauce

2 tablespoons tomato paste

2 tablespoons nutritional yeast

¼ teaspoon freshly ground black pepper

2 teaspoons minced fresh dill

2. Meanwhile, prepare the sauce. Place a large sauté pan over medium-high heat. Place the oil, onion, garlic, and chile in the pan and cook for 3 minutes, stirring constantly. Lower the heat to medium, add the carrot, parsnip, and celeriac, and stir well.

3. Add the wine and stir well, scraping the bottom of the pan. (This technique is called deglazing.) Add the vegetable stock and cook for 10 minutes, stirring frequently. Add the remaining ingredients, except the dill, and stir well. Remove from the heat.

4. Carefully transfer the contents of the pan to a blender and blend until just creamy. Return to the pan to low heat.

5. Place the tempeh cutlets in pan and allow them to cook in the sauce for at least 5 minutes, up to 15 minutes. Serve each cutlet with a liberal topping of sauce. Garnish with dill and enjoy!

Variation

- Replace the tempeh with tofu or a Gardein "chicken" cutlet (see page xxii).

Chef Patrick Recommends:
Cabernet Sauvignon or Merlot

Stuffed Apples (Bratapfeln)

A traditional Christmas and winter delicacy throughout Germany, this is a super simple recipe that is quite a healthful dessert (it is naturally fruit-sweetened). Numerous variations are possible. Be bold and replace the apples with pears or persimmons. Serve warm with a scoop of vegan ice cream or Cashew Cream (page 90) topped with Cherry Sauce (page 206).

SERVES 8

4 apples (such as Jonagold or Gala; see page 245)

½ cup rolled oats

½ cup finely chopped hazelnuts

½ teaspoon ground cinnamon

¼ teaspoon ground nutmeg, ground cardamom, and/or ground allspice

Pinch of sea salt

1 cup raisins or dried currants

¼ cup plus 2 tablespoons date syrup (see page 264), or 2 tablespoons maple syrup plus ¼ cup water

4 tablespoons vegan butter (optional but oh so good)

½ cup apple juice, or ¼ cup water plus ¼ cup date syrup (see page 264)

1. Preheat the oven to 425°F. Remove the core from each apple and scoop out a ½-inch hole. Slice each apple in half across its equator.

2. Combine the remaining ingredients, except the apple juice, in a small bowl and mix well. Fill each apple with about ¼ cup of the stuffing, forming a mound over the top.

3. Place the apples in a well-oiled 8-inch casserole dish. Pour the apple juice into the casserole dish and over the apples, and bake covered until the apples are just soft, about 20 minutes, depending upon the size and variety of the apples. Serve warm with the Cashew Cream.

Bread Pudding with Chocolate Sauce

Hold onto your glockenspiel, as you will find yourself swooning with the combination of warm sweet bread with a luscious chocolate sauce, closely related to French toast. The idea of using leftover bread to create a delectable sweet dessert may trace its origins back to ancient Roman times. Serve warm and top with a dollop of Cashew Cream (page 90).

SERVES 6 TO 8

4½ cups bread that has been cut into ½-inch cubes, about half of a loaf (see box)

½ cup raisins

½ cup toasted hazelnuts (see page 188), roughly chopped

2½ cups soy or coconut creamer

½ cup organic sugar or pure maple syrup

2 tablespoons vegan butter

2 teaspoons vanilla extract

¾ teaspoon ground cinnamon

½ teaspoon ground nutmeg

Pinch of sea salt

2 tablespoons arrowroot dissolved in 3 tablespoons water

1. Preheat the oven to 425°F. Place the bread cubes, raisins, and hazelnuts in a large bowl and mix well.

2. Place the creamer in a saucepan over medium-high heat. Add the sugar, vegan butter, vanilla, cinnamon, nutmeg, and salt, and cook for 5 minutes, whisking occasionally. If the mixture begins to boil, lower the heat. Add the arrowroot mixture and cook until the mixture thickens, about 3 minutes, whisking well constantly.

3. Pour the mixture into the bowl with the bread cubes and mix well. Transfer to well-oiled 8-inch casserole dish and bake for 15 minutes.

continues

Bread Pudding with Chocolate Sauce *continued*

CHOCOLATE SAUCE

¼ cup plus 2 tablespoons pure maple syrup or agave or coconut nectar

3 tablespoons unsweetened cocoa powder

1 teaspoon vanilla extract

¼ teaspoon ground cinnamon

2 tablespoons soy, rice, or coconut milk, or soy creamer

4. Meanwhile, prepare the Chocolate Sauce by combining all the ingredients in a mixing bowl and whisking well. To serve, drizzle the sauce over each serving.

Variations

- Replace the hazelnuts with walnuts, pecans, almonds, or your favorite nuts or seeds.
- Replace the raisins with any dried fruit, or vegan chocolate or carob chips— yum! If you do use the chocolate or carob chips, you can omit the chocolate sauce.
- You can also replace the raisins with fresh fruit such as berries or chopped banana, apples, pears, or peaches.
- Replace the soy creamer with soy, coconut, rice, almond, or macadamia milk (see page 259).
- For a gluten-free version, use gluten-free bread.

Chef's Tips and Tricks

A plain white, sourdough, or spelt flour bread works best for this recipe. Steer clear of the heavier whole-grain breads. I cringe at the use of stale bread in recipes, though traditionally many bread puddings are used with leftover bread. It's your call!

Apple Strudel

What apple pie is to Americans, strudel is to Germany and Austria. (Incidentally, I place *strudel* with *schnitzel* in the "fun words with which to practice your German accent" category.) Apples are an abundant crop in the region. Experiment with the many varieties of apples available. This vegan version of the iconic dish is best enjoyed warm with a hearty serving of vegan ice cream or Cashew Cream (page 90).

SERVES 8 TO 10

FILLING

3 apples (such as Jonagold or Gala), peeled and sliced thinly (4½ cups)

3 tablespoons white spelt or gluten-free flour

½ cup raisins

½ cup sugar or sweetener of choice, or to taste, depending upon sweetness of the apples (see page 245)

3 tablespoons freshly squeezed lemon juice

1 teaspoon lemon zest

1 teaspoon vanilla extract

2 teaspoons poppy seeds

1½ teaspoons ground cinnamon

¼ teaspoon ground cardamom

Pinch of sea salt

continues

1. Preheat the oven to 425°F. Oil or place parchment paper on a large baking sheet. Place the filling ingredients in a large bowl and mix well.
2. Place the dry dough ingredients in a large bowl and mix well. Place the wet dough ingredients in another bowl and mix well. Add the wet dough ingredients to the dry and mix well.
3. Transfer the dough onto a flour-dusted clean surface, and using a flour-dusted rolling pin, roll into a rectangle about 12 inches long and 8 inches wide. Add small amounts of vegan butter, if necessary, to have a pliable dough. Transfer to the prepared baking sheet.
4. Place the filling in the center of the dough, leaving about 1 inch on the ends and 3 inches on either side. Lift the two sides and fold them up and over until they meet in the middle. Create a seam across the top and seal well. Baste with additional vegan butter or coconut oil.
5. Bake until the dough is thoroughly cooked and golden brown, about 15 minutes. Baste again and bake for an additional 5 minutes. Enjoy warm or chilled.

continues

Apple Strudel *continued*

DOUGH (DRY)

3 cups white spelt flour

2 tablespoons sugar (optional)

½ teaspoon baking powder

Pinch of sea salt

DOUGH (WET)

⅓ cup soy creamer or soy milk

8 tablespoons vegan butter or
coconut oil, unmelted

1½ tablespoons ground flaxseeds
mixed with 5 tablespoons water

Additional vegan butter or coconut
oil for basting

Confectioners' sugar (optional)

Variations

- Replace the apples with other fruit, such as pears, peaches, or nectarines.
- Top with confectioners' sugar and fresh berries.
- For a quicker version, you can replace the dough with 5 or 6 phyllo sheets. Lay a sheet on a clean, dry surface and baste with melted vegan butter or coconut oil. Place the second sheet on top of the first sheet and baste well. Repeat with the remaining sheets. Follow steps 4 and 5 above to complete the recipe.

Black Forest Parfait

The dessert poster child for German cuisine, the Black Forest Cake is traditionally a multilayered chocolate cake with whipped cream and cherries. The real deal contains a cherry brandy (Kirschwasser) that is indigenous to the Black Forest region and is what gives the cake its name. Believe it or not, there is actually a law that requires this liquor to be included for the cake to be labeled as a Black Forest Cake. We are a bit more laid back in 30-Minute Vegan world and no alcohol is required. Enjoy with a glass of Six-Herb Botanical Juice (page 207)

SERVES 12

CAKE (DRY)

1½ cups white spelt flour

1 teaspoon baking soda

¼ teaspoon sea salt

½ teaspoon ground cinnamon

¼ teaspoon ground nutmeg

½ cup unsweetened cocoa powder

1½ cups organic sugar (see page xxi)

CAKE (WET)

1 cup soy milk or soy creamer

2 teaspoons raw apple cider vinegar

½ cup Vegan Sour Cream (page 226)

1 teaspoon vanilla extract

½ teaspoon almond extract (optional)

2 tablespoons ground flaxseeds mixed with ¼ cup cold water

continues

1. Preheat the oven to 400°F. Well oil a 9 by 13-inch baking sheet or casserole dish. Place the dry cake ingredients in a large bowl and whisk well. Place the wet cake ingredients in another bowl and mix well. Add the wet cake ingredients to the dry and mix well. Pour into the baking sheet and bake for 20 minutes.

2. Meanwhile, prepare the cream layer by placing the frosting ingredients in a strong blender or food processor and processing until creamy. The strength of your blender will determine how much liquid you need to accomplish this. Add more if necessary to create a creamy yet not liquidy consistency. Transfer to a bowl.

3. Prepare the cherry sauce by placing a small pot over medium-high heat. Place the cherries, cranberry concentrate, and almond extract and cook for 2 minutes, stirring constantly. Add the arrowroot dissolved in water and cook until the sauce thickens, about 3 minutes. Stir continuously to ensure that the arrowroot is thoroughly dissolved. Remove from the heat.

continues

Black Forest Parfait *continued*

CREAM LAYER

3 cups raw cashews

1½ cups soy, coconut, or almond milk (see page 259)

¼ cup agave nectar, coconut nectar, or light-colored sweetener of choice, or to taste depending upon the sweetness of the milk (see page 261)

1 teaspoon vanilla extract

Pinch of sea salt

CHERRY SAUCE

2 (10-ounce) packages frozen cherries, thawed, or fresh and pitted cherries (4 cups)

1 cup frozen cranberry or apple juice concentrate, thawed

¾ teaspoon almond extract

4 tablespoons arrowroot powder dissolved in ½ cup cold water

Fresh mint leaves

4. To assemble, set aside twelve parfait glasses. Slice the cake into twenty-four equal-size pieces. Place one piece at the bottom of each parfait glass. Add a couple of tablespoons of the cherry sauce, then a couple of tablespoons of the cream topping. Add the remaining pieces of cake to each glass. Top with a couple of tablespoons of the sauce, then a couple of tablespoons of the cream layer, and finish off with a tablespoon of the cherry sauce. Garnish with mint leaves before serving.

Variations

- You can also serve this as a Black Forest Cake. To do so, once the cake cools, top with the cream sauce and cherry topping and give a hearty *danke schön* before slicing into individual pieces.
- If you happen to have some Kirschwasser, a clear alcohol distilled from cherries, you can add 2 to 3 tablespoons to the cherry sauce.

Six-Herb Botanical Juice ♥

Combining six popular herbs and one of Germany's most popular juices, this refreshing beverage is simple to prepare. Check out the bulk herb or tea section of your local natural foods store to locate the herbs. Please do not be deterred if you do not have all six; you can alter the combination and quantity to suit your fancy. Enjoy as a between-meal elixir or while feasting on Black Forest Parfait (page 205).

SERVES 4

4 cups water

2 tablespoons fennel seeds

2 tablespoons dried lemongrass

2 tablespoons dried rose hips

2 tablespoons dried hibiscus flowers

2 tablespoons dried chamomile
    flowers

2 teaspoons dried peppermint leaves

3 cups freshly juiced apple juice

Sweetener of choice

1. Bring the water to a boil in a small pot over high heat. Remove from the heat.
2. Add the herbs, stir well, and allow to steep for 20 minutes. Strain well.
3. Add the juice and mix well. Add the sweetener to taste and mix well. Pour into four glasses with ice.

Variations

- If you have more time, allow to chill for 30 minutes or longer in the refrigerator before serving.
- Replace the apple juice with your favorite fruit juice.
- Create a sparkling beverage by adding 1 cup of sparkling water to the juice and mixing well before serving.

Vegan Oktoberfest

The epic festival of Germany held annually in Munich since 1810, Oktoberfest is a celebration of food and beer that takes place for roughly two weeks, beginning in late September. A lot of *Wurst* and beer are consumed, as you can imagine. Here is a vegan Oktoberfest feast you can enjoy all year long:

Beer Soup

Beer-Braised Greens

Brussels Sprouts and Red Cabbage

Roasted White Asparagus with Nutmeg
    Cream Sauce

German Potato Salad

Notwurst (Vegan Bratwurst) with
    Spaetzle Noodles

Baked Vegan Schnitzel

Apple Strudel

Black Forest Parfait

Rote Grütze Red Berry Pudding

Credits: Mark Reinfeld

Quicker and Easier Germany
by contributing chef Surdham Daniele Goeb

Cabbage Salad with Pink Pepper ♥ _____

½ green cabbage (or pointed cabbage, if you can find it)
2 tablespoons sunflower oil
3 tablespoons white wine vinegar
1 teaspoon freshly ground pink pepper
Sea salt

▶ Cut the cabbage into the thinnest slices possible and mix with the rest of the ingredients. Let the salad sit for 10 minutes and add salt to taste. This salad is an ultra-quick side dish, German style. The pink pepper gives it an extravagant note and color.

Rote Grütze Red Berry Pudding _____

Feel free to substitute the following berries for those that are
available locally and organically.
½ cup fresh black currants
½ cup fresh red currants
½ cup fresh raspberries
½ cup agave nectar, or sweetener of choice to taste
Seeds of ½ vanilla bean, or 1 teaspoon vanilla extract
1½ teaspoons cornstarch

▶ Wash, clean, and dry the fruit. Heat a skillet over medium heat and briefly cook the berries with the agave nectar. As soon as the fruit is giving off juice, remove from the heat and drain the berries in a colander. Whisk the cornstarch and vanilla into the juice; watch out for lumps. Heat the juice to a boil and let it cool a little before you gently stir in the fruit again.

PART SEVEN

EUROPE FUSION

*This is the miracle that happens every time to those who really love:
the more they give, the more they possess.*

—Rainer Maria Rilke

It's a bit audacious to attempt to cover the culinary traditions of a dozen countries within a small recipe section, when each country could justifiably have its own section. What made it easier to narrow down the choices is that, while each region highlighted does have a vast food history, the vegan revolution is still making its way into this part of the world.

When researching recipes for this section, I discovered that there is a great deal of similarity among popular dishes in various countries. For instance, there are many variations of a mashed potato–based dish throughout Europe. Potato cakes popular in Scotland resemble Eastern European latkes, which is similar to Norwegian *lefse*. A Transylvanian stew bears a similarity to Hungarian goulash and even an Irish stew. In the end, I decided to include a wide array of dishes that I felt balanced out the other sections of the book.

Included here are recipes from Poland, Finland, Iceland, Romania, Czechoslovakia, Hungary, Sweden, Switzerland, the Netherlands, and recipes of Eastern European origin that have been passed down through the Jewish culinary traditions. Creating vegan versions of some of the recipes I grew up with as a child, such as Kasha Varnishkes, Stuffed Cabbage, blintzes, and latkes, was particularly rewarding. These dishes made their way from my ancestors in Eastern Europe, all the way to the Lower East Side of New York, where my family landed in the United States.

I have also included some Mediterranean-themed dishes, such as a Mediterranean Green Smoothie and a Mediterranean Hot Sauce, which use ingredients popular throughout the region. The highlight of these recipes is the Mediterranean Pistachio-Crusted Tofu with Saffron Quinoa Pilaf, which was selected as Recipe of the Year for 2011 by Vegan.com.

As you experiment with the recipes in this section, allow them to be a starting point for your own exploration into Fusion meals. Think outside of the box—way outside the box—in terms of combining ingredients from different ethnic cuisines. You will be surprised at the level of creativity that will awaken!

Credit: Mark Reinfeld

Baked Potato Latkes

No Hanukkah meal would be complete without latkes, or potato pancakes. Of Eastern European origin and traditionally made with eggs, here ground flaxseeds hold everything together. Please see below for a few of the many variations that are possible. Take a break from spinning the dreidel and serve with Vegan Sour Cream (page 226) or apple sauce.

MAKES 8 LARGE LATKES

1 large russet potato, peeled and grated (2 cups)

¼ teaspoon minced yellow onion

¼ cup plus 1 tablespoon white spelt flour

1 tablespoon ground flaxseeds mixed with 3 tablespoons water

¾ teaspoon sea salt

A pinch of crushed red pepper flakes (optional)

¼ teaspoon paprika (optional; try smoked)

1. Preheat the oven to 400°F. Oil a baking sheet well. Place all the ingredients in a large bowl and mix well. You can speed this process up by using the grater attachment on a food processor for the potatoes.
2. Scoop about ¼ cup of the mixture for each latke onto the prepared baking sheet. Flatten to about ¼ inch thick. Bake for 8 minutes.
3. Flip the pancakes and bake until golden brown, about 8 minutes, before serving.

Variations

- Make smaller latkes by using 2 tablespoons instead of ¼ cup of the batter for each pancake.
- Replace 1 cup of grated potato with grated sweet potato or yam.
- Add 1 tablespoon of minced fresh dill, parsley, or basil.
- Add 2 tablespoons of finely chopped green onion.
- Add 1 pressed or minced garlic clove and ½ teaspoon of seeded and diced chile pepper.

continues

Baked Potato Latkes *continued*

Variations *(continued)*

- Add ½ cup of peeled and grated parsnip or carrot.
- Create Italian latkes by adding 1 tablespoon of Italian Spice Mix (page 51).
- Go Mexican by adding 1 tablespoon of minced fresh cilantro and 1 teaspoon each of chile powder and ground cumin.
- Add ½ cup of grated vegan Cheddar- or mozzarella-style cheese for an over-the-top latke experience.
- For a gluten-free version, replace the spelt flour with brown rice flour.

If You Have More Time

Allow the batter to sit for at least 10 minutes before shaping the pancakes and baking.

For traditional latkes, you can fry the pancakes in a liberal amount of oil. Cook until both sides are golden brown, about 5 minutes, pressing down with a spatula and flipping occasionally to ensure even coating. Place on a paper towel after frying, to absorb some of the oil.

Potato Pierogi

Of Polish origin and gracing tables throughout Eastern Europe, these delights are sure to turn your next potluck into a rocking pierogi party! The fewer (and larger) pierogi you make, the closer you will be to fitting this into a 30-minute time frame. Serve as festive appetizers along with Baked Potato Latkes (page 213) and Vegan Sour Cream (page 226) and Pesto Magnifico (page 31).

SERVES 6

FILLING

1 potato, chopped small (1½ cups)

2 teaspoons oil

½ cup diced yellow onion

2 garlic cloves, pressed or minced

¼ cup vegan cream cheese or
  Vegan Sour Cream (page 226)

1 to 2 tablespoons vegan butter

½ teaspoon sea salt

⅛ teaspoon freshly ground black
  pepper

2 tablespoons nutritional yeast
  (optional)

1 tablespoon minced fresh dill

⅛ teaspoon crushed red pepper
  flakes (optional)

DOUGH: DRY

1½ cups white spelt flour

¼ teaspoon sea salt

DOUGH: WET

1 tablespoon ground flaxseeds
  mixed with 3 tablespoons water

¼ cup water

2 tablespoons coconut oil or vegan
  butter, softened

1. Fill a large pot with water and bring to a boil. Lower the heat to medium while you prepare the remainder of the dish. You will need the water at the end to cook the pierogi.

2. Prepare the filling: Place a steamer basket in another pot filled with about 1 inch of water. Place over high heat. When the water boils, add the potatoes to the steamer basket and cook covered until just soft, about 10 minutes. Drain well.

3. Meanwhile, place a small sauté pan over medium-high heat. Place the oil, onion, and garlic in the pan and cook for 3 minutes, stirring constantly. Lower the heat to low, and cook until the potatoes are done cooking, stirring occasionally. Place in a bowl with the remaining filling ingredients, including the potatoes, and mash well with a fork or a strong whisk.

4. Prepare the dough: Place the dry ingredients in a large bowl and whisk well. Place the wet ingredients in another bowl and mix well. Add the wet to the dry and mix well. Transfer to a flour-dusted cutting board or clean, dry surface and roll into a 10-inch log. Slice into twelve equal-size pieces.

5. Roll each portion with a flour-dusted rolling pin or use your hands to press down to create 3-inch circles. You can also make smaller pierogi, if you wish.

continues

Potato Pierogi *continued*

6. Place 1 rounded tablespoon of the filling in the center of each pierogi, fold in half, and pinch the edges together to seal. You can also seal the edges with a fork.

7. Bring the large pot of water back to a boil. Carefully drop the pierogi into the water and cook until they float to surface, about 5 minutes. Depending upon the size of your pot, you may wish to do this in two batches. Remove with a mesh strainer and place on a serving platter. You can serve as is, or with Vegan Sour Cream (page 226) and topped with fresh dill.

Variations

- Replace the dill with fresh flat-leaf parsley and/or basil.
- Mix in ¾ cup of Pesto Magnifico (page 31) with the potatoes once they are cooked.
- Add 1 cup of finely diced mushrooms or seeded and finely diced peppers to the filling along with the onion.
- Replace the potato with sweet potato or roasted squash.
- Try sautéing ½ cup of diced onions for a few minutes before adding the pierogi.
- You can also bake the pierogi on a well-oiled baking sheet at 425°F for 5 minutes before serving.

If You Have More Time

For optimal flavor and for a more authentic pierogi experience, after boiling, you can sauté the pierogi in oil until golden brown, about 8 minutes, gently flipping midway through.

Borscht

With origins in the Ukraine and popular throughout Eastern Europe, borscht has made its way across the Atlantic and all the way to the Catskill Mountains in New York, popularly referred to as the Borscht Belt. The base of the soup is the humble beet, which was immortalized in the book *Jitterbug Perfume,* and which will be sure to let your cutting board, and your hands, know that it was used in the dish. For the full effect, serve with a dollop of Vegan Sour Cream (page 226). Have an Eastern European feast along with Tempeh Stroganoff (page 233) and Icelandic Red Cabbage (page 220).

SERVES 6

1 tablespoon oil

1 yellow onion, diced (1½ cups)

¾ cup sliced celery

3 garlic cloves

1 cup small-diced potato

1 cup diced carrot or parsnip (or ½ cup of each)

3 beets, chopped into ¼-inch chunks (about 3 cups)

5½ cups heated vegetable stock (see page 253) or water

2 tablespoons freshly squeezed lemon juice

1 tablespoon red wine vinegar

1 tablespoon wheat-free tamari or other soy sauce (optional)

1¾ teaspoons sea salt

¼ teaspoon freshly ground black pepper

½ teaspoon celery seeds (optional)

1 tablespoon finely chopped fresh dill

1 tablespoon finely chopped fresh flat-leaf parsley

About ½ cup Vegan Sour Cream (page 226)

Black sesame seeds

Dill sprigs

1. Place a large pot over medium-high heat. Place the oil, onion, celery, and garlic in the pan and cook for 2 minutes, stirring constantly. Add the potato, carrot, beets, and vegetable stock and cook until the beets are just soft, about 15 minutes, stirring occasionally.

2. Add the lemon juice and vinegar, the soy sauce, if using, and the salt, pepper, and celery seeds, if using, and stir well. Carefully transfer to a strong blender and blend until creamy. Return the mixture to the pot. Add the dill and parsley and stir well.

3. Garnish each bowl with a dollop of sour cream, a sprinkle of black sesame seeds, and a sprig of fresh dill.

Variations

- For an added layer of flavor, add 2 tablespoons of tomato paste along with vegetable stock.
- Add ½ teaspoon of liquid smoke along with vegetable stock.

Polish Kielbasa Soup

The sausage of Poland, traditional kielbasa, comes close to topping the list of the foods that will lead you to a cardiologist. This heart-healthy version is a variation of *krupnik,* or Polish barley soup. If you have more time, go for the *krupnik,* following the instructions below. Go Fusion and serve with Pommes Frites (page 68) and Radicchio and Endive with Shaved Fennel and Italian Vinaigrette (page 13).

SERVES 6

1 tablespoon oil

1 yellow onion, diced (1¼ cups)

¾ cups thinly sliced celery

3 garlic cloves, pressed or minced

½ teaspoon seeded and diced hot chile pepper

5 cups heated vegetable stock (see page 253) or water

2 bay leaves

¾ cup diced carrot

¾ cup diced mushrooms

7 ounces vegan kielbasa-style sausage, cut into ½-inch slices

1½ cups thinly sliced cabbage

1½ tablespoons finely chopped flat-leaf parsley

1 tablespoon balsamic vinegar

1 teaspoon minced fresh dill

1 teaspoon sea salt

1 teaspoon caraway seeds

¼ teaspoon freshly ground black pepper

2 teaspoons wheat-free tamari or other soy sauce (optional)

1. Place a large pot over medium-high heat. Place the oil, onion, celery, garlic, and chile pepper in the pot and cook for 2 minutes, stirring constantly.
2. Add the vegetable stock, bay leaves, carrot, and mushrooms and cook for 10 minutes, stirring occasionally. Add the vegan kielbasa and cook for 5 minutes, stirring occasionally.
3. Add the cabbage and cook for 5 minutes, stirring occasionally. Add the remaining ingredients and cook for 5 minutes, stirring occasionally. Remove the bay leaves before serving.

Variations

- If you have more time, turn this soup into *krupnik.* Before adding the cabbage, add ½ cup of barley and 2 additional cups of water. Cook for 45 minutes, or until the barley is just soft. Add the cabbage and the remaining ingredients.
- Replace the carrot and mushrooms with other vegetables, such as zucchini, broccoli, bell peppers, or cauliflower.
- Replace the vegan sausage with tofu that has been marinated with liquid smoke and then roasted (see page 252).

Coleslaw

A staple of picnics and potlucks in every nation, this cold, cabbage-based salad is said to originate in Holland, where it is traditionally made with an oil and vinegar base. Eastern European versions, including those in Serbia and Hungary, likewise go for the oil and vinegar approach to slaw. The American version adds mayonnaise and is a regional favorite in the Southeast. Serve as a Fusion side dish with Babe's Bocadillos (page 106), Baked Vegan Schnitzel (page 196), or Quiche Monet (page 85).

SERVES 6

3 cups shredded extremely thinly sliced green cabbage

1½ cups shredded red cabbage

1 teaspoon celery seeds

1 tablespoon minced fresh dill, or 2 tablespoons minced fresh flat-leaf parsley

DRESSING

3 tablespoons olive oil

2 tablespoons apple cider vinegar

2 tablespoons freshly squeezed lemon juice

1½ tablespoons vegan Dijon or stone-ground mustard (optional)

2 teaspoons agave nectar, pure maple syrup, or sweetener of choice (see page 261)

1 garlic clove, minced or pressed (optional)

½ teaspoon sea salt

¼ teaspoon freshly ground black pepper

¼ teaspoon crushed red pepper flakes

1. Combine the green cabbage, red cabbage, celery seeds, and dill in a large bowl and mix well.
2. Combine the dressing ingredients in a small bowl and mix well. Add the dressing to the large bowl and mix well. For best results, chill for 20 minutes or more before serving.

Variations

- To Americanize the dish, add ¼ cup of vegan mayonnaise (Vegenaise or homemade; see page 261).
- Add 1 cup of grated veggies of choice, such as carrot, daikon, jicama, or beet.
- Replace the dill with other fresh herbs, such as basil, flat-leaf parsley, or cilantro.

Icelandic Red Cabbage

I love purple foods. In the "eat a rainbow" theory of nutrition, they are the violet and highest-vibration area of the spectrum. This is a traditional Icelandic dish and a rumored favorite of Bjork. While the yellow tomatoes add a nice color contrast, feel free to replace them with your favorite variety of red tomato. Serve as a side dish along with Tempeh Sauerbraten (page 198), Grilled Tofu with Horseradish Sauce (page 141), or Lemon Tempeh with Creamy Asparagus Sauce (page 40).

SERVES 6

½ cup diced yellow tomato

½ cup diced and seeded cucumber

¼ teaspoon sea salt

⅛ teaspoon freshly ground
    black pepper

2 tablespoons olive oil

1 small yellow onion, sliced thinly
    (1 cup)

5 cups very thinly sliced red cabbage

3 tablespoons red wine vinegar

1 tablespoon freshly squeezed
    lemon juice

1 tablespoon vegan butter
    (optional)

1. Place the tomatoes and cucumber in a small bowl with a pinch of salt and pepper and mix well.

2. Place the oil in a large sauté pan over medium-high heat. Add the onion and cook for 8 minutes, stirring frequently and adding small amounts of water if necessary to prevent sticking. Add the cabbage, lower the heat to medium and cook for 5 minutes, stirring occasionally. Add the remaining ingredients, stir well, and cook until the cabbage is just soft, about 3 minutes, stirring occasionally.

3. Top with tomatoes and cucumber before serving. May be enjoyed warm or cold.

Transylvanian Roasted Eggplant–Stuffed Tomatoes

This is an authentic Gypsy recipe passed down from my friend Harvey Goldstein's grandmother from the Old Country. The filling bears a striking resemblance to the popular Middle Eastern eggplant dish baba ghanoush, and is irresistible when served as spread for Bruschetta (page 4) or as a dip for crudités. Serve the stuffed tomatoes as a starter before indulging in your Hungarian Goulash (page 225) or Tempeh Stroganoff (page 233).

SERVES 4

3 small eggplants (½ pound)

2 medium-size tomatoes

1 tablespoon olive oil

¼ cup diced yellow onion

4 to 6 garlic cloves, minced

1 tablespoon freshly squeezed lemon juice

¼ to ½ teaspoon sea salt

⅛ teaspoon cayenne pepper (optional)

⅛ teaspoon freshly ground black pepper

Paprika (try smoked)

2 teaspoons finely chopped fresh flat-leaf parsley

4 to 8 green or black olives, quartered

1. Poke several holes in each eggplant with a fork. Place on a baking sheet in the oven on the HIGH BROIL setting. Broil for 25 minutes, or until the eggplant is shriveled and the inside is soft, periodically flipping the eggplant with tongs to ensure even cooking.

2. Meanwhile, slice the tomatoes in half across the equator, and scoop out and discard the insides.

3. Place the oil in a small sauté pan over low heat. Add the onion and cook for 15 minutes, stirring occasionally. Add the garlic, and cook for 5 minutes, stirring frequently and being careful not to let too much color develop on the garlic. Transfer to a bowl with the lemon juice, salt, cayenne if using, and pepper and mix well.

4. When the eggplant is done cooking, scoop out the insides into a measuring cup to yield 1 cup. Place in the bowl with the onion and mix well.

5. Stuff the tomatoes with the eggplant mixture and top with a pinch of paprika, parsley, and the quartered olives.

Variations
- Top each serving with roasted red pepper (see page 19).
- If you have more time, you can roast the eggplants for a longer period time at a lower temperature. Try roasting at 400°F for about 50 minutes, or until the skin is shriveled and the inside is soft. The length of time will depend upon the size of the eggplants.

Dutch Stamppot

When I asked my friends in Holland what recipe would be the iconic Dutch dish, they all replied with a resounding, *"Stamppot."* A very grounding and filling dish made with mashed potatoes and kale, many versions also include sausage. Once again, we are rescued by the availability of vegan sausages that enable us to replicate this dish with an even higher degree of authenticity. Have a Fusion feast by serving with Onion Gravy (page 147) along with Red Lentil Soup (page 161) and mixed wild greens and Toasted Hazelnut Vinaigrette (page 188).

SERVES 2 TO 4

1½ cups chopped potato
(¼ to ½-inch pieces)

2 teaspoons oil

1 small yellow onion, chopped small
(1 cup)

7 ounces vegan sausage, sliced thinly
(1 cup)

2 cups rinsed, finely chopped kale,
pressed firmly

½ teaspoon sea salt

1½ teaspoons wheat-free tamari or
other soy sauce

1 tablespoon vegan butter
(optional)

2 tablespoons unsweetened soy,
rice, coconut, or almond milk
(see page 259)

2 tablespoons vegan mayonnaise
(Vegenaise or homemade; see
page 261; optional)

2 teaspoons vegan Dijon mustard

1. Place a steamer basket in a covered large pot filled with about 1 inch of water. Place over high heat and bring to a boil. Place the potato in the steamer basket, lower the heat to medium-high, and cook covered until just soft, about 10 minutes.

2. Meanwhile, place a large sauté pan over medium-high heat. Place the oil and onion in the pan and cook for 2 minutes, stirring constantly. Add the vegan sausage and cook for 5 minutes, stirring frequently. Add the kale and cook until the kale is just tender and still a vibrant green, about 4 minutes, stirring frequently. Lower the heat to low.

3. When the potato is done cooking, remove from the heat, drain well, and place in a bowl with the remaining ingredients. Mash with a fork or a sturdy whisk. Transfer to the sauté pan and mix well before serving.

Variations
- Replace the vegan sausage with Field Roast or roasted tofu or tempeh (see page 252).
- Experiment with different types of potato, including yam or sweet potato.
- Replace the kale with your favorite green, such as spinach, arugula, chard, or collards.

Kasha Varnishkes

Kasha, or toasted buckwheat groats, is an ancient dish of Eastern European and Slavic origin. Kasha varnishkes, where the buckwheat is mixed with bowtie pasta and fresh minced herbs, was a regular staple of my childhood. You might be surprised to learn that buckwheat is actually a seed that is not related to wheat and is entirely gluten-free. The eggs in the traditional dish are replaced with ground flaxseeds and water. Serve as a side with grilled or roasted tofu or tempeh (page 252) and Onion Gravy (page 147).

SERVES 4 TO 6

12 ounces bowtie pasta

1½ teaspoons sea salt, or to taste

2 tablespoons olive oil

1 yellow onion, diced (1½ cups)

3 to 5 garlic cloves, pressed or minced

¼ teaspoon freshly ground black pepper

1 teaspoon paprika (try smoked)

1 cup uncooked kasha (see box)

2 tablespoons ground flaxseeds mixed with ¼ cup water

2¾ cups vegetable stock (see page 253) or water

¼ cup tightly packed chopped fresh flat-leaf parsley

1. Bring water to a boil in a large pot. Add the bowtie pasta and ¾ teaspoon of the sea salt and cook according to the package instructions until the pasta is just tender, about 8 minutes, depending upon the brand. Drain well and place in a large bowl.

2. Meanwhile, place the olive oil in a large sauté pan over medium-high heat. Add the onion, garlic, remaining ¾ teaspoon of sea salt, pepper, and paprika, and cook for 3 minutes, stirring frequently.

3. Place the kasha in a small bowl with the flaxseed mixture and stir well. Add to the sauté pan and cook for 2 minutes, stirring frequently. Lower the heat to medium, add the vegetable stock, stir well, and cover. Cook until all the liquid is absorbed and the kasha is tender, about 15 minutes.

4. Add to the bowl with the pasta, add the parsley, and gently stir well.

continues

Kasha Varnishkes *continued*

Variations

- Replace the bowtie pasta with your pasta of choice.
- Replace the parsley with an equal amount of fresh herbs, such as basil or cilantro, or 2 tablespoons of minced dill.

Chef's Tips and Tricks

Both raw and toasted versions of buckwheat are available in many natural foods stores. You want to make sure you are using the toasted version, or kasha, for this recipe. If no kasha is available, you can toast your own. To do so, place a large sauté pan over high heat. When the pan is hot, add the raw buckwheat groats. Cook until the groats become dark brown, about 5 minutes, stirring constantly.

Hungarian Goulash

A dish that tastes much better than it sounds, goulash was traditionally made in a cast-iron pot over a fire, and has paprika as a key ingredient. *Goulash* means "herdsman" or "cattle stockman" in Hungarian, and apparently this was such workers' cooking method of choice. This cow-friendly version is made with seitan and topped with Vegan Sour Cream. Serve over rice noodles, quinoa, or rice along with Radicchio and Endive with Shaved Fennel and Italian Vinaigrette (page 13), Provençal Vegetable Salad (page 67) or Watercress with Raspberry Vinaigrette (page 131).

SERVES 4 TO 6

2 tablespoons olive oil

1 small yellow onion, sliced thinly (1½ cups)

4 garlic cloves, pressed or minced

8 ounces beef-style seitan

2 tablespoons paprika (try smoked)

1¼ cups water

1¼ cups diced parsnips or carrots

1 small potato, cut into ¼-inch dice (1½ cups)

1 bay leaf

1 small green bell pepper, seeded and diced (¾ cup)

1 (14.5-ounce) can fire-roasted tomatoes, or 1¾ cups diced tomatoes with juice

⅛ teaspoon cayenne pepper

1½ teaspoons caraway seeds (optional)

1 teaspoon sea salt

⅛ teaspoon freshly ground black pepper

1 tablespoon minced fresh dill

2 tablespoons nutritional yeast (optional)

continues

1. Place the oil in a large pot over medium-high heat. Add the onion, garlic, and paprika, and cook for 3 minutes, stirring frequently.
2. Add the seitan and cook for 3 minutes, stirring frequently. Add the water, parsnip, potato, bay leaf, green pepper, and tomatoes and cook covered until the potato is just tender, about 15 minutes, stirring occasionally. If you have more time, and for optimal flavor, allow to simmer for an additional 15 minutes over low heat, stirring occasionally.
3. Remove the bay leaf, add the cayenne, the caraway seeds, if using, salt and pepper, and nutritional yeast, if using, and mix well.
4. Combine the Vegan Sour Cream ingredients in a small bowl and stir well. Serve the goulash with a dollop of the sour cream and top with fresh dill.

continues

Hungarian Goulash *continued*

VEGAN SOUR CREAM

¾ cup vegan mayonnaise (Vegenaise or homemade; see page 261)

1 tablespoon freshly squeezed lemon juice

¼ teaspoon minced fresh dill, or a pinch of dried dill (optional)

Variations

- Replace the potato, parsnip, and green peppers with an equal amount of other vegetables, such as carrots, celery, broccoli, cauliflower, mushrooms, or turnips.
- Replace the seitan with vegan sausage or Field Roast.
- For a gluten-free variation, replace the seitan with cubed extra-firm or super-firm tofu, tempeh, or chopped portobello mushrooms.
- Try using a smoked paprika.

If You Have More Time

As the flavor of this dish improves with time, cook over a low heat for up to 45 minutes, for the full experience.

Stuffed Cabbage 🕐

This recipe really takes me back to my roots. I can almost see my grandfather (and wonderful chef) Benjamin Bimstein preparing these rolls at our family feasts. Popular throughout Eastern Europe and Scandinavia, and a cornerstone of Jewish cooking for possibly two thousand years, they traditionally include meat. This recipe will admittedly push the 30-minute time frame. For a quicker version, you can leave out the sauce and the baking, and simply serve your rolls with a portion of Vegan Sour Cream (page 226). To go all out, serve with Borscht (page 217) and Coleslaw (page 219).

SERVES 4 TO 6

1 large green cabbage

RICE

¾ cup uncooked white basmati rice

1½ cups vegetable stock (see page 253) or water

½ teaspoon sea salt

FILLING

1 tablespoon oil

¾ cup diced yellow onion

2 garlic cloves, pressed or minced

4 ounces tempeh, chopped finely (¾ cup)

¼ cup water

3 tablespoons tomato paste

¾ teaspoon sea salt, or to taste

¼ teaspoon freshly ground black pepper

½ teaspoon seeded and diced hot chile pepper

1 tablespoon finely chopped fresh flat-leaf parsley

1 tablespoon minced fresh dill

2 teaspoons paprika (try smoked)

2 tablespoons raisins (optional)

continues

1. Preheat the oven to 425°F. Oil an 8-inch casserole dish well. Cut the very bottom portion off of the cabbage. Carefully peel away six to eight of the largest leaves. Place a steamer basket in a large pot with about 1 inch of water. Place over high heat. When the water boils, add the cabbage leaves to the steamer basket and cook covered until just soft, about 5 minutes. Carefully remove the leaves and place on a plate to cool.

2. Place another pot over medium-high heat. Add the rice, vegetable stock, and salt, and bring to a boil. Lower the heat to low, cover, and cook until all the liquid is absorbed, about 10 minutes. Remove from the heat and allow it to continue to cook for another 5 minutes or so.

3. Meanwhile, place a large sauté pan over medium-high heat. Place the oil, onion, and garlic in the pan and cook for 2 minutes, stirring constantly. Add the tempeh and cook for 3 minutes, stirring frequently and adding small amounts of water if necessary to prevent sticking. Add the remaining filling ingredients and cook for 5 minutes, stirring frequently and adding small amounts of water if necessary to prevent sticking. Remove from the heat.

4. When the rice is done cooking, add to the sauté pan and mix well.

continues

227

Stuffed Cabbage *continued*

SAUCE

3 tablespoons tomato paste

¾ cup water

1 teaspoon sweetener of choice

½ teaspoon sea salt, or to taste

½ teaspoon minced fresh dill
(optional)

⅛ teaspoon cayenne pepper
(optional)

2 tablespoons raisins (optional)

5. Place the sauce ingredients in a small bowl and mix well. Place one-quarter of the sauce in the prepared casserole dish.

6. Create your cabbage rolls by placing a small amount of filling at the center of each cabbage leaf, toward the bottom. Fold in the sides and roll tightly away from you. Place in the casserole dish. Top with the remaining sauce. Cover and bake for 10 minutes.

Variation

- Replace the basmati rice with brown rice, millet, or quinoa (see page 255).

Mediterranean Pistachio-Crusted Tofu

I am excited to share this recipe, which, along with the Saffron Quinoa Pilaf, is the winner of Vegan.com's 2011 "Recipe of the Year" award. This is a recipe to prepare when you want to impress folks with the wonderful culinary potential of tofu. It is a creative and colorful dish with several layers of delicious flavor and an amazing texture, which lends itself to many variations. Because tomatoes figure prominently in the topping, be sure to choose the freshest ones possible for the most auspicious results. Serve with the Saffron Quinoa Pilaf (page 231).

SERVES 4

2 tablespoons wheat-free tamari or other soy sauce

1 tablespoon olive oil or your favorite (optional)

1 tablespoon water

14 ounces extra-firm tofu

TAHINI SPREAD

2 tablespoons sesame tahini

1 teaspoon wheat-free tamari or other soy sauce

1 teaspoon freshly squeezed lemon juice

2 tablespoons water, or more depending on the consistency of the tahini

CRUST

¾ cup roasted, unsalted pistachio nuts

1 tablespoon minced fresh flat-leaf parsley, basil, or herb of your choosing

½ teaspoon dried oregano

¼ teaspoon dried thyme

¼ teaspoon crushed red pepper flakes

⅛ teaspoon sea salt, or to taste

⅛ teaspoon freshly ground black pepper

continues

1. Preheat the oven or a toaster oven to 375°F. Place the soy sauce, olive oil, if using, and water in a baking dish and stir well. Slice the tofu into four cutlets and place in the baking dish. Marinate for at least 5 minutes or up to 30 minutes, flipping periodically.

2. While the tofu is marinating, prepare the tahini spread: Place its ingredients in a small bowl and whisk well. You are looking for a smooth, spreadable consistency. Since the consistency of tahini varies greatly, you may need to add a bit more water.

3. Place the tofu, along with its marinade, in the oven and roast for 10 minutes. While the tofu is cooking, prepare the crust: Pulse-chop the pistachio nuts in a food processor until they are coarse crumbs. Be careful not to overprocess or it will turn into a paste. Transfer to a bowl with the remaining crust ingredients and mix well.

4. Meanwhile, combine the topping ingredients in a mixing bowl and gently mix well. Combine the dressing ingredients in a small bowl and stir well. Add to the topping and gently mix well.

continues

Mediterranean Pistachio-Crusted Tofu *continued*

MEDITERRANEAN VEGETABLES

¾ cup chopped artichoke hearts, chopped

2 tomatoes, chopped into ½-inch chunks (1½ cups)

½ cup finely chopped arugula or spinach

3 tablespoons finely chopped kalamata olives

2 tablespoons diced green onion

1 tablespoon thinly sliced or shaved, and chopped fennel

1 tablespoon capers

2 tablespoons chiffonaded basil

2 teaspoons minced fresh oregano, or ½ teaspoon dried

½ teaspoon fresh thyme, or ¼ teaspoon dried

¼ teaspoon lemon zest

DRESSING

2 tablespoons olive oil

1 tablespoon freshly squeezed lemon juice

2 teaspoons balsamic vinegar

1 garlic clove, pressed or minced

¼ teaspoon sea salt, or to taste

¼ teaspoon freshly ground black pepper

5. Remove the tofu from the oven and coat the top of the cutlets with the tahini spread, using a spoon. Liberally top the cutlets with the crust mixture and bake for an additional 10 minutes.

6. To serve, slice the cutlets into triangles (for smaller servings, you can slice each of these triangles into two smaller triangles) and place on a platter or individual plates. Top each cutlet with a small scoop of the Mediterranean Vegetables and serve alongside the Saffron Quinoa Pilaf, optionally using a ring mold or half-cup measuring cup to form the pilaf. Decorate the plates with arugula or wild salad greens.

Variations

- So many are possible. You can replace the tofu with tempeh, portobello mushrooms, or eggplant or zucchini steaks.
- All or a portion of the pistachio nuts can be replaced with macadamia nuts, walnuts, pecans, or cashews.
- Try adding 3 tablespoons of dried coconut to the crust mixture.
- Experiment with your favorite spices and herbs.
- Feel free to increase the quantity of fennel, olives, garlic, or herbs, depending on your preferences.

Saffron Quinoa Pilaf

Creating a pilaf by adding vegetables and herbs to a grain is a simple way to take the flavor of your dish to the next level. The saffron adds a beautiful color and unique dimension to the quinoa (for more on saffron, see page xxx). If saffron is not available, feel free to leave it out—you will still have a lovely pilaf to complement the Mediterranean Pistachio-Crusted Tofu Cutlets (page 229).

SERVES 4 TO 6

1¼ cups uncooked quinoa, rinsed and drained well

2¼ cups vegetable stock (see page 253) or water

½ teaspoon sea salt, or to taste

½ teaspoon saffron threads

¼ cup thinly sliced green onion

1 tablespoon freshly squeezed lemon juice

½ teaspoon lightly packed lemon zest (optional)

2 to 3 tablespoons finely chopped fresh flat-leaf parsley or chiffonaded basil

1. Place the quinoa, vegetable stock, salt, and saffron threads in a pot over high heat. Bring to a boil.
2. Cover, lower the heat to low, and simmer until all the liquid is absorbed, about 15 minutes. Allow to sit for 5 minutes longer.
3. Add the remaining ingredients and gently mix well.
4. To serve, place quinoa in a ramekin, ring mold, or 1-cup measuring cup and press down firmly. Flip onto each serving plate before adding Pistachio Tofu and Mediterranean Vegetables.

Variations
- Add ½ cup of nuts such as pine nuts or slivered almonds or chopped walnuts, pistachios, or pecans after cooking.
- Add ¼ cup of dried fruit such as currants or cranberries after cooking.
- Add 1 teaspoon of lemon zest after cooking.
- Replace the saffron with 1 teaspoon of grated fresh turmeric.

continues

Saffron Quinoa Pilaf *continued*

Chef's Tips and Tricks

This Mediterranean Pistachio Crusted Tofu with Saffron Quinoa Pilaf is a perfect example of a template recipe whereby, by altering any of the components, you can create a new dish.

Tofu component: the tofu can be replaced with tempeh, portobello mushrooms, eggplant, or zucchini steaks.

Marinade component: add additional ingredients, such as pure maple syrup, balsamic vinegar, brown rice vinegar, mirin, curry paste, or your favorite fresh herbs.

Tahini spread component: replace the tahini with almond butter, peanut butter, or other nut butter. Replace the lemon juice with lime juice. Add additional ingredients, such as minced garlic, ginger, or various ethnic spices.

Crust component: the pistachio nuts can be replaced with any nut or seed, such as macadamias, walnuts, pecans, hazelnuts, sunflower seeds, pumpkin seeds, or sesame seeds. These can be raw or roasted. You can replace the herbs with your favorites, such as cilantro, basil, or dill. You can also create various ethnic crusts by adding spices from various cuisines (Mexican: chili powder, cumin, oregano; Italian: basil, parsley, oregano, rosemary, thyme; Indian: curry powder, cumin powder, ground coriander).

Pilaf component: replace the quinoa with other grain, including millet, any variety of rice, even brown rice pasta. Add herbs of choice to pilaf.

Mediterranean Vegetable component: these vegetables can be replaced with your favorites—either raw, steamed, roasted, sautéed, or grilled.

Tempeh Stroganoff

Originating in Russia and popular throughout Europe, including Nordic countries as well as the United Kingdom, stroganoff is typically a sour cream–based sauce. This version uses vegan mayonnaise mixed with lemon to create a homemade sour cream. Serve over rice pasta, quinoa, or brown rice along with Horta (page 181), Beer-Braised Greens (page 189), or Raw Kale Salad with Cranberries and Walnuts (page 132).

SERVES 4 TO 6

TEMPEH MARINADE

2 tablespoons olive oil

2 tablespoons wheat-free tamari or other soy sauce

2 teaspoons pure maple syrup

3 tablespoons water

A few drops of liquid smoke

16 ounces tempeh, cut into ½-inch cubes

STROGANOFF

1 tablespoon olive oil

1 yellow onion, sliced thinly (1½ cups)

3 garlic cloves, pressed or minced

1 teaspoon paprika (try smoked)

8 ounces mushrooms, halved or quartered (try cremini)

1 tablespoon freshly squeezed lemon juice

¾ cup vegan mayonnaise (Vegenaise or homemade; see page 261)

¾ cup soy, rice, or almond milk (see page 259)

¾ teaspoon sea salt, or to taste

½ teaspoon freshly ground black pepper

¼ teaspoon cayenne pepper, or to taste

¼ cup thinly sliced green onion

1 tablespoon minced fresh dill

1. Preheat the oven to 375°F. Place all of the marinade ingredients in a 9 by 13-inch casserole dish and mix well. Add the tempeh and mix well. Allow to sit for 5 minutes, stirring occasionally to ensure an even coating. Bake for 15 minutes.

2. Meanwhile, place the oil in a large sauté pan over medium-high heat. Add the onion, garlic, and paprika, and cook for 3 minutes, stirring frequently. Add the mushrooms and lemon juice, and cook for 3 minutes, stirring frequently. Lower the heat to medium, add the vegan mayonnaise, soy milk, salt, pepper, and cayenne and mix well.

3. Add the tempeh cubes and the contents of the casserole dish, and cook for 5 minutes, stirring occasionally. Garnish with the green onion and dill before serving.

Variations

- Replace the tempeh with tofu or seitan.
- Replace the dill with a fresh herb of your choosing, such as basil, cilantro, or flat-leaf parsley.

Romanian Mămăligă

When in Romania, do as the Romanians do. This creamy polenta dish is all the rage in Bucharest. Satisfying and grounding, and a favorite of Gypsies around the world, *mămăligă* is perfect for a cold winter morning. Top with sliced bananas or berries and serve warm with an Espresso Smoothie (page 49).

SERVES 2 TO 4

3½ cups soy, rice, or almond milk
  (page 259)

1 teaspoon sea salt, or to taste

1 cup polenta

2 tablespoons vegan butter
  (optional)

Pinch of ground cinnamon

Pinch of ground cardamom

1. Place the soy milk in a large pot over high heat. When the milk begins to boil, lower the heat to low, add the salt, and slowly whisk in the polenta.

2. Cook for 5 minutes, whisking constantly. Add the vegan butter, if using, and spices, cover, and cook for 10 minutes, stirring occasionally.

Variations
- For a cheesy variation, add ¼ cup of grated vegan mozzarella- or Cheddar-style cheese or 2 tablespoons of nutritional yeast.
- For a savory variation, add 1½ cups of corn, a pinch of crushed red pepper flakes, and 2 tablespoons of minced fresh flat-leaf parsley, cilantro, or basil after the polenta has cooked.

Blueberry Blintzes 🕐

This dish evokes many childhood memories of when we would lovingly defrost the frozen blintzes with great fanfare and reheat them for a special meal. To make them from scratch, and to make them vegan, was a true revelation. Of Slavic origins, blintzes are part of the Eastern European culinary tradition. Many fillings and toppings are possible for both sweet and savory versions. Here is one of the most popular. For a healthier blintz, you can leave out the sautéing at the end. Serve at your next Hanukkah Party along with Baked Potato Latkes (page 213) and Vegan Sour Cream (page 226).

MAKES 6 BLINTZES

1 recipe Crepes (see page 87)

Oil for sautéing

Confectioners' sugar (optional)

Fresh mint leaves (optional)

FILLING

7 ounces extra-firm tofu

8 ounces vegan cream cheese (try Tofutti brand)

1 tablespoon nutritional yeast

2 tablespoons tahini

1 to 2 tablespoons freshly squeezed lemon juice

¼ cup organic sugar (see page xxi)

¼ teaspoon sea salt

BLUEBERRY SAUCE

8 ounces frozen or fresh blueberries

½ cup water (add ¼ cup more water if fresh blueberries)

2 tablespoons organic sugar, or to taste

⅛ teaspoon ground cardamom

1 tablespoon arrowroot powder dissolved in 2 tablespoons cold water

1. Prepare the crepes and stack them on a plate.
2. Prepare the filling: Place a steamer basket in a pot filled with 1 inch of water over high heat and bring to a simmer. Place the tofu in the steamer basket, cover, and cook for 5 minutes. Remove the tofu and rinse well under cold water.
3. Meanwhile, place the remaining filling ingredients in a bowl and mix well. Crumble the tofu into the bowl with the filling ingredients and mix well.
4. Prepare the sauce by placing all the ingredients, except the arrowroot mixture, in a small pot over medium heat and stir well. Cook for 5 minutes, stirring occasionally. Add the arrowroot mixture, lower the heat to low, and stir well. Cook over low heat until the blintzes are finished cooking, stirring occasionally.
5. To prepare the blintzes, place about 3 tablespoons of the filling along the edge closest to you of a crepe, leaving about a 1-inch margin at that edge without filling. Fold the margin over the filling, and then fold both sides in toward the center. Roll the whole blintz away from you, making a tight packet, leaving the seam on the bottom. Repeat with the remaining crepes, reserving about ½ cup of the filling to garnish the blintzes.

continues

Blueberry Blintzes *continued*

6. Heat a small amount of oil in a large sauté pan. Place the blintzes in the pan and cook for 3 minutes on each side. Serve warm topped with confectioners' sugar, if using, plus a liberal amount of sauce and a dollop of the filling. Garnish with mint leaves, if using.

Variations

- For potato blintzes, use the mashed potato filling from the Shepherdess's Pie (see page 145).
- Replace the blueberries with strawberries, peaches, mangoes, or your favorite fruit.

Finnish Aland Pancakes

How do you say *yum* in Finnish? A favorite at IHOFP, the International House of Finnish Pancakes, and with origins in the Aland Islands between Sweden and Finland in the Baltic Sea, these *pannukakku* are simple to prepare. They are baked instead of cooked on a griddle. For a more custardy pancake, include the silken tofu. Enjoy yours as a light breakfast with Mediterranean Green Smoothie (page 242) or as an exotic dessert topped with Cashew Cream (page 90).

MAKES 6 TO 8 SERVINGS

DRY

1¼ cups semolina flour

½ cup organic sugar (see page xxi)

⅛ teaspoon sea salt

½ teaspoon baking soda

¼ teaspoon plus ⅛ teaspoon ground cardamom

WET

1½ cups soy, rice, or almond milk (page 259)

1 (12.5-ounce) package silken firm tofu (optional)

2 tablespoons ground flaxseeds mixed with 6 tablespoons water

1 tablespoon vegan butter (optional)

¼ cup raisins

TOPPINGS

Vegan butter

Almond butter

Jam

1. Preheat the oven to 425°F. Oil an 8-inch casserole dish well. Place the dry ingredients in a large bowl and whisk well.
2. Place the wet ingredients in a blender and blend until smooth. Add the wet to the dry and mix well.
3. Transfer to the prepared casserole dish and bake until slightly browned on top, about 20 minutes.
4. Slice into individual pieces and serve warm with vegan butter, almond butter, and jam.

Variations

- Top with a drizzle of freshly squeezed lemon juice and some maple syrup.
- Prepare a simple fruit topping: Place 1 cup of frozen berries and ¾ cup of water in a small saucepan and simmer until reduced by half. Mash up the berries with a fork, add a pinch of salt, and sweeten to taste. Top each pancake with a few spoonfuls of this nectar!
- For gluten free, replace the flour with a gluten-free mix (page 260).

Czechoslovakian Fruit Dumplings
(Ovocne Knedliky)

I am sure everybody has heard of *ovocne knedliky* before. So it will be no surprise to you that these fruit-filled dumplings are quite easy to prepare. You can create an infinite array of these easily pronounceable treats by changing out the fruit filling. Serve with Swedish Thumbprint Cookies (page 239) and a cup of mint tea.

MAKES 12 TO 14 DUMPLINGS

DRY

1¼ cups white spelt flour

¼ cup organic sugar (see page xxi)

⅛ teaspoon sea salt

½ teaspoon ground cinnamon

⅛ teaspoon ground nutmeg

WET

1 tablespoon ground flaxseeds
    mixed with 3 tablespoons water

2 tablespoons vegan butter,
    softened, or coconut oil

2 tablespoons soy milk

12 to 14 strawberries or raspberries,
    fresh or frozen, or pieces of
    other fresh fruit such as apricot
    or peach, about ¾ inch diameter

1. Bring a large pot of water to a boil over high heat. Lower the heat to medium while you prepare the remainder of the recipe.
2. Place the dry ingredients in a large bowl and whisk well. Place the wet ingredients in another bowl and mix well. Add the wet to the dry and mix well.
3. Transfer to a flour-dusted cutting board or clean surface and roll into a 10-inch log. Slice into twelve to fourteen equal-size pieces.
4. Press each piece into a small circle, add a piece of fruit to the center, and then fold in the sides. Create a ball by rolling in your hands so the fruit is totally surrounded by the dough.
5. Bring the large pot of water back to a boil. Place the dumplings in the pot and cook for 10 minutes. Remove with a mesh strainer and place on serving platter.
6. Place the confectioners' sugar and cocoa powder in separate small bowls. Roll half of the dumplings in each topping.

Variations
- For optimal flavor, after boiling, you can also sauté the dumplings for a few minutes in oil, or bake on a well-oiled baking sheet for 10 minutes at 400°F.
- For additional color and flavor, you can roll the dumplings in shredded dried coconut or finely minced nuts or seeds.

Swedish Thumbprint Cookies (Rosenmunnar)

I never realized that these jelly-filled cookies were of Swedish origin. Popular throughout Scandinavia, these treats are very simple to prepare. There is no end to the amount of variations possible by changing the jam filling. Serve with Amsterdam Mintade (page 241) for a lovely snack.

MAKES 12 COOKIES

8 tablespoons vegan butter, softened, or coconut oil

½ cup organic sugar (see page xxi)

2 tablespoons soy milk

2 teaspoons freshly squeezed lemon juice (optional)

½ to 1 teaspoon lemon zest (optional)

2 cups white spelt flour

⅛ teaspoon sea salt

¼ teaspoon ground cardamom

¼ cup fruit jam (try raspberry, strawberry, or blueberry)

1. Preheat the oven to 375°F. Oil a baking sheet well or line with parchment paper.
2. Place the butter, sugar, soy milk, lemon juice, if using, and lemon zest, if using, in a bowl and mix well.
3. Place the flour, salt, and cardamom in another bowl and whisk well. Add the dry to the wet and mix well.
4. Form about twelve small balls, using about 2 tablespoons of dough each. Place on the prepared baking sheet.
5. Press down to form cookies about 3 inches in diameter. Using the back of a teaspoon, make a 1-inch-diameter compression in the center of each cookie. Bake for 10 minutes. Remove from the oven.
6. Place about 1 teaspoon of jam in the center of each compression. You may need to press the compression down again before adding the jam, depending upon how the cookie baked.
7. Return the pan the oven and bake for an additional 8 minutes. Remove from the oven and let cool on the pan for a few minutes, then transfer to a cooling rack or a flat serving platter. Allow the cookies to cool before handling as they may crumble . . . and nobody likes a crumbled cookie!

Variations

- Replace the lemon zest and juice with lime or orange.
- Replace the cardamom with ground cinnamon, nutmeg, or allspice.
- Try replacing the jam with the Chocolate Hazelnut Spread from the Crepes (see page 87).

Swiss Chocolate Fondue

Fondue has a fascinating history. The cheese version originated as a peasant dish in Switzerland. The fondue phenomenon experienced its heyday in the United States in 1950s, with the chocolate version arriving on the scene in the 1960s. Fondue is an amazing party dish. Many people will find a colorful fondue pot, one of the least-used wedding gifts, packed away in their attic. Let your imagination run wild when it comes to the dippables. Serve with pretzels, sliced bananas, strawberries, pear or apple slices, candied ginger, vegan brownies, or cookies. Bonus: when allowed to cool and solidify, this makes a wonderful chocolate frosting.

MAKES ABOUT 2 CUPS FONDUE

2 cups vegan dark chocolate chips

¾ cup soy creamer (try French vanilla), coconut creamer, or soy milk

2 teaspoons vanilla extract

3 tablespoons vegan butter

2 tablespoons creamy almond or peanut butter plus 2 tablespoons additional creamer

1. Melt the chocolate chips in a double boiler. If you do not have a double boiler, place water in a small pot and bring to a boil. Lower the heat to a simmer. Place chocolate chips in a stainless-steel or glass bowl and place on top of the pot with the simmering water. Be sure to keep water out of the bowl that contains the chocolate chips, as moisture can interfere with creating a smoothly melted chocolate.

2. When the chips are melted, add the remaining ingredients and stir well until a smooth consistency is attained.

3. Transfer to a fondue pot and dip away!

Chef's Tips and Tricks

Chocolate chips with a lower cacao content (less than 50 percent) tend to work better in this recipe.

Amsterdam Mintade ♥

This is my take on a highly refreshing beverage called Lemonada I had while visiting Amsterdam. The lemon, mint, and ice combo delivers every time, especially when you are looking for a recharge on a hot day. Enjoy with any of the meals in this book.

MAKES TWO 10-OUNCE SERVINGS

3 cups crushed ice or ice cubes

1 cup water

½ cup loosely packed fresh mint leaves

¼ cup plus 1 tablespoon freshly squeezed lemon or lime juice

¼ cup sweetener of choice, or to taste (see page 261)

1. Place all the ingredients in a strong blender and blend until the ice is thoroughly blended. For more of a tang, add more lemon juice.

Variations

- Blend 3 tablespoons of finely chopped fresh ginger with the water. Strain well and discard the pulp. Return the water to the blender with the remaining ingredients and blend well.
- Replace the lemon juice with lime.
- Replace the water with coconut water.

Mediterranean Green Smoothie ♥

Green smoothies have become the symbol for healthy beverages. Featuring nutrient-rich kale, it is a wonderful way to start the day. Here is a version that uses ingredients abundantly available throughout the Mediterranean.

MAKES TWO 12-OUNCE SMOOTHIES

2 large, ripe pears

1 cup frozen berries

1 large banana

6 to 8 large basil leaves

6 sprigs flat-leaf parsley

2 to 3 leaves kale, stemmed

2 pitted dates (optional, for sweetening)

Small amount of water or ice cubes

A few fresh mint leaves (optional)

Place all the ingredients in a strong blender and blend well.

Variations

- You can also peel and freeze bananas to have on hand to add to your smoothies. A frozen banana works well in this recipe.
- You can add pure maple syrup, agave nectar, or sweetener of choice, if desired.
- Try adding ½ cup of vegan yogurt.
- Replace the pears with peaches, mangoes, papayas, or pineapple.
- Replace the kale with chard, spinach, or romaine lettuce.

Mediterranean Hot Sauce ♥

Nothing says "Mediterranean" quite like vibrant red chiles strung together by a cord and gracing the outside of buildings in the region. This simple hot sauce is for those who like to live on the edge. For those who like to live beyond the edge, leave in the seeds for a hot hot hot sauce.

MAKES ¾ CUP SAUCE

3 sun-dried tomatoes

1 cup assorted hot chile peppers, sliced

¼ cup plus 1 tablespoon sun-dried tomato soaking water

2 tablespoons freshly squeezed lime juice

2 teaspoons red wine or apple cider vinegar

¼ teaspoon sea salt

½ teaspoon raw sugar or sweetener of choice (optional)

1 garlic clove (optional)

½ teaspoon smoked paprika (optional)

1 tablespoon olive oil (optional)

1. Soak the sun-dried tomatoes in hot water for 15 minutes, or until soft.
2. Place in a blender with the remaining ingredients, including the measured amount of sun-dried tomato soaking water, and blend until smooth. Store in a glass jar in the refrigerator for up to a week.

Quicker and Easier Europe Fusion

Charoset ♥

Of Eastern European origins, this simple and popular dish is served during the Jewish holiday of Passover. Combine two apples, cored and chopped small, in a bowl with ½ cup of chopped walnuts, ¼ teaspoon of ground cinnamon, a pinch of ground nutmeg and/or ground cardamom, ½ cup of grape juice or red wine, and 2 tablespoons of agave nectar (or to taste, depending upon the sweetness of the apples.) You can also add ½ cup of pitted and chopped dates and ¼ cup of orange juice. For best results, allow to chill in the refrigerator for 20 minutes or longer before serving.

Norwegian Cucumber Salad ♥

Combine the following in a bowl and mix well: one thinly sliced cucumber, 1 tablespoon of white vinegar, 1 teaspoon of organic sugar (see page xxi), 1 tablespoon of finely chopped fresh flat-leaf parsley, a pinch of crushed red pepper flakes, and sea salt and freshly ground black pepper to taste. For best results, allow to sit in the refrigerator for 20 minutes before serving.

Credits: Mark Reinfeld

244

APPENDIX A

Taste of Europe Pantry

This section highlights popular ingredients used in European cuisine, many of which are part of the culinary traditions of several countries.

Part 1: European Ingredients

Apples. Apples are a favorite fruit in many European countries. Some of the many varieties of apple include Fuji, Cortland, Pink Lady, Gala, Granny Smith, Braeburn, McIntosh, Jonathan, Pippin, and Red Delicious. Popular apples for eating raw are Red Delicious, Pippin, and Pink Lady. The best for jellies and jams are crabapples, and the popular apples for cooking are Cortland, Granny Smith, Jonathan, and Pink Lady. There are many more to experience, and all of them have a slightly distinct flavor, though some are a cross of two varieties.

Apple cider vinegar. Made from apples; look for the raw variety, which preserves many of its nutrients and is considered to have beneficial healing qualities.

Balsamic vinegar. Slightly sweet, fruity flavor, and mild acidity. Traditional balsamic vinegar is made from the last grapes of the season and is aged at least twelve years in casks made from oak, cherry, chestnut, ash, or mulberry. Most are used for salad dressings or marinades. There are two varieties, *condimento* and *tradizionale*; the *tradizionale* version is often aged longer and has higher standards, and as such is used in smaller quantities to enhance the flavor of the food with which it is paired.

Capers. A peppercorn-size flower bud of a bush, *Capparis spinosa*, native to the Mediterranean and parts of Asia. Capers are usually sun dried and pickled in vinegar brine to bring out their lemonlike flavor. They impart a tangy, salty flavor to dishes, and are popular in Mediterranean and Italian cuisine as a garnish or seasoning.

Champagne vinegar. Champagne vinegar is made using the same grapes as for champagne, to achieve a light and crisp flavor.

Grapeseed oil. Produced from the seeds of grapes used in wine making, this is a great oil for high-temperature cooking because of its high burning point. It is lighter than olive oil, and is used in dressings and infusions, as well as many cosmetics.

Hazelnuts. Hazelnuts, also called filberts, are dark brown nuts used in sweets and flavorings, usually roasted. They are produced in the largest quantities in Turkey, Italy, and Greece.

Olives. The olive tree is native to the coastal Mediterranean region as well as northern parts of Iran. In Italy alone, are over three hundred types of olives, and there are thousands total. Kalamata olives are served in vinegar or wine as a table olive and are named after Kalamata, Greece. Manzanilla olives, or "little apples," originated in Seville, Spain, and are known for their large oval shape and strong taste. Olive oil has been popular since ancient Greek times, when it was called "liquid gold" by Homer for its medicinal properties.

Onions. There are three many types of onion, each with its own varieties—yellow, white, and red. Yellow onions range in sweetness, from the Yellow Ebenezer to the Candy Yellow and the Savannah Sweet. These are better for storing long term and best for cooking, and are the onion choice for French onion soup. Red onions, such as the Red Delicious and Salad Red, are crispy and semisweet, and best on sandwiches or in salads—both raw and grilled. White onions are common in Mexican cuisine and have a sweet flavor when sautéed. Green onions are onions that are harvested at an immature stage, before the bulb forms. Scallion is a separate variety from green onions, latter of which are young onions and have a rounded end; scallions are cylindrical all the way down. They are commonly used in many cuisines around the world.

Potatoes. Many different varieties of potato are used for certain purposes. Often the russet potato, more common in North America, is used for mashing, frying, or eating whole as a baked potato. In Europe, they are also fried to make chips, the larger version of the American French fry. They are a staple starch in many traditionally European dishes, such as shepherd's pie, latkes (potato pancakes), and potato soups and salads. Other varieties of potato include Yukon Gold, red, creamer, fingerling, purple, and Caribe potatoes. Russet, Goldrush, Idaho, and other starchy potatoes are best for baking and mashing. Yukon Gold, Peruvian Blue, Superior, and Kennebec potatoes are all-purpose potatoes, good for roasting and in soups and gratins. Waxy potatoes, such as Round white and red, Red La Rouge,

Yellow Finnish, Red Bliss, and Ruby Crescent, are best for boiling, salads, casseroles and roasting.

Pine nuts. The edible seeds of some varieties of pine tree, though in Europe the stone pine is most commonly harvested. Pine nuts are very high in protein, thiamine, and fiber. They are a culinary nut and botanically a seed. Pine nuts are used extensively in Mediterranean cuisine and are a main ingredient in pesto. In Spain they are used in coffee and a variety of desserts, as well.

Red wine vinegar. The most commonly used vinegar in the Mediterranean and Central areas of Europe. Wine quality plays a major role in the quality of the vinegar, but vinegars aged for at least two years are considered to be better quality. Red wine vinegar has a tangy flavor and is used in vinaigrettes and marinades. Vinegar is used often for pickling, mixing in sauces, marinades, and other flavorings.

Sherry vinegar. Sherry vinegar is made from the fermentation of sherry wine, and has a stronger flavor than does wine vinegar. It is often used in marinades and dressings. It is linked to the production of Jerez wines, originally in the Andalusia region of Spain.

Tomatoes. Rich in lycopene, an antioxidant that has been linked with good heart health and offers protection against various other diseases. No other food has as much of this important nutrient as does the tomato. Centuries ago, the French believed that tomatoes had aphrodisiac qualities and named them pommes d'amour (love apples). Make sure to use organic tomatoes whenever possible.

Tomatoes, heirloom. A nonhybrid, open-pollinated tomato that produces a large variety of color and size in the fruit. The tomato of choice for many chefs.

Tomatoes, Roma. Originating in Italy, the Roma is a pear- or egg-shaped tomato that is easy to grow. It is often used in sauces and in salads, for example.

Tomatoes, sun-dried. Tomatoes that are placed in the sun and may lose up to 93 percent of their weight, but retain their nutritional value. Sun-dried tomatoes retain their vitamin C, lycopene, and antioxidant levels. They are often preserved in oil with spices.

Conversion Chart

- The recipes in this book have not been tested with metric measurements, so some variations might occur.
- Remember that the weight of dry ingredients varies according to the volume or density factor: 1 cup of flour weighs far less than 1 cup of sugar, and 1 tablespoon doesn't necessarily hold 3 teaspoons.

General Formulas for Metric Conversion

Ounces to grams	❯ ounces $\times$ 28.35 = grams
Grams to ounces	❯ grams $\times$ 0.035 = ounces
Pounds to grams	❯ pounds $\times$ 453.5 = grams
Pounds to kilograms	❯ pounds $\times$ 0.45 = kilograms
Cups to liters	❯ cups $\times$ 0.24 = liters
Fahrenheit to Celsius	❯ (°F − 32) $\times$ 5 ÷ 9 = °C
Celsius to Fahrenheit	❯ (°C $\times$ 9) ÷ 5 + 32 = °F

Linear Measurements

½ inch	=	1½cm
1 inch	=	2½ cm
6 inches	=	15 cm
8 inches	=	20 cm
10 inches	=	25 cm
12 inches	=	30 cm
20 inches	=	50 cm

Volume (Dry) Measurements

¼ teaspoon = 1 milliliter
½ teaspoon = 2 milliliters
¾ teaspoon = 4 milliliters
1 teaspoon = 5 milliliters
1 tablespoon = 15 milliliters
¼ cup = 59 milliliters
⅓cup = 79 milliliters
½ cup = 118 milliliters
⅔ cup = 158 milliliters
¾ cup = 177 milliliters
1 cup = 225 milliliters
4 cups or 1 quart = 1 liter
½ gallon = 2 liters
1 gallon = 4 liters

Volume (Liquid) Measurements

1 teaspoon = ⅙ fluid ounce = 5 milliliters
1 tablespoon = ½ fluid ounce = 15 milliliters
2 tablespoons = 1 fluid ounce = 30 milliliters
¼ cup = 2 fluid ounces = 60 milliliters
⅓ cup = 2⅔ fluid ounces = 79 milliliters
½ cup = 4 fluid ounces = 118 milliliters
1 cup or ½ pint = 8 fluid ounces = 250 milliliters
2 cups or 1 pint = 16 fluid ounces = 500 milliliters
4 cups or 1 quart = 32 fluid ounces = 1,000 milliliters
1 gallon = 4 liters

Oven Temperature Equivalents, Fahrenheit (F) and Celsius (C)

100°F = 38°C	350°F = 180°C
200°F = 95°C	400°F = 205°C
250°F = 120°C	450°F = 230°C
300°F = 150°C	

Weight (Mass) Measurements

1 ounce = 30 grams
2 ounces = 55 grams
3 ounces = 85 grams
4 ounces = ¼ pound = 125 grams
8 ounces = ½ pound = 240 grams
12 ounces = ¾ pound = 375 grams
16 ounces = 1 pound = 454 grams

APPENDIX B

Preparation Basics

This section goes over some of the basic principles of vegan natural food preparation used in the recipes in the book.

Techniques

Toasting Spices, Nuts, and Seeds

Toasting is a method to bring out a deeper flavor of ingredients. There are two methods I commonly use.

1. **Dry sauté pan.** For this method, place the food in a pan, place over high heat, and cook until the item turns golden brown, stirring constantly. This method is good for spices, grains, and small quantities of nuts or seeds.

2. **Oven.** Preheat your oven to 350°F. Place the food on a dry baking sheet, and leave in the oven until golden brown, stirring occasionally and being mindful to avoid burning. This method is best for nuts, seeds, and shredded coconut. Nuts become crunchier after cooling down. As mentioned earlier, if you have more time, you can enhance the flavor even more by roasting at lower temperatures for longer periods of time. Nuts, for instance, roasted at 200°F for 45 minutes have a richer, toastier flavor than when roasted at a high temperature for shorter periods of time.

Working with Tofu

Tofu is processed soy bean curd and has its origins in ancient China. It is sold in a number of different forms, including extra-firm, firm, soft, and silken. There is even a super-firm variety available as well as sprouted tofu, which is said to be easier to digest.

Each different form lends itself to a particular type of food preparation. The recipes will describe which form of tofu is required for the dish.

Silken: may be blended and used to replace dairy products in puddings, frostings, dressings, creamy soups, and sauces.

Soft: may be used cubed in soups or pureed in sauces, spreads, or dips.

Medium and firm: may be scrambled, grated in casseroles, or cubed in stir-fries.

Extra-firm and super-firm: may be grilled or baked as cutlets, or it may be cubed and roasted. It may also be steamed and used in steamed veggie dishes.

Leftover tofu should be rinsed and covered with water in a glass container in the refrigerator. Changing the water daily is recommended. Use within 4 days. Firm and extra-firm tofu may be frozen for up to 3 months. Frozen tofu, once defrosted, has a spongy texture that absorbs marinades more than does tofu that has not been frozen.

How to press tofu: Some recommend pressing tofu to remove excess water, create a firmer tofu, and to help the tofu absorb marinades more effectively. Pressing is generally not needed for the super-firm and many extra-firm varieties. If you would like to press your tofu, place the block of tofu on a clean surface, such as a plate, baking sheet, or casserole dish. Place a clean plate on top of the tofu and weight down with a jar or other weight. Allow it to press for 15 to 45 minutes, draining the liquid periodically.

To make tofu cutlets: Slice a block of extra-firm tofu into thirds or fourths. If you wish, you can then cut these cutlets in half to yield six or eight cutlets per pound. You can also cut the tofu diagonally to create triangular cutlets. Cutlets can be marinated and then roasted or grilled.

To make tofu cubes: To make medium-size cubes, slice the tofu as you would for three or four cutlets. Then make four cuts along the length and three cuts along the width of the tofu. You can make the cubes larger or smaller by altering the number of cuts.

Working with Tempeh

Tempeh is originally from Indonesia. It consists of soybeans fermented in a rice culture, then cooked. Many different varieties are created by mixing the soybeans with grains such as millet, wheat, or rice together with sea vegetables and seasonings. Tempeh has a heavier, coarser texture than tofu does. It usually has a mild, slightly fermented flavor. Its color is usually tan with a few dark gray spots. Tempeh needs to be thoroughly cooked, by either steaming, sautéing, roasting, or grilling. For storage, tempeh may be frozen or refrigerated.

Tempeh is typically available in an 8-ounce package. Several varieties come in a thick, square block; others come as a thinner rectangle. Some recommend steaming the tempeh before using in dishes, to remove the bitterness. To do so, place a steamer basket in a large pot filled with about 1 inch of water. Place over high heat. Cover, bring to a boil, and add the tempeh. Lower the heat to medium, and cook covered for 10 minutes. Store leftover tempeh in a sealed glass container in the refrigerator for up to 3 days.

To make tempeh cutlets: You can slice the square block in half to create a thinner block, and then cut it in half or into triangles. The longer block may also be sliced into thinner cutlets. These cutlets may then be cut into cubes.

Tempeh Bacon

Use this recipe instead of purchasing a bacon alternative.

SERVES 4

2 to 3 tablespoons wheat-free tamari or other soy sauce

3 tablespoons water

1 tablespoon pure maple syrup or agave nectar

¼ teaspoon liquid smoke

½ teaspoon garlic powder

½ teaspoon onion powder

8 ounces tempeh, sliced into ⅛-inch or thinner strips

1. Place all the ingredients, except the tempeh, in a shallow dish and whisk well. Add the tempeh and marinate for 10 minutes, flipping frequently.
2. You have two options for cooking. A healthier version is to preheat the oven or toaster oven to 375°F and place the tempeh on a well-oiled baking sheet. Bake for 8 minutes, flip, and bake for another 7 minutes.
3. For the full, crispy, almost-like-bacon effect, place 2 tablespoons of coconut oil or your favorite oil in a medium-size sauté pan. Sauté the tempeh over medium-high heat until crispy, flipping occasionally to cook both sides evenly.

Variations

- You can replace the tempeh with 8 ounces of thinly sliced, extra-firm tofu. To create the slices, cut the block of tofu in half and then slice thinly.
- Replace the liquid smoke with 1 teaspoon of smoked paprika

Roasting Tofu and Tempeh

Tofu and tempeh cubes can be marinated, roasted, and then stored for a couple of days in a glass container in the refrigerator to be used in salads, stir-fries, or on their own as a snack.

To roast tofu and tempeh cutlets and cubes follow these three simple steps:

1. Preheat the oven or toaster oven to 375°F. Cut the tofu or tempeh into cutlets or cubes as described previously.
2. Place them in a marinade of your choosing. Allow them to sit for at least 5 minutes and up to overnight. If marinating overnight, store in an airtight container in the refrigerator.
3. Place on a well-oiled baking sheet or casserole dish. Roast until golden brown, 15 to 20 minutes, stirring the cubes occasionally to ensure even cooking. As brands and oven temperatures differ, check periodically to attain your desired level of doneness. If making cutlets, you can flip them after 10 minutes. Try a convection oven or use a BROIL setting for a crispier crust.

I prefer to use a toaster oven for small quantities of up to 1 pound of tofu or tempeh. This amount conveniently fits in the baking tray. Be aware that food tends to cook faster in a toaster oven than in a regular oven. Depending on the toaster oven, you can typically roast the tofu or tempeh in 15 minutes instead of 20.

Working with Seitan

Originating in ancient China, seitan is sometimes referred to as "meat of wheat." It is wheat gluten dough that has been cooked in a broth with different types of seasonings. Seitan can be used as an animal product replacement in virtually any dish. Several brands available. Experiment with them all to find your favorite. If you are ambitious and wish to make your own, go to www.about.com and enter "making seitan," which brings you to step-by-step instructions. Note that seitan is pure wheat gluten—it's definitely not the dish for the gluten intolerant!

Grilling

Consider grilling tempeh and tofu cutlets, as well as many vegetables, such as portobello mushrooms, corn, onions, baby bok choy, carrots, bell peppers, asparagus, zucchini, coconut meat, or eggplant. You can even grill fruit, such as pineapple slices, apples, or pears. If you wish, for added flavor, place the food in a marinade from a few minutes to overnight

before grilling. Baste or brush lightly with oil, brushing occasionally and grilling until char marks appear and the item is heated thoroughly, flipping periodically. If using a gas grill, avoid placing items over a direct flame.

Another grilling option is to use a stovetop grill. Kitchen supply stores sell cast-iron and nonstick pans that are flat, straddle two burners, and have a griddle on one side and a grooved side for grilling. The grilled flavor is similar and you get the fancy char marks without having to fuss with (or own) a grill.

To grill tofu (stick with extra-firm or super firm) or tempeh, follow the instructions on page 250 or page 251 for creating cutlets. Preheat a grill on high. Place the cutlets in a marinade and grill until the cutlet is cooked through and char marks appear on both sides, 3 to 5 minutes per side, depending upon the heat of the grill. You can baste the cutlets with a marinade or a simple basting sauce of oil, salt, and pepper.

Steam Sautéing

Steam or water sautéing may be used by those wishing to eliminate the use of heated oils in their diet. Water or stock is used instead of oil in the initial cooking stages for dishes that are sautéed. Place a small amount of water or stock in a heated pan, add your vegetables, and follow the recipes as you would if using oil. Add small amounts of water at a time if necessary to prevent sticking. Lemon juice or tamari may also be mixed in with the water for added flavor.

Creating Soup Stock

Soup stock adds depth to dishes and is an innovative and efficient way to use vegetable trimmings from the preparation of other dishes. Stock is a versatile ingredient to have on hand. Use it for sauces, sautéing, consommés, and a warm broth or in any of the recipes calling for vegetable stock.

For a simple soup stock: Save the clippings and scraps of vegetables used in preparing other recipes. Place them in a large, heavy-bottomed stockpot on low heat with water to cover and simmer until all veggies are completely cooked. Cook until the liquid is reduced to 75 to 50 percent of the original volume. Their flavor will be imparted to the broth. Experiment with different vegetables and herbs until you discover your favorite combinations. Strain well, and add salt and pepper to taste.

Try using trimmings from potatoes, celery, carrots, onions, parsley, mushrooms, parsnip, zucchini, leeks, corn cobs, and garlic. Many avoid using vegetables that become bitter, such as bell peppers, radishes, turnips, broccoli, cauliflower, and Brussels sprouts. It is not necessary to add dried herbs or spices to a stock as it becomes flavorful unto itself.

Some use bouquet garni and then remove it. The stock may be frozen and thawed for future use. You can even pour the stock into ice cube trays, freeze, and use as needed.

Cooking Grains

Simply follow these instructions and you will always have perfectly cooked grains.

1. Rinse the grain thoroughly and drain the excess water.
2. Bring the measured amount of grain and liquid (either vegetable stock or filtered water) to a boil. You may wish to add a pinch of sea salt.
3. Cover with a tight-fitting lid, lower the heat to low, and simmer for the recommended time. Because the grain is being steamed, do not lift the lid until the grain is finished cooking.

Cooking times may vary, depending upon altitude and stove cooking temperatures. The grain is generally finished cooking when it is chewy and all of the liquid is absorbed.

Enhance the flavor of your grain dishes by adding such ingredients as minced garlic or fresh ginger, diced onion, a couple of bay leaves, or crushed lemongrass while cooking.

If you wish to use a rice cooker, Miracle puts out a stainless-steel version. Steer clear of aluminum rice cookers.

Grain Cooking Chart				
Grain	Liquid per cup of grain (cups)	Approx. cooking time (minutes)	Approx. yield (cups)	Comments
Amaranth	2½	25	2½	Ancient grain of Aztecs, higher in protein and nutrients than most grains.
Barley, pearled	3	45	3½	Good in soups and stews.
Buckwheat	2	15	2½	Hearty, nutty flavor. When toasted, it's called kasha and takes less time to cook. Also used as a breakfast cereal.
Cornmeal	3	20	3½	From ground corn—a staple of Native Americans; use in corn bread or grits
Couscous	1½	15	1½	A North African staple made from ground semolina.
Kamut	3	60	3	An ancient variety of wheat that many with wheat allergies are able to tolerate.
Millet	2½	20	3	A highly nutritious grain that is used in casseroles, stews, and cereals. Especially tasty with flax oil.
Oats				A versatile grain that is popular as a cereal, for baking, and for milk.
Steel cut	3	30 to 40	3	
Groats	3	60	3	
Rolled	3	10	3	
Quick	2	5	2	
Polenta	3	10	3	A type of cornmeal used in Italian cooking. To cook, bring liquid to a boil. Lower the heat to a simmer and whisk in the polenta, stirring until done.
Quinoa	2	20	2½	Ancient grain of the Inca. High in protein and nutrients. Has a delicate, nutty flavor. One of our favorites!

continues

255

Grain Cooking Chart *continued*

Grain	Liquid per cup of grain (cups)	Approx. cooking time (minutes)	Approx. yield (cups)	Comments
Rice				Rice has a high nutrient content and is a staple in many of the world's cultures, to say the least. Basmati rice has a nutty flavor and is used in Indian cooking. We prefer brown short-grain rice for its taste and nutritional value.
Brown basmati	2	35 to 40	2¼	
White basmati	1½	20	2	
Brown long grain	2	45	3	
Brown short grain	2	45	3	
Wild	3	60	4	
Jasmine	1¾	20	3½	
Sushi	1¼	20	3	
Rye				A staple grain throughout Europe. Used as a cereal or ground to make breads, including pumpernickel.
Berries	4	60	3	
Flakes	3	20	3	
Spelt	3½	90	3	Spelt is the purest and one of the most ancient forms of wheat. It contains much more protein and nutrition than wheat does and is more digestible.
Teff	3	20	1½	From Ethiopia, the smallest grain in the world, and the main ingredient for *injera* flatbread.
Wheat				A primary bread grain. Bulgur is used in Middle Eastern dishes, such as tabbouleh. Cracked may be used as a cereal.
Whole	3	120	2¾	
Bulgur	2	15	2½	
Cracked	2	25	2½	

Cooking Legumes

Before you cook legumes, it is recommended to pick over them thoroughly (remove any stones or debris), rinse them well, and soak them overnight. This improves their digestibility and reduces gas. Other methods for improving digestibility include adding some fennel seeds, a handful of brown rice, or a small strip of the sea vegetable kombu to the legumes while cooking. If you forget to soak beans overnight, a quick method is to bring the beans and four times the amount of water to a boil, remove from the heat, cover, and allow to sit for a few hours.

After soaking the legumes or boiling them in this fashion, drain them and discard the soaking water. Place the beans and the measured amount of vegetable stock or filtered water in a heavy-bottomed pot, bring to a boil, cover, lower the heat to simmer, and cook until tender. Please see the following legume cooking chart. The times in the chart are for cooking dried legumes. Please reduce the cooking time by 25 percent if legumes are presoaked.

Do not add salt to the cooking liquid; it can make the legumes tough. The beans are done cooking when they are tender but not mushy. They should retain their original shape.

	Dried Bean Cooking Chart			
Legume	Liquid per cup of legume (cups)	Approx. cook time (hours)	Approx. yield (cups)	Comments
Aduki beans	3¼	45 min.	3	Tender red bean used in Japanese and macrobiotic cooking
Anasazi beans	3	2	2	Means "the ancient ones" in Navajo language; sweeter and meatier than most beans
Black beans (turtle beans)	4	1¼	2½	Good in Spanish, South American, and Caribbean dishes
Black-eyed peas	4	1¼	2	A staple of the American South
Chickpeas (garbanzo beans)	4	3 to 4	2	Used in Middle Eastern and Indian dishes. Pureed cooked chickpeas form the base of hummus.
Great northern beans	4	1½	2	Beautiful, large white beans

continues

257

Dried Bean Cooking Chart *continued*

Legume	Liquid per cup of legume (cups)	Approx. cook time (hours)	Approx. yield (cups)	Comments
Kidney beans	4	1½	2	Medium-size red beans. The most popular bean in the United States; also used in Mexican cooking.
Lentils	3	45 min.	2¼	Come in green, red, and French varieties. A member of the pea family used in Indian dal dishes and soups.
Lima beans baby limas	3 3	1½ 1½	1¼ 1¾	White beans with a distinctive flavor; high in nutrients.
Mung beans	3	45 min.	2¼	Grown in India and Asia. Used in Indian dal dishes. May be soaked and sprouted and used fresh in soups and salads.
Navy beans (white beans)	4	2½	2	Hearty beans used in soups, stews, and cold salads
Pinto beans	4	2½	2	Used in Mexican and Southwestern cooking. Used in soups and as refried beans in burritos.
Split peas	3	45 min	2¼	Come in yellow and green varieties. Used in soups and Indian dals.
Soybeans	4	3+	2	Versatile, high-protein beans widely used in Asia. May be processed into tofu, tempeh, miso, soy milk, soy sauce, and soy cheese.

Basic Recipes

Basic Nut or Seed Milk

Recipe courtesy of *The 30-Minute Vegan*

Use this base recipe to create countless varieties of nut and seed milks. Each combination will provide its own unique flavor. Partake of this milk in all recipes that call for milk, or on its own as a refreshing beverage. If you have more time and for best results, see the chart at the end of the recipe for recommended soaking times.

MAKES 1 QUART MILK

1 cup nut or seeds
4 cups water

▶ Rinse the nuts or seeds well and drain. Place them in a blender with the water and blend on high speed for 30 seconds, or until creamy. Strain the milk through a fine-mesh strainer, cheesecloth, or a mesh bag. If using a fine-mesh strainer, use a spoon or rubber spatula to swirl the nut or seed meal around, which allows the milk to drain faster. If desired, sweeten with agave nectar or pure maple syrup to taste.

Note: This recipe also works for rice milk. Just follow the ratios, using uncooked brown rice and water. It's a convenient way to save on packaging; it's fresh and tastes better!

Nut, seed, and rice milks will last for 3 to 4 days when stored in a glass jar in the refrigerator.

If You Have More Time

Soaking Chart

Rinse nuts or seeds well and place them in a bowl or jar with water in a 1 part nut or seed to 3 or 4 parts water ratio. Allow them to sit for the recommended time before draining, rinsing, and using in recipes.

Nut/Seed	Soak time (hours)	Nut/Seed	Soak time (hours)
Almonds	4 to 6	Pecans	4 to 6
Macadamia nuts	1 to 2	Pine nuts	1 to 2
Hazelnuts	4 to 6	Sesame seeds	1 to 4
Cashews	1 to 2	Pumpkin seeds	1 to 4
Brazil nuts	4 to 6	Sunflower seeds	1 to 4
Walnuts	4 to 6		

Gluten-Free Flour Mix

Use this to replace the flour called for in the recipes.

▶ Combine equal parts of sorghum flour, brown rice flour, and tapioca flour. Use ¼ teaspoon of xanthan gum for each cup of flour in cookies and pies, and ½ teaspoon of xanthan gum per cup of flour for cakes, muffins, or scones.

Marinades

Marinade ingredients greatly determine the flavors of a dish. Simply by placing something like tofu or a portobello mushroom in different marinades creates dramatically different taste sensations.

Creating marinades is both fun and rewarding. Following are a couple of our favorite marinades. Place the items in the marinade for a minimum of 10 minutes. The longer it sits in the marinade, the more flavor it will acquire. We like to marinate our tofu (as well as vegetables) overnight, if possible. These are simple marinades that make enough for 1 pound of tofu or tempeh or two servings of veggies

Be bold in your exploration of different marinades. Please use the following marinades as a starting point on your own voyage of discovery. Some of my favorite marinade ingredients include: toasted sesame oil, mirin, mustard, brown rice vinegar, horseradish, minced garlic or fresh ginger, pure maple syrup, balsamic vinegar, and a variety of spices and herbs.

Maple Balsamic Marinade

MAKES ABOUT ¾ CUP MARINADE

½ cup filtered water
3 tablespoons wheat-free tamari or soy sauce
2 tablespoons olive or coconut oil
1 tablespoon pure maple syrup or agave nectar
2 teaspoons balsamic or red wine vinegar
1 teaspoon minced garlic or fresh ginger
1 tablespoon minced fresh herbs (optional)
Pinch of cayenne pepper

▶ Place all the ingredients in a bowl and whisk well.

Lemon Dijon Marinade

MAKES ABOUT ¾ CUP MARINADE

½ cup freshly squeezed lemon juice
¼ cup filtered water
2 tablespoons minced fresh herbs (try thyme, oregano, and parsley)
1½ teaspoons vegan Dijon or stone-ground mustard
½ teaspoon sea salt
¼ teaspoon freshly ground black pepper
1 tablespoon olive oil (optional)
¼ teaspoon cayenne pepper (optional)

▶ Place all the ingredients in a bowl and whisk well.

Vegan Mayonnaise

Use this egg-free mayonnaise in any recipe that calls for mayo.

MAKES 2¼ CUPS MAYONNAISE

1½ cups safflower oil
¾ cup soy milk
½ teaspoon vegan Dijon mustard
1 teaspoon agave nectar (optional)
¾ teaspoon sea salt, or to taste
1½ teaspoons freshly squeezed lemon juice

▶ Combine all the ingredients, except the lemon juice, in a blender and blend until smooth.
▶ Slowly add the lemon juice through the top while blending, until the mixture thickens.

Natural Sweeteners

Many people believe that eating foods with refined white sugar can lead to certain health problems, including emotional disorders, obesity, diabetes, and tooth decay. It is believed that because refined sugars are missing the nutrients contained in naturally sweet whole foods, the body is drained of its own store of minerals and nutrients in its efforts to metabolize the sugar.

Vegan Fusion natural food preparation makes use of various naturally occurring and minimally processed sweeteners. You can replace traditional white sugar with raw cane sugar or organic sugar at a one-to-one ratio without making any changes to your recipes. You can also replace the white sugar with any of the following sweeteners. These sweeteners are superior to white sugar, but it is still believed that most of them need to be used in moderation.

The following chart indicates how much of a sweetener is needed to replace 1 cup of refined white sugar. The chart indicates how much liquid to delete from the recipe to maintain its consistency if the sweetener is a liquid.

Sweetener	Replace 1 cup of refined sugar with	Reduce liquids by	Comments
Agave nectar	¾ cup	⅓	A natural extract from a famous Mexican cactus, with a low glycemic index. There is a bit of a controversy surrounding agave and its similarity to high-fructose corn syrup.
Barley malt syrup	¾ cup	¼	Roughly half as sweet as honey or sugar. Made from sprouted barley; has a nutty, caramel flavor.
Brown rice syrup	1 cup	¼	A relatively neutral-flavored sweetener that is roughly half as sweet as sugar or honey. It's made from fermented brown rice.
Blackstrap molasses	½ cup	¼	This syrup is a liquid by-product of the sugar refining process. It contains many of the nutrients of the sugar cane plant. Has a strong, distinctive flavor.
Coconut crystals	1 cup	0	Air-dried coconut nectar creates a nutrient-rich granulated sugar that is our recommended sweetener for the recipes in this book. It has a dark, rich flavor with a lower glycemic index than cane sugar. Manufactured by Coconut Secret.
Coconut nectar	¾ cup	⅓	A mildly flavored sweetener manufactured by Coconut Secret, which is a wonderful replacement for agave nectar. It has a low glycemic index and is loaded with vitamins, minerals, amino acids, and other nutrients.
Date sugar	⅔ cup	0	A granulated sugar produced from drying fresh dates
Fruit syrup	1 cup	¼	The preferred method of sweetening involves soaking, then blending, raisins and dates with filtered water, to create a sweet syrup. Try ½ cup of raisins with 1 cup of water and experiment to find your desired sweetness.

continues

Sweetener	Replace 1 cup of refined sugar with	Reduce liquids by	Comments
Lucuma powder	1 cup	0	A raw, low-glycemic sweetener with a slight maple flavor. Comes from the lucuma fruit, grown in the Peruvian Andes and referred to as the "gold of the Inca."
Maple syrup	¾ cup	¼	Forty gallons of sap from the maple tree are needed to create 1 gallon of maple syrup. It is mineral rich and graded according to color and flavor. Grade A is the mildest and lightest, Grade C is the darkest and richest. Good for baking. Use only pure maple syrup, not table or pancake syrup.
Sucanat	1 cup	0	Abbreviation for "sugar cane natural." It is a granular sweetener that consists of evaporated sugar cane juice. It has about the same sweetness as sugar. It retains most of the vitamins and minerals of the sugar cane.
Stevia (powdered)	1 teaspoon	0	Stevia is a plant that originated in the Brazilian rainforest. The powdered form is between 200 and 400 percent sweeter than white sugar. It is noncaloric, does not promote tooth decay, and is said to be an acceptable form of sugar for diabetics and those with blood sugar imbalances. For baking conversions, please visit www.ehow.com/how_2268348_substitute-stevia-sugar-baking.html.
Xylitol	1 cup	0	A naturally occurring sugar substitute found in the fibers of fruits and vegetables, such as berries, corn husks, oats, plums, and mushrooms. Originally extracted from birch trees in Finland in the nineteenth century. Said to promote dental health and to be a safe sweetener for diabetics because of its low glycemic index.
Yacón	¾ cup	⅓	This tuber is a distant relative of the sunflower. From the Andean region of South America, mineral-rich yacón syrup has a dark brown color and is used as a low-calorie sweetener.

Chef's Tips and Tricks

Date Syrup ♥

This is probably one of the most healthful, least processed sweeteners you can use. Use it to replace maple syrup, agave nectar, or other concentrated sweeteners.

MAKES ABOUT 1 CUP

¼ cup dates
1 cup water

Combine the dates and water in a strong blender and blend until smooth. Store in a glass jar in the refrigerator for up to 4 days.

APPENDIX C

Supplemental Information

Why Vegan?

Nothing will benefit human health and increase
the chances for survival of life on Earth
as much as the evolution to a vegetarian diet.

—ALBERT EINSTEIN

In the years since the first 30-Minute Vegan book was published in 2009, there has been an explosion of interest in vegan foods. In addition to former president Bill Clinton, there are a slew of celebrities (from Ellen DeGeneres to Alicia Silverstone), high-performance athletes (triathlete Brendan Brazier), powerful entrepreneurs (hip-hop mogul Russell Simmons and Twitter cofounder Biz Stone), and folks from every walk of life who are experimenting with this transformational lifestyle.

The reasons people choose to enjoy vegan foods are many. First and foremost, these foods taste incredible! People also turn to vegan foods for weight loss and disease prevention. There are now numerous studies demonstrating that many serious illnesses, such heart disease, obesity, and diabetes can be prevented and reversed by enjoying more plant-based foods. Please check out the movie *Forks over Knives* if you are interested in learning more about the many health benefits of a vegan diet.

Want to be Earth friendly? In addition to providing an out-of-this-world culinary experience, eating vegan also happens to be one of the most effective steps we can take to protect the environment. The UN's Food and Agriculture Organization estimates that meat production accounts for nearly a fifth of global greenhouse gas emissions—more than the entire world's transportation industry combined. We do more for the environment by switching meals to vegan than by trading in our gas-guzzlers for an electric car or jogging to work.

Optimal Health

I went on essentially a plant-based diet. I live on beans,
legumes, vegetables, fruits. I drink a protein
supplement every morning. No dairy. I lost 24 pounds
and I got back basically to what I weighed in high school . . .
I'll become part of this experiment. I'll see if I can
be one of those that can have a self-clearing mechanism.

—President Bill Clinton

There is a true revolution occurring in the medical world regarding the benefits of vegan foods. Renowned doctors, such as Dr. Caldwell Esselstyn Jr. and Dr. Dean Ornish, have successfully reversed instances of heart disease with programs that incorporate vegan foods. Dr. John McDougall, Dr. Gabriel Cousens, Dr. Neal Barnard, and Joel Fuhrman have likewise had success reversing certain forms of diabetes.

The evidence continues to mount that overconsumption of the saturated fat and cholesterol in animal products leads to serious health problems, such as obesity, heart disease, diabetes, hypertension, gout, kidney stones, and certain forms of cancer.

In addition, animals raised on factory farms are routinely given hormones to accelerate their rate of growth for maximum profit. Antibiotics are used to protect their health as they are housed and transported in less than sanitary conditions. These drugs inevitably make their way into the body of the humans that consume them.

In 2009, the American Dietetic Association restated their position that "well-planned vegan and other types of vegetarian diets are appropriate for all stages of the life cycle, including during pregnancy, lactation, infancy, childhood, and adolescence." It is the association's official opinion, as well as that of the Dietitians of Canada, that "appropriately planned vegetarian diets, including total vegetarian or vegan diets, are healthful, nutritionally adequate, and may provide health benefits in the prevention and treatment of certain diseases."

May this forever dispel the myth that a vegan diet is nutritionally lacking in any way. For anyone concerned about this, please rest assured that vegan foods provide all of the protein, calcium, iron, and all other vital nutrients needed for us to thrive.

Preserving the Environment

In terms of immediacy of action and the feasibility of bringing about [green house gas] reductions in a short period of time, it clearly is the most attractive opportunity. Give up meat for one day [a week] initially, and decrease it from there.

—Dr. Rajendra Pachauri, chair of the Nobel Prize–winning United Nations Intergovernmental Panel on Climate Change

The environmental footprint of a vegan diet is a fraction of that of a meat-based diet. Vegan foods represent the best utilization of the earth's limited resources. It takes 16 pounds of grain and 2,500 gallons of water to produce 1 pound of beef. It's astonishing to realize this when we see so much in the news about food and water shortages and people going to bed hungry.

We must use the resources of our planet wisely if we are to survive. World scientists agree that global warming poses a serious risk to humanity and life, as we know it. The key to reducing global warming is to reduce activities that produce the greenhouse gases that cause the Earth's temperature to rise. According to a 2006 UN Report, "Livestock's Long Shadow," raising livestock for food consumption is responsible for 18 percent of all greenhouse gases emitted. That's a lot of gas!

Here are some additional topics to consider for those wishing to go green:

The livestock population of the United States consumes enough grain and soybeans each year to feed over five times the human population of the country. Animals are fed over 80 percent of the corn and 95 percent of the oats that are grown on our soil.

According to the USDA, 1 acre of land can produce 20,000 pounds of vegetables. This same amount of land can only produce 165 pounds of meat.

It takes 16 pounds of grain to produce 1 pound of meat.

If Americans were to reduce meat consumption by just 10 percent, it would free up 12 million tons of grain annually.

It takes approximately 2,500 gallons of water to produce a single pound of meat. It takes 300 gallons to provide a day's worth of food for a person's plant-based diet.

To support cattle grazing, South and Central America are destroying their rainforests. These rainforests contain close to half of all species of life on Earth, including many medicinal plants. Over a thousand species per year are becoming extinct, most of these from rainforest and tropical settings. This practice also causes the displacement of indigenous peoples who have been living in these environments for countless generations.

Over 60 million people die of starvation every year. This means that we are feeding grain to animals while our fellow humans are dying of starvation in mind-staggering numbers.

For those concerned about our environment, it all boils down to the question of sustainability. What is the most sustainable way for us to feed and support the growing human population? When you look at the disproportionate amount of land, water, and resources it takes to support a meat-based diet, it makes a lot of sense for us to introduce more plant-based foods into our way of life. Whether by going completely vegan or simply including more vegan meals each week, every little bit helps.

It's Still Cool to Be Kind

I've become an animal rights activist . . . I'm taking care
of myself for the rest of my life. I've changed my will to
show my concern for animal rights. Animal-based food kills people.
This way by going vegan . . . we get healthy and save animals.

STEVE WYNN

Wynn is a hotel magnate who went vegan after watching the movie *Eating*. He was so inspired that he purchased 10,000 copies of the DVD for all of his executives, chefs, and employees, and has added a vegan menu to all of his hotel restaurants. He also happened to lose 15 pounds since going vegan!

Many people adopt a vegan diet out of a commitment toward nonviolence. For them, we are meant to be stewards and caretakers of the Earth and its inhabitants, and do not wish to support practices that inflict suffering on any creature that has the capacity to feel pain.

The small family farm where husbandry practices engendered a certain respect for the animals that were used for food is becoming a thing of the past. Today, most of the world's meat, dairy, and egg production occur on massive factory farms that are owned by agribusiness conglomerates. This has brought about practices that view the raising and transportation of farm animals solely in terms of their ability to generate profits.

Animals are routinely given chemicals and antibiotics to keep them alive in these conditions. To increase the weight of cows, many are fed sawdust, plastic, tallow, grease, and cement dust seasoned with artificial flavors and aromas. Mother pigs on factory farms are kept to crates that are so small they are unable to turn around. Dairy cows are forced to remain pregnant most of their lives and are injected with hormones to increase milk production.

Male calves born from these cows are often confined as newborns to a crate that is so small that they are unable to turn around. They are fed diets that are deliberately iron deficient, a practice that induces anemia and allows the flesh to remain white. After four months or so in these conditions, the calf is slaughtered to produce veal. Simply put, choosing to go vegan or to eat fewer animal products is good for the environment, good for the animals, and good for you. That's the best sort of kindness.

Go Organic

The Organic Trade Association states, "Organic farming is based on practices that maintain soil fertility, while assisting nature's balance through diversity and recycling of energy and nutrients. This method also strives to avoid or reduce the use of synthetic fertilizers and pest controls. Organic foods are processed, packaged, transported, and stored to retain maximum nutritional value, without the use of artificial preservatives, coloring or other additives, irradiation, or synthetic pesticides."

Wondering whether it's worth it to buy organic? Consider that many of the chemicals in commercial pesticides and fertilizers have not been tested for their long-term effects on humans. Is it worth it to take that chance with your health and the health of your family? Organically grown foods represent a cycle of sustainability that improves topsoil fertility, enhances nutrition, and ensures food security.

Organic farmers employ farming methods that respect the fragile balance of our ecosystem. This results in a fraction of the groundwater pollution and topsoil depletion that's generated by conventional methods. Most people have also found the taste and nutrient quality of organic products superior to those of conventionally grown food.

Purchasing local, seasonal, and organically grown food is also an extremely effective way to reduce your environmental impact. Buying local saves the huge amount of energy it takes to transport food—sometimes across oceans and continents.

Another reason to support organic farmers has to do with the health of the farmworkers themselves. Farmworkers on conventional farms are exposed to high levels of toxic pesticides on a daily basis. Organic farmworkers don't have to encounter these risks.

Lastly, by supporting organic farmers, we are supporting small, family farms. This once prevalent method of farming is rapidly disappearing. This is due to the small farmer's inability to compete with the heavily subsidized agribusiness farms that use synthetic soil, pesticides, crop dusters, and heavy machinery on lands that encompass thousands of acres.

For more information on organic farming, visit your local farmers' market and talk to the farmers. You can also check out the websites for the International Federation of Organic Agriculture Movements, the Organic Consumers Association, and the Organic

Trade Association listed in Appendix D. You can identify organic produce by looking at the PLU, which should begin with a "9."

Not all produce is created equal. The organization called the Environmental Working Group put together a list of those commercially grown foods with the highest level of pesticides, and those with the lowest levels of pesticides.

Those with the highest levels of pesticides are referred to as "The Dirty Dozen," which tested positive for 47 to 67 different pesticides. Always purchase these organically:

celery	sweet bell peppers
peaches	spinach, kale, and collard greens
strawberries	cherries
apples	potatoes
domestic blueberries	imported grapes
nectarines	lettuce

"The Clean 15" had little to no traces of pesticides:

onions	cabbage
avocados	eggplant
sweet corn	cantaloupe
pineapples	watermelon
mango	grapefruit
sweet peas	sweet potatoes
asparagus	sweet onions
kiwi fruit	

GMO Must GO

A GMO (genetically engineered and modified organism) is a plant, animal, or microorganism that has had its genetic code altered—typically by introducing genes from another organism. This process gives the GMO food characteristics that are not present in its original form. Many feel this practice goes against nature and poses a profound threat to people, the environment, and our agricultural heritage.

GMO seed manufacturers maintain that this makes the seed more pest resistant, promotes higher yields, or enhances nutrition. The fact is that the long-term effects of these seeds on the consumer and our genetic pool are still unknown. This untested engineering is dangerous to human health in the long term. By definition, eating organic foods eliminates GMO from our food supply.

Many communities around the world have succeeded in becoming GMO-free. Please join us in this critical movement to move our agriculture away from genetic engineering and toward truly sustainable agriculture. For more information, you may visit the Non-GMO Project at www.nongmoproject.org. You can tell if your produce has been genetically modified by looking at the PLU label. Numbers beginning with "8" indicate a GMO product.

Composting: The Cycle of Life

Composting is the method of breaking down food waste, grass trimmings, and leaves to create nutrient-rich and fertile soil. It's the next step we can take toward creating a more sustainable method of growing our food. Compost contains nitrogen and micronutrients to keep the soil healthy and can be used as a mulch and soil amendment. When the soil is healthy, plant yields are higher and fertilizers and pesticides aren't as necessary.

Composting completes the cycle of life from seed to table and back to the earth. Many communities sponsor composting programs and can give you all the tools and instructions you need to succeed. Check out www.compostguide.com for a complete guide to composting.

APPENDIX D

Additional Resources

Further Reading

Want to learn more? Explore this section to deepen your knowledge of the information touched upon in *the 30-Minute Vegan's Taste of Europe.*

Barnard, Neal, MD. *Breaking the Food Seduction: The Hidden Reasons Behind Food Cravings—And 7 Steps to End Them Naturally.* New York: St. Martin's Griffin, 2004.

Brazier, Brendan. *The Thrive Diet: The Whole Food Way to Lose Weight, Reduce Stress, and Stay Healthy for Life.* New York: Da Capo Press, 2007.

Campbell, T. Colin, and Thomas M. Campbell II. *The China Study: The Most Comprehensive Study of Nutrition Ever Conducted and the Startling Implications for Diet, Weight Loss, and Long-term Health.* Dallas, TX: Benbella Books, 2006.

Davis, Brenda, RD, and Vesanto Melina, MS, RD. *The Complete Guide to Adopting a Healthy Plant-Based Diet.* Summertown, TN: Book Publishing Company, 2000.

Esselstyn, Caldwell. *Prevent and Reverse Heart Disease.* New York: Avery Publishing, 2007.

Fuhrman, Joel, MD. *Eat to Live: The Revolutionary Formula for Fast and Sustained Weight Loss.* Boston, MA: Little, Brown, and Company, 2005.

Hever, Julieanna. *The Complete Idiot's Guide to Plant-Based Nutrition.* Indianapolis, IN: Alpha Books, 2011.

Klaper, Michael, MD. *Vegan Nutrition: Pure and Simple.* Summertown, TN: Book Publishing Company, 1999.

Krizmaniac, Judy. *A Teen's Guide to Going Vegetarian.* London, UK: Puffin, 1994.

Jacobson, Michael, PhD. *Six Arguments for a Greener Diet: How a Plant-Based Diet Could Save Your Health and the Environment.* Washington, DC: Center for Science in the Public Interest, 2006.

Lyman, Howard. *Mad Cowboy: Plain Truth from the Cattle Rancher Who Won't Eat Meat.* New York: Scribner, 2001.

Marcus, Erik. *Vegan: The New Ethics of Eating.* Ithaca, NY: McBooks Press, 2001.

Norris, Jack, and Virginia Messina. *Vegan for Life: Everything You Need to Know to Be Healthy and Fit on a Plant-Based Diet.* Boston, MA: Da Capo Lifelong, 2011.

Ornish, Dean. *Dr. Dean Ornish's Program for Reversing Heart Disease: The Only System Scientifically Proven to Reverse Heart Disease Without Drugs or Surgery.* New York: Ivy Books, 1995.

Pitchford, P. *Healing with Whole Foods.* Berkeley, CA: North Atlantic Books, 1993.

Reinfeld, Mark, and Jennifer Murray. *The 30-Minute Vegan.* Boston, MA: Da Capo Lifelong, 2009.

Reinfeld, Mark, and Jennifer Murray. *The 30-Minute Vegan's Taste of the East.* Boston, MA: Da Capo Lifelong, 2010.

Reinfeld, Mark, and Bo Rinaldi. *Vegan Fusion World Cuisine.* New York: Beaufort Books, 2007.

Reinfeld, Mark, Bo Rinaldi, and Jennifer Murray. *The Complete Idiot's Guide to Eating Raw.* Indianapolis, IN: Alpha Books, 2008.

Robbins, John. *Diet for a New America.* Tiburon, CA: HJ Kramer, 1987.

Robbins, John. *Healthy at 100.* New York: Random House, 2006.

Robbins, John. *The Food Revolution: How Your Diet Can Help Save Your Life and Our World.* Newburyport, MA: Conari Press, 2001.

Robbins, John. *The New Good Life: Living Better Than Ever in an Age of Less.* New York: Ballantine Books, 2010.

Stuart, Tristram. *The Bloodless Revolution: A Cultural History of Vegetarianism from 1600 to Modern Times.* New York: W. W. Norton, 2007.

Tuttle, Will, PhD. *World Peace Diet: Eating for Spiritual Health and Social Harmony.* Brooklyn, NY: Lantern Books, 2005.

Online Resources

Here are some of the more popular websites and blogs promoting a vegan and sustainable way of life. We also list some go-to sites for kitchen equipment and to stock up your European pantry.

Vegan and Veg Friendly Websites

www.earthsave.org

Founded by John Robbins, EarthSave is doing what it can to promote a shift to a plant-based diet. It posts news, information, and resources and publishes a magazine.

www.happycow.net

Happy Cow is a searchable guide to vegetarian restaurants and natural health food stores, with information on vegetarian nutrition, raw foods, and vegan recipes.

www.veganessentials.com

The ultimate vegan superstore, with everything from cosmetics, to clothing, to household products, supplements, and more. When it comes to vegan—you name it, they have it.

www.animalconcerns.org

Animal Concerns Community serves as a clearinghouse for information on the Internet related to animal rights and welfare.

www.farmusa.org

Farm Animal Reform Movement (FARM) is an organization advocating a plant-based diet and humane treatment of farm animals through grassroots programs.

www.hsus.org

The Humane Society of the U.S (HSUS) wishes to create a world where humans relate to animals with compassion.

www.vegweb.com

A vegetarian mega site with recipes, photos, articles, online store, and more.

www.brendanbrazier.com

Brendan Brazier is an Ironman Triathlete, speaker, and author of *The Thrive Diet*. You can find his book and his calendar of events here on this website.

www.vegtv.com

This is the site for Veg TV video production company, producing and streaming original content about vegetarian and vegan food, health and nutrition, and eco-travel.

www.vegan.com

The popular site of Erik Marcus, geared toward the aspiring and long-term vegan, which features articles, interviews, product evaluations, book reviews, and more.

www.vegan.org

Vegan Action is a nonprofit grassroots organization dedicated to educating people about the many benefits of a vegan lifestyle.

www.veganpassions.com

Vegan Passions is a free online dating site for meeting single vegans.

www.vrg.org

The Vegetarian Resource Group (VRG) is a nonprofit organization dedicated to educating the public on vegetarianism including information on health, nutrition, ecology, ethics, and world hunger.

www.vegdining.com

This vegetarian dining guide includes an international search option, a monthly veggie restaurant contest, and the opportunity to purchase a VegDining card for discounts at participating veggie restaurants.

www.vegan.meetup.com

Meet up with other vegans in your town!

www.veganoutreach.com

An amazing resource for aspiring vegans, Vegan Outreach is a wonderful organization dedicated to pamphleting and other educational activities.

www.keepkidshealthy.com

This guide for raising vegan children carries advice on providing your child with an early start on leading a long and healthy life.

www.veganfitness.net

Vegan Fitness is a community-driven message board seeking to provide a supportive, educational, and friendly environment for vegans, vegetarians, and those seeking to go vegan.

www.vegansociety.com

The Vegan Society promotes ways of living free of animal products for the benefit of people, animals, and the environment.

www.veganpet.com.au

Veganpet provides nutritionally complete and balanced pet food and information on raising vegan pets.

www.vegfamily.com

This is a comprehensive resource for raising vegan children, including pregnancy, vegan recipes, book reviews, product reviews, message board, and more.

www.veganbodybuilding.com

Vegan Body Building and Fitness is the website of vegan body builder Robert Cheeke and features articles, videos, products, and a forum for the active vegan.

www.vegsource.com

This site features over ten thousand vegetarian and vegan recipes, discussion boards, nutritionists, medical doctors, experts, authors, articles, newsletter, and the vegetarian community.

www.pcrm.org

The Physicians Committee for Responsible Medicine (PCRM) is a nonprofit organization that promotes preventive medicine, conducts clinical research, and encourages higher standards for ethics and effectiveness in research.

www.ivu.org

The World Union of Vegetarian/Vegan Societies has been promoting vegetarianism worldwide since 1908.

www.vegetarianteen.com

This online magazine has articles on vegetarian teen lifestyle, activism, nutrition, social issues, and more.

www.johnrobbins.info

This comprehensive website has podcasts, videos, resources, and a blog by vegan pioneer and best-selling author John Robbins.

Organic and Gardening Websites

www.ota.com

The Organic Trade Association website will tell you anything you want to know about the term *organic,* from food to textiles to healthcare products. The OTA's mission is to encourage global sustainability through promoting and protecting the growth of diverse organic trade.

www.organicconsumers.org

The Organic Consumers Association is an online, grassroots, nonprofit organization dealing with issues of food safety, industrial agriculture, genetic engineering, corporate accountability, and environmental sustainability.

www.organicgardening.com

Find out where to get your soil tested, manage pests without using chemicals, and read vegetable and flower growing guides.

www.avant-gardening.com

This site advocates organic gardening with information on composting, soil building, permaculture principles, botany, companion and intensive planting, and more.

www.wwoof.org

World-Wide Opportunities on Organic Farms (WWOOF) is an association helping those who wish to volunteer on organic farms internationally.

www.gefoodalert.org

GE Food Alert Campaign Center is a coalition of seven organizations committed to testing and labeling genetically engineered food.

www.earthflow.com

Earthflow is an all-natural approach to permaculture design, offering garden tours and training programs, including permaculture courses.

www.biodynamics.com

The Biodynamic Farming and Gardening Association supports and promotes biodynamic farming, the oldest nonchemical agricultural movement.

www.kidbean.com

This site sells organic, earth-friendly, and vegan products for families.

www.veganorganic.net

This is a source of articles and information about green, clean, cruelty-free living and organic growing.

Environmental and Sustainability Websites

www.conservation.org

Conservation International is involved in many conservation projects worldwide. On its site you can calculate your carbon footprint, based on your living situation, car, travel habits, and diet.

www.greenpeace.org

Greenpeace focuses on the most crucial worldwide threats to our planet's biodiversity and environment.

www.nrdcwildplaces.org

Natural Resources Defense Council (NRDC) is an environmental action group with over 1 million members working to safeguard the American continents' natural systems.

www.dinegreen.com

The Green Restaurant Association (GRA) is a national nonprofit organization that provides a convenient way for all sectors of the restaurant industry, which represents 10 percent of the U.S. economy, to become more environmentally sustainable.

www.ran.org

Rainforest Action Network is working to protect tropical rainforests around the world and the human rights of those living in and around those forests.

www.childrenoftheearth.org

Children of the Earth United is a children's environmental education website that educates the public on ecological concepts and aims to provide a forum for people to share knowledge and ideas.

Specialty Foods and Products

www.goldminenaturalfood.com

This online source carries a vast selection of organic foods, raw foods, macrobiotic, vegan, gluten-free, Asian, gourmet, and specialty foods as well as natural cookware and home products.

www.amazon.com

Amazon.com is perhaps the world's largest superstore. Check it out to order a gnocchi board, spaetzle maker, and any other kitchen equipment or specialty food items.

Eco-Friendly Products and Services

www.foodfightgrocery.com

Food Fight! Grocery is an all-vegan convenience store located in Portland, Oregon, with an online market that emphasizes junk foods, imports, and fun stuff.

www.vitamix.com

Find the latest Vita-Mix blenders here on the official site, including factory-reconditioned models that still come with a seven-year warranty. For free shipping in the continental United States, enter code 06–002510.

www.877juicer.com

This website carries way more than juicers, including everything kitchen related, plus air purifiers, books, and articles.

www.greenpeople.org

Green People provides a directory of eco-friendly products and services.

www.ecoproducts.com

Ecoproducts is the premier site for biodegradable and compostable food service products and environmentally friendly household supplies.

www.vegbay.com

This is a free online auction site for environmentally friendly, eco-conscious individuals, organizations, and small businesses. Animal products are prohibited.

www.pureprescriptions.com

Pure Prescriptions is an online superstore for high-quality nutritional products, complete with free consultations and a health library.

Raw Food Lifestyle Websites

www.livesuperfoods.com

This is the go-to site for all of your raw food needs, from food and supplements, to appliances and books.

www.goneraw.com

Gone Raw is a website created to help people share and discuss raw, vegan food recipes from around the world.

www.rawfoods.com

Living and Raw Foods is the largest raw online community with appliances for the raw foodist, chat rooms, blogs, articles, classifieds ads, and recipes.

www.gliving.tv

The G Living Network is a hip and modern green lifestyle network, with videos and articles on living in an earth-friendly way, including raw recipes, sustainable fashion, technology, and household design.

www.highvibe.com

This great site dedicated to the raw lifestyle offers an online store, recipes, fasting information, testimonials, interviews, and much more.

www.rawfamily.com

On this website, Victoria Boutenko and her entire family share recipes and their secrets on life as a raw family.

www.living-foods.com

The largest online community dedicated to educating the world about the power of raw and live foods. This site is jam-packed with information, classifieds, personals, books, homepages, and much more.

Contributor Bios

JENNIFER MURRAY, *Contributing Chef*
Jennifer Murray is the coauthor of three cookbooks, including *The 30-Minute Vegan*, *The 30-Minute Vegan's Taste of the East*, and *The Complete Idiot's Guide to Eating Raw*. She currently offers culinary classes on the Garden Island of Kauai through her company Nourish Kauai. You can reach her at NourishKauaiCooking @gmail.com.

PATRICK BREMSER, *Contributing Chef*
Patrick Bremser has had his hands in a mixing bowl since he could see into one. With twenty-plus years of professional experience in the culinary arts, Patrick appreciates and experiences cuisine as not only a dance on the palate, but also as the essential foundation for vibrant health and a thriving community. When he's not in the kitchen, you can find him in the garden, in the surf, on a trail, or in meditation. See more at www.ShriCuisine.com.

COLIN PATTERSON, *Contributing Chef*
Colin's chef career started in 1996 at Western Culinary Institute, where he learned the basic science of the alchemy of food. In 2008,

he, along with his wife and some friends, opened Sutra—a vegan restaurant that serves a four-course prix-fixe menu based on local organic ingredients. He focuses on sourcing consciously, working with whole foods, and making food that is delicious, beautiful, and takes care of your temple (the body). Learn more at www.sutraseattle.com.

DEBORAH BROWN PIVAIN,
Contributing Chef
The Gentle Gourmet in Paris and the Paris Vegan Day Festival were created by Deborah Brown Pivain and Alex and Caroline Pivain to promote veganism in Paris and the rest of France by means of a restaurant, bed-and-breakfast accommodation, cooking classes, and special events, such as the 2011 New Years Eve's Eve Cruise and an annual festival that has become Europe's largest specifically vegan event, attracting more than 8,000 visitors. www.gentlegourmetcafe.com

SURDHAM DANIELE GOEB,
Contributing Chef
Surdham is the vegan organic chef who started Zerwirk, the first all-vegan restaurant in Germany, in 2005. Luxury dining experiences are now available for catering,

private cooking, and coaching private or for businesses. He grew up in Italian catering, and his lineage goes back five generations in the hospitality business. Cooking and understanding of food is in his blood. Extensive traveling and meditation have given him a new depth and a unique style in his field. See more at www.web.me.com/surdham.

FAWNE FRAILEY AND SEBASTIAN ROMERO, *Food Photographers*

Fawne Frailey and Sebastian Romero, of Sea Light Studios, celebrate life together doing what they love—capturing the beauty of the moment. They specialize in lifestyle photography on the island on Kauai. They enjoy living a healthy lifestyle and nurturing their bodies with delicious vegan cuisine. www.sealightstudios.com

AMAYA GREEN, *Food Stylist*

Amaya is the award-winning photographer for *Vegan Fusion World Cuisine* who makes her home on the beautiful island of Kauai. Her love for the creative expression of food is evident in all of her works. She can be contacted at greenleafkauai@gmail.com.

LISA PARKER, *Recipe Tester*

An alchemist at heart, Lisa loves plants, colors, flavors, textures, and smells. She loves measuring and stirring and filling the kitchen with delectable fragrances. Lisa has been cooking and concocting ever since she received an Easy-Bake Oven for her seventh birthday. These days, she cooks a lot for friends and family, has a botanical

body product business, and works with her husband to create a tropical food forest and sanctuary at their home on Kauai. www.greensongbotanicals.com

ROLAND BARKER, *Recipe Tester*

As a young musician, Roland's working in restaurants was a good way to make a living, and as his knowledge and appreciation of food grew, it became a lifelong passion. Roland is inspired by nature's abundance and ability to nourish and heal us, and as a cook, he tries to add to that his intention for healing and joy in the preparation of natural, whole foods. Xnau Web design—www.xnau.com

SUZANNE RUDOLPH, *Recipe Tester*

An avid world traveler with a lifelong passion for food, Suzanne's palate has been strongly influenced by the cuisines she has eaten while on trips to over thirty countries. Suzanne divides her time with catering and teaching classes for home cooks at the Auguste Escoffier School of Culinary Arts in Boulder. www.rudymademeals.com, www.examiner.com/user-suzannerudolph

DAWN JEWELL, *Vegan Fusion Proofreader*

Dawn Jewell first began working with Mark Reinfeld and Vegan Fusion in 2004, while living on the Hawaiian island of Kauai. She has been dubbed the "Princess and the Pea Proofreader." Dawn is also a community and media activist, disc jockey, and a performing singer-songwriter. auroradawn33@yahoo.com

Acknowledgments

As I type the final pages of the manuscript I feel deep and profound gratitude. I am so grateful for the love and support of all of my family and friends. Thanks go to my mother, Roberta Reinfeld, and sisters Jennifer and Dawn Reinfeld. Also to Roger Vossler, Richard Slade, Bill Townsend, Cody Martin Townsend, and Sierra Molly Townsend.

Many thanks to all of those whose incredible contributions have made this book possible. Kudos to my rock star recipe testers Lisa Parker, Roland Barker, Suzanne Rudolph, Joanna Faso, and Alana Layne Greenberg. Also to contributing chefs Jennifer Murray, Patrick Bremser, Colin Patterson, Surdham Daniele Goeb, and Deborah Brown Pivain. Special thanks to Jennifer Murray for her contributions to the other books in the 30-Minute Vegan series: *The 30-Minute Vegan*, and *The 30-Minute Vegan's Taste of the East*, as well *The Complete Idiot's Guide to Eating Raw*.

Props to the stellar food photographers Fawne Frailey and Sebastian Romero of Sea Light Studios. I am also honored to have had the help of Amaya Green as the food stylist. Amaya was the food photographer for our first cookbook, the multiple award–winning *Vegan Fusion World Cuisine*. Thanks also to Engelica Desamparado for her help during the photo shoots.

Thanks to all of the recipe tasters and feedback givers—both in Colorado and in Hawaii—Roberta Reinfeld, Roger Vossler, Dawn Reinfeld, Bill Townsend, Suki Halevi, Lani Starr of LaniStarr.com, Smita Khatri, and Erik Marcus of Vegan.com, to name a few.

Thanks to Dawn Jewell, the "Princess and the Pea Proofreader," as well as Sara Jelley of Curvy Fitness for assisting with the research for the book.

Giving thanks for my amazing literary agent Marilyn Allen, and to my friend Daniel Rhoda, who introduced me to her. Special thanks to my editor at Da Capo, Renée Sedliar, whose patience and flexibility gave me the space to create the book. Thanks also to everyone on the production and marketing team at Da Capo, including former editor Matthew Lore who first believed in the 30-Minute Vegan concept—you rock!

Deep thanks to my partners in Vegan Fusion, Bo and Star Rinaldi, for their continual love and support.

ACKNOWLEDGMENTS

And while the *Taste of Europe* is dedicated to my grandfather Benjamin Bimstein, who instilled in me the love of the culinary arts, I also would like to dedicate it to the memory of my father, Martin Reinfeld. His love and desire for my personal freedom allowed me to embark upon the life of a world traveler—something that has filled me with a richness and an appreciation for life that continues to deepen.

About the Author

Mark Reinfeld is the winner of Vegan.com's Recipe of the Year Award for 2011 and has over twenty years' experience preparing creative vegan and raw food cuisine. Mark is described by VegCooking.com as being "poised on the leading edge of contemporary vegan cooking." He is the founding chef of the Blossoming Lotus Restaurant, winner of Honolulu Advertiser's Ilima Award for "Best Restaurant on Kauai." Mark is also the recipient of a Platinum Carrot Award for living foods—a national award given by the Aspen Center of Integral Health to America's top "innovative and trailblazing healthy chefs."

Mark received his initial culinary training from his grandfather Ben Bimstein, a renowned chef and ice carver in New York City. He developed his love for world culture and cuisine during travel journeys through Europe, Asia, and the Middle East. In 1997, Mark formed the Blossoming Lotus Personal Chef Service in Malibu, California. To further his knowledge of the healing properties of food, he received a master's degree in holistic nutrition.

His first cookbook, *Vegan Fusion World Cuisine*, coauthored with Bo Rinaldi and with a foreword by Dr. Jane Goodall, has won several national awards, including "Cookbook of the Year," "Best New Cookbook," "Best Book by a Small Press," and a Gourmand Award for "Best Vegetarian Cookbook in the USA." In addition, Mark coauthored *The 30-Minute Vegan's Taste of the East*, *The 30-Minute Vegan*, and *The Complete Idiot's Guide to Eating Raw*.

Mark specializes in vegan recipe development and offers chef training and consulting services internationally. He conducts online vegan culinary lessons at veganfusion.com as well as vegan and raw food workshops, immersions, and culinary tours worldwide.

Index